SPACE CRAFT DIGEST

THEORIES OF ELECTRICAL FLY

COLLECTED EDITION (1958-59)

William Gordon Allen

SAUCERIAN PUBLISHER

ISBN: **978-1-955087-14-8**

© 2022, Saucerian Publisher

Al rights reserved. No part of this publication maybe reproduced, translate, distribute, store in a retrieval system, or transmitted in any form or by any means, electronic, mechanical, photocopying, recording or otherwise, without prior written permission from the publisher.

Prologue

It is generally a good idea to return to the classics in any genre. This also goes for UFO literature. Rereading a book after ten or twenty years is a rewarding experience. You will discover new data and ideas you didn´t notice before. The reason, of course, is that you are, in many ways, not the same person reading the book the second or third time. Hopefully, you have advanced in knowledge, experience, intellectual and spiritual discernment. A good starting point is to reread the UFO classics of the 1960s and 70's in order to understand the deeper mystery involved in what happened during that era.

Space Craft Digest. Theories of Electrical Fly was a saucer letter size magazine published as a mimeographed newsletter by W. Gordon Allen from Salem, Oregon, under the banner of the *Pacific Lemurian Society*. The main idea behind **Space Craft Digest**, like many similar publications of that time, was to create a forum for UFO experience and saucer sightings for the purpose of the investigation of spacecraft, extra-terrestrial travel, and other subjects relating to these matters in order to encourage public support of projects in connection with these phenomena.

Saucerian Publisher was founded with the mission of promoting books in Ufology, Paranormal, and the Occult. Our vision is to preserve the legacy of literary history by reprint editions of books which have already been exhausted or are difficult to obtain. Our goal is to help readers, educators and researchers by bringing back original publications that are difficult to find at reasonable price, while preserving the legacy of universal knowledge. Very rare **Space Craft Digest**,edition! This is a rare set of **Space Craft Digest** issues published by

Pacific Lemurian Society., between 1958-59. These are VERY hard to come across these days.These are **UNIQUE ISSUES!** We decided to published them as a collected edition as a set to make it easier for someone to add them to their flying saucer/UFO collection. This title is an authentic reproduction of the original printed text in shades of gray. **THIS IS NOT A COMPLETED COLLECTIONS. SOME ISSUES ARE MISSING. IMPORTANT:** Despite the fact that we have attempted to accurately maintain the integrity of the original work, the present reproduction may have minor errors beyond our control like: missing and blurred pages, poor pictures and readers' pencil markings from the original scanned copy. **HOWEVER**, because this book is culturally important, we have made available as part of our commitment to protect, preserve and promote knowledge in the world. These issues are an authentic reproduction of the issues of the **SENTINEL** for the years: 1958-59. Great, but unpretentious, these issues are extraordinarily rare symbols by themselves of what was going on in those early years of the modern UFO era. This collected edition has the following issues of **Space Craft Digest: Spring, 1958; Summer, 1958; Fall, 1958; Spring-Summer, 1959.**

Editor
Saucerian Publisher, 2022

SPACE CRAFT Digest

SPRING ISSUE 1958

Theories of Electrical Flight

published by the PACIFIC LEMURIAN SOCIETY

FOUNDER

W. Gordon Allen

W. Gordon Allen became interested in the fantastic story of MU while a Naval Radar officer in the Pacific in the second World War. Allen saw many remains of the ancient civilization in the different island areas. In editing the SPACE CRAFT DIGEST he uses the approach of his background of engineering (he graduated in electrical engineering with additional work at Princeton and MIT).

He is now in the radio business in the Pacific Northwest and has built some eight commercial broadcast stations.

In founding the LEMURIAN SOCIETY he hopes to unravel the mysteries of the ancient civilization and to complete work on an observatory and astrophysical center through increased membership in the society.

Members already are scattered over the world and the size of the SPACE CRAFT DIGEST is to be increased next issue.

EDITORIAL

The SPACE-CRAFT DIGEST promotes the editorial conception that pure electrical flight in space is possible and that now the U.S. is on the wrong road in attempting Moon or Mars flight with rockets dragging tank cars full of fuel with them in space flight.

In the near future, someone on this planet is going to streak ahead a thousand years with one brilliant flash of discovery of fundamental universal principles. If this is not a citizen of the U.S. we may find our whole western civilization in jeopardy. The group that makes this discovery can do with the planet as it may wish.

Further, there is the question of why great civilizations in the past disappeared from the face of the earth. Today we are not immune to such a fate. It bears us well to study every item of knowledge about these peoples and profit from their demise. LEMURIA . . . MU . . . the motherland was one such continent. That is why the PACIFIC LEMURIAN SOCIETY carries on the work of re-discovery and tabulation of this lost knowledge.

Also, it is felt that those who can conceive of the real connection between the esoteric and physical schools of thought have a duty to explain the correlation to those who do not yet conceive that in the cosmos all is interconnected into one great universe of knowledge and motion.

The PACIFIC LEMURIAN SOCIETY headquarters is in Salem, Ore., USA, the still existing eastern boundary of the ancient lost continent of MU. The Society hopes in the near future to begin construction of the LEMURIAN ASTROPHYSICAL CENTER and is now soliciting subscriptions from those who will wish to be members of an esoteric and scientific group that is to be independent of the world's dogmas . . . as much as it is possible to be.

Bulletin

San Antonio, Texas...... 18 Feb. INS..... The air force chief of staff of space medicine says many more tests will be necessary to prove conclusively the hypothesis that man is capable of space flight.

But Lt. Col. George R Steinkamp of the Randolph Field school of aviation medicine, director of the space xperiment with airman Donald Farrel, says that the barrier to space flight belongs to the engineers.

COMMENT BY ED..... " the much publicized trip to the moon by the airman was nothing more than a stunt, in our opinion. The gravity problem was not encountered, nor was that of high acclerations. The USSR was certanly not fooled---only the nation's news editors who hung on every respiration as if it were REALLY A TRIP TO THE MOON.

IN CAMBRIDGE, MASS. THE US NAVY isimmersingmice in a liquid and has found that a mouse wrapped in a liquid space-suit with stood over 1500 G's for about a minute....."still the same old track, however, no matter how you wrap the animal gelatin-mass it still may be smashed by gravity.....so let's spend more of our money looking for a real gravitic understanding.....Ed."

Los Angeles..17 Feb. INS....PLANS ARE ON THE DRAWING BOARD TODAY FOR A NUCLEAR ROCKET WHICH WILL POSSIBLY CARRY THE FIRST MAN INTO OUTER SPACE. THE AIR FORCE AND NORTH AMERICAN AVIATION'S ROCKETDYN DIVISION HAVE ANNOUNCED THAT SUCH A ROCKET IS UNDER DEVELOPMENT HERE. ALTHO THE PROJECT IS STILL IN THE RESEARCH STAGE IT IS A DEVELOPMENT THAT WILL ONE DAY BE A REALITY A ROCKETDYN SPOKESMAN SAID.

Buenos Aires, Argentina...COMISION OBSERVAT DORA DE OBJECTOS VOLADORES NO INDENTIFICADOS......Casilla de Correo 2560 ...publishes an eight page mimeographed bulletin for 1957 giving a chronology of UFO sitings over Argentina last year. The publication is in Spanish, but is not too difficult to translate ....24 excellent reports thru the year are logged such as that of Dr. Juan A Siffredi.." .... at 1800 hours in the plaza of the federal capital he saw an oval object of an aluminum color at about 2,000 meters. There were also 6 or 7 other objects of the same brilliant metal. The objects hovered over the plaza....." Most of the sightings are quoting professional men such as Doctors and other citizens of professional responsibility. The objects are of most of the familiar types found in the UFO literature.

FLYING SAUCER REVIEW....excellent publication...(English) can be obtained from Allen's Book Shelf 11056 Sierra Avenue, Fontana, California. Six issues $3.75....."promises in the Mar-April issue to have an article from a man in Warwiskshire who has 'talked to A MAN FROM ANOTHER WORLD".....HERT'S, ENGLAND, in the same publication said that school children saw a glittering silver disc (and-or) ball of fire hovering in the sky at mid-day in December (9th) 1957.

NATIONAL INVESTIGATIONS COMMITTEE
ON AERIAL PHENOMENA
WASHINGTON 6, D. C.

TELEPHONE: NORTH 7-9434
CABLE ADDRESS:
SKYLIGHT

MAJOR DONALD E. KEYHOE
USMC (RET.) DIRECTOR

Subscribe....$7.50 t
NICAP

ADMINISTRATIVE OFFICES:
1536 CONNECTICUT AVE., N. W.
Washington, D.C.

CONFIDENTIAL BULLETIN —
to: SPACE-CRAFT DIGEST

March 5, 1958

(by Major Donald E. Keyhoe)

Dear Member:

Since the Armstrong TV show, when I was cut off the air, there have been important developments affecting you as a NICAP member. First, you should know that there was AF pressure during the Armstrong rehearsals which caused censorship of my script. The section deleted listed four AF documents never officially released but which had been confirmed by Capt. E. J. Ruppelt, former chief of Project Blue Book, and another former Project officer. These were:

1. A September 1947 ATIC conclusion that the flying saucers were real.
2. A 1948 top secret ATIC conclusion that the UFOs were spaceships.
3. An AF Intelligence analysis of UFO maneuvers, with the same conclusion.
4. A secret report by a scientists' panel at the Pentagon in January 1953 which urged
    a) that the AF quadruple its UFO project, and
    b) that they give the American people all UFO information, including AF conclusions.

According to an Armstrong official, the AF officer on the show warned them the AF would immediately deny the documents' existence if I were permitted to name them. This would also include denouncing the quoted source—their former Project chief—though his book with these items was cleared by AF Security and Review. This threat, which appears to be censorship by intimidation, caused my statement to be cut out. Though Armstrong producers tried to be impartial, AF insistence on most of the program time forced me to delete many vital items including: Official orders which silence armed forces personnel, and an AF letter to NICAP by Maj. Gen. Joe Kelly, Director of Legislative Liaison, USAF, refusing to release UFO reports and admitting they are classified "for official use only."

Because of this pressure, I tried to ad-lib the following statement on the Armstrong program: "In the last six months, we (NICAP) have been working with a Senate committee investigating official secrecy on UFOs. If open hearings are held, I feel it will prove beyond doubt that the flying saucers are real machines under intelligent control."

Though this had been discussed with a sponsor's representative, who reacted favorably, the producer later told me that since he was not informed he had to cut me off, under CBS rules. However, this does not alter the fact of Air Force censorship before the show.

Since then, there have been intensified attacks on NICAP and its Director. I hope to cover the items omitted on the Armstrong show on next Saturday, March 8, when I am scheduled to be interviewed by Mike Wallace of the ABC network at 10 pm EST; also when I appear on the "Long John" program on Station WOR after midnight following the Mike Wallace show. I hope to offset one serious effect of the Armstrong show.

A privately supported fact finding body serving the national public interest

The Truth of the U.S. Missiles Failure - - -

The German V-2 could have put a "moon" into Orbit in 1943!
Quoting Dr. I.M. Levitt -- director Fels Planetarium.

During the nationwide jubilation that followed the successful launching of America's Explorer satellite a fascinating story was overlooked....the TRUT

Hardly anyone realized the army scientists made desperate by the failure of the Navy's Vanguard rocket' decided figuratively to go primitive and blast a satellite into orbit by hook or crook.

The scientists called it the "quick and dirty" system. The launching also pointed up the difference between the Jupiter C and the Vanguard. They decided to fire a rocket using EXPLOSIVES which is like propelling an auto by exploding dynamite charges just back of the rear wheels.

HERE IS THE STORY OF THE HODGEPODGE..........The Redstone is just a souped-up version of the German V-2 (15 years old in development) which develops 78'000 pounds of thrust compared to the V-2's 56,000 lbs. But it had a thoroly reliable guidance system. (good enough to be hitting a certain section of London regularily in the second world war).

ON TOP OF THIS V-2 was piled three more rocket systems which were of the solid fuel type. ELEVEN WAC Sergeants were mounted in a circle as the next stage. This "stalk" was followed by three more mounted as the next stage. ON TOP a single rocket to "set" the 30 pound payload into orbit (18,'000 mph). It takes 2200 pounds of fuel and hardware per payload of satellite! ***************end of quote.

DEMOS WATCH G.O.P.......(From Democratic Digest)... "Well, almost before the reluctant American Sattellite made its first reluctant turn around the earth, Republican Congressmen began popping up on TV stations all across the country with films explaining the new scientific achievement. Of course, just to sure they could get on TV in time to take advantage of the excitement caused by our first satellite, the films were made in advance. This resulted in one little flaw. The films were about the WRONG sattelite? While our explorer was circling overhead, the GOP congressmen were basking in their self-styled limelight with a film about the still grounded Vanguard! NEWSWEEK... said....as it corrected the GOP.
The film said 20" in diameter (actually it is 80" long)....further....the film said it was a three stage rocket (it was a four stage) ....it said the first stage shot the rocket 35 miles (actually 60 miles) ....now from the Demo. Digest " We can say from long experience that it was nothing for the Republicans to tell 20 million people how they launched the Vanguard while it was still on the ground at Cape Canaveral!"
****

Salem, Oregon.....March 5,1958.... Mrs. Elinor Prink, 4347 Macleay Rd. reports seeing a fiery blue streak trailed by a flashing red area about the size of a red large star traveling East at terrific speed at 11:45 PM........
Must have been a jet plane because UFO's do not exist says the USAF.

Space Craft Bulletins   -------from around the planet.

UFO INVESTIGATOR ---1536 Connecticut avenue--Washington, D.C. states that Maj. Gen. J.W. Kelly of the USAF admits that the AIR FORCES are intentionally deceiving the American Public.
****

OCTOBER 6th 1957, TOLEDO, OREGON, Rufus B. Wood, (excerpt from letter) ".... two nights ago Newport(Ore.)people reported seeing about 20 flying objects make a complete turn over the city at about 10:30PM. a large object with fire all over it came down out of the clouds made a turn and flew up the coast."
****

NEWSWEEK....In the second report of their continuing study of man's exposure to radiation and especially radio-active Strontium 90 the deadly debris of H-bomb fallout. Three Columbia University scientists J. Laurence Kulp, Walter Eckelman, and Arthur R. Schulert---have analyzed over a 1,000 cadaver bone samples collected from over six continents the last five years and in the current issue of SCIENCE they draw some disturbing conclusions:

THE BODY'S LEVEL OF "STRONTIUM 90" A SUBSTANCE
WHICH IS SOAKED UP BY BONE CALCIUM AND RESULTS
IN BONE CANCER HAS RISEN 33% IN THE LAST YEAR!
****

KITCHENER ONTARIO, PO, BOX 21.....Homer Schafer...."...on June 7,1957, about 11:45 PM I observed the gigantic BRIDGE ON THE MOON thru my 6" reflector telescope......"Letter 1 Feb. 1958
****

SEATTLE POST INTELLIGENCE...11 February 1958....Columnist Frank Lynch.."...Shortly after Sputnik blazed across the sky there was a package in our mailbox. It was post-marked from Everett, and there was no other clue to the identity of the sender. THERE WERE FOUR PHOTOS IN THE PACKAGE THE FIRST WAS SAID TO BE A VIEW OF THE MOON FROM 120,000 miles, the second a snap of the moon from 50,000 miles. THE THIRD WAS A VIEW FROM JUST 10,000 MILES OUT----THE FOURTH BORE THIS CAPTION "...CLOSE UP OF PLANT LIFE ON THE MOON"... The photog went on to point out that in each of the photos the outer air was dotted by flying saucers.. "he goes on to ask....."is there a flying saucer in Everett or vicinity?
****

SEAFORD, NEW YORK, Feb 21, 1958.....Mysterious antics of bottles and other objects finally proved to be too much today for the James Herrmann family. They quit their home to live with relatives.

A flying sugar bowl and a leaping inkwell last night served as the final straws to the nerve wracked mother and father of two children 12 and 13. For 18 days the family has been plagued by such things as: a bottle of bleaching liquid blew its scre top: a porcelain figurine danced off the table; A bowl of sugar flew off the table and made a dent a fifth of an inch thick in the wood of the floor."........POLTERGEISTS AT WORK?.......certainly a highly concentrated force field of some psychic nature seems to be responisble for this type of phenomena that science cannot yet understand or explain, BUT never-the-less these things happen and certainly are from beyond our present state of knowledge, but they do give us a hint of other force fields beyond our senses, do they not?(Ed)

The Real Truth Behind the U.S.A.-U.S.S.R. Frantic Race to the Moon

Those who are careful students of what astronomers have really seen near the moon, as well as other students of Metaphysics and other simply careful observers have almost all come to the conclusion that over the years there has been a lot of traffic in the vicinity of the Moon. Even though "authorities" have taught for hundreds of years that Luna is a very dead planetoid (in the earth-moon binary system) these phenomena keep on happening and with modern methods of communication, even the dogmatists cannot succeed in keeping these stories out of the public fund of knowledge.

> BULLETIN...
> Any hour now the US. or USSR may send a reaction-powered vehicle to the moon. This is an easier "shot" than the perfect timing required to "set" a satellite in an orbit BUT REMEMBER....that it is a projectile, not a space-craft and that the earth-moon is a single unit binary system. No matter how wonderful our publicity makes it look, it will not be space flight but just a crude, small projectile which has broken free of the earth's "gravity" field. Do not be taken in by the publicity. Man has still much to learn about the fundamentals of the cosmos...(Ed.)

The year of 1957 found these interesting Lunar Traffic Items:

STOCKHOLM, Sweden – 31 December, '57 ... A report by a Swedish officer of a shining object traveling on a spiral course toward the Moon was under examination at Sweden's defense headquarters Monday.

The best guess so far seems to be that it might have something to do with the USSR satellite or middle experiment, a staff officer said.

"We know that it is no airplane, nor any meterological balloon," he said. "And the Stockholm Observatory has told us that it is no meteor?

He said the observation was made Sunday by a Swedish army captain at Kortedala, near Goteborg, on the Swedish west coast.

"The captain reported he watched the object through his field glasses for 20 minutes."

"We are taking this report seriously since it came from a competent observer. All details are being forwarded to the FOA (scientific research institute of Sweden's armed forces).

"The captain described the object as a FLATTENED SPHERE circling moonwards."

"Its sides were somewhat elongated and there was a flickering glow as if from burning exhaust gases from one side."

The Swedish defense staff spokesman said the captain had not been able to estimate the altitude but had reported the "object moved one degree a second on the scale of his field glasses."

From his position at Kortedala the captain saw the object in a S.S.W. direction.

The object was certainly not possibly Sputnik, as it is outside all possible schedules," the spokesman concluded.

So ends this Swedish army report of what most open-minded observers would say is an amazing UFO report.

In the November, 1957 issue of SKY AND TELESCOPE, published in conjunction with the activities of the Harvard Observatory is this report:

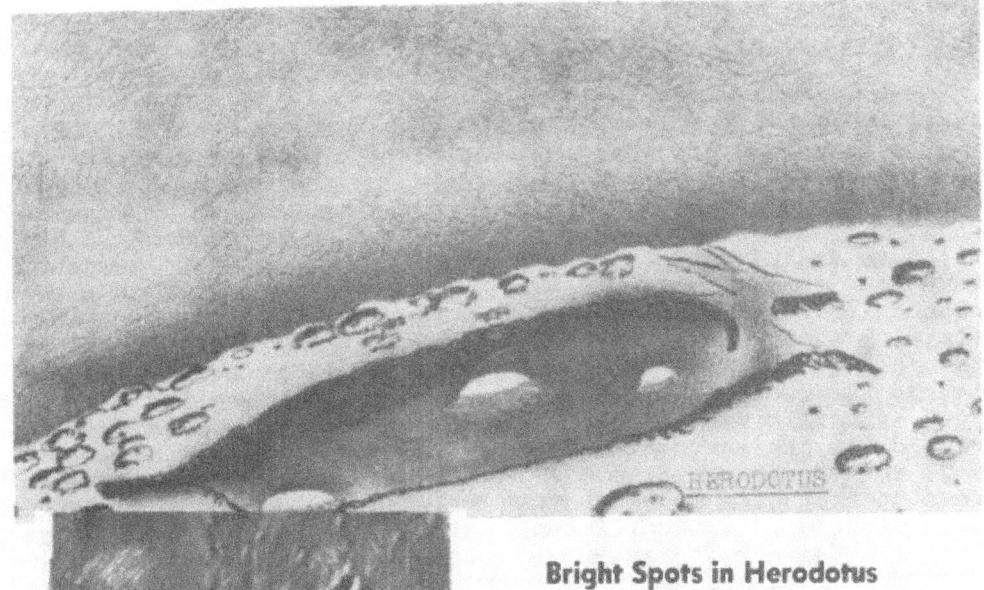

Bright Spots in Herodotus

"Sketches made on several nights indicate that no fewer than 26 craterlets of bright spots were drawn. For one brief instant of perfect seeing the dark velvety floor of Plato appeared to be covered with still other minute spots"

In the July issue of the same astronomical publication James C. Bartlet saw three bright spots in the Lunar crater HERODOTUS. Earlier observers had not seen these spots.

In the U.S. there are several observatories with Lunar Viewing contracts. SPACE CRAFT DIGEST has found that these "secret" archives have kept from the public the amazing truth that high officials in the U.S. and the USSR cannot rest until they know the real secrets of space travel, for the nation that has this great secret will rule this planet !.. THAT'S THE REAL SECRET BEHIND THE USSR-USA FRANTIC RACE TO THE MOON. ROCKETS ARE ALREADY OBSOLETE AND ALL WORLD PROPULSION EXPERTS KNOW IT :

Open Pit Mine?

Under a sketch of the Lunar crater Plato (see also illustration of HERODOTUS) Patrick McIntosh of RR 2, Box 231 of Robinson, Ill. writes:

"Jackson T. Carle's article THE THREE RIDDLES OF PLATO in the April, 1955 (S and T) encouraged me to begin the observations of the details on the floor of this crater, using an 8 in. f 7.5 reflector

The small moon "spirit" observed in the Astral travels of Immanuel Swedenborg of the 1700's perfectly describes the crewman of a flying saucer or UFO which crash-landed near Mexico City in January, 1952 and is shown above as a corpse on display between two German biochemists. It shows also his approximate size. This is stamped "secret" in the U.S. but the picture was obtained from West Germany. Is this the type of being which might be living IN the Moon? Certainly there is a great deal of activity in certain craters of the Moon which shows up to close Lunar observers.

YET these sightings are in no way different than what has been seen on the moon for a long, long time - in fact, for.........

For the last hundred years and more responsible observers from various national observatories over the world as well as competent amateurs have seen any number of indications that the nearest neighbor in the universe to the earth, the moon, has plenty of activity.

This activity varies from bright lights, thru various colored lights, to white and jet black spots. Peculiar reticulations are seen not only by amateurs, but also they are shown with clarity by the 200 inch telescope of Mt. Palomar. These moon pictures that take the observer to within 25 miles of the moon clearly show that something is making deep trails in the moon dust outside of the craters. Objects are seen to be moving across the moon and some 1600 or more instances of lights near the surface of the moon have been recorded. Many of the objects crossing the moon are seen to cast shadows. Lights from the dark portion of the moon have often been seen.

The very strong indications are that all of the Lunar traffic here recorded means nothing less than the amazing possibility that other entities might well have been using Luna as an earth-orbit space station long before man struggled into his own atmosphere via the airplane. Countless reference to flying saucer, UFO's or spacemen appear all thru written history from the time of Amenhotep III in 1500 B.C. These might well have been, and could be now, based in the moon. They might well be from Mars or Venus. Mars has two small satellites of its own 9 and 11 miles in diameter. Mars seems to have "answered" the moon lights with light signals of its own.

BODIES CROSSING THE MOON

SCIENCE July 31, 1896. Mr. W. R. Brooks, director of the Smith Observatory, saw a dark round object pass slowly across the moon in a horizontal direction; apparent diameter 1/30th that of the moon's; crossed the disc in three or four seconds.

Dr. F. B. Harris (POPULAR ASTRONOMY 20-398) Jan. 27, 1912. Saw upon a moon an intensely black object estimated to be 250 miles long and 50 miles wide.

(L'Anne Scientific 1860-25). Vast numbers of bodies were seen by M. Lamey to cross the moon. Issue (1874-62) Messier reports an immense number of black spherical bodies.

POPULAR SCIENCE 34-158. Serviss tells of a shadow that Schroeter saw in 1788 in the Lunar Alps. First he saw a light, but then when this region was illuminated he saw a round shadow where the light had been and "that he saw a luminous object near the moon: that that part of the moon became illuminated and the object was lost to view; but then its shadow underneath was seen!"

MONTHLY NOTICES OF THE ROYAL ASTRONOMICAL SOCIETY (8-132) — "Remarkable appearances during the total eclipse of the moon on 19 March, 1848). At the time of the predicted total eclipse that the moon shown with about three times the mean intensity of the eclipsed lunar disc . . . rather tinged with red and being as perfect with light as if there were not an eclipse at all."

POPULAR ASTRONOMY—Prof. Swift of Mattoon, Illinois, during an eclipse of the sun on August 7, 1869; objects moving in two directions across the moon and each moving in parallel lines.

ASTRONOMICAL REGISTER—23-205. Prof. Schafarik of Prague writes that on April 24, 1874, he saw an object of such peculiar size that "I do not know what to make of it" . . . slowly traversing the disc of the

How the Saucers Fly -----

To understand how the UFO is propelled one must discard the conventional conception of the atom composed of a central proton around which revolve electrons in the manner of the planets of the solar system.

Substitute the thought that Isaac Newton was right when he stated "space is absolute" and that all throughout the universe is an all pervading ether -- or fields --or field situation. Then "something" in "some" manner is able to seize a bit of this space or ether and whirl it in the manner shown in the illustration of the vortex atom. The NUTRINO will be just one of the uncharged doughnut shapes whirling in the vortex motion. TWO will produce the fundamental form of the primary <u>ether pump</u> which assumes a charge and acts as the fundamental of the atom.

The NUTRINO is not affected by "gravity" or charge and can penetrate the most dense substances with ease. When a charge is added it responds to both the electrostatic and the electromagnetic fields. BUT the gravitational field does not have any effect at the atomic level. This would seem to indicate that when this little "ETHER PUMP" of a vortex atom is in action that the effect of gravity is negated by the difference of "ether pressure" at the two sides of the whirling vortex.

The TRENT UFO (see diagram) is considered by the author to be one of the most significant UFO pictures in existence. Farmer TRENT on the Oregon coast snapped two UFO pictures in 1950. The pictures are some of the best saucer photographs ever taken and are genuine, beyond a doubt. The author has seen the remainder of the roll of film taken at a family picnic near McMinnville, Oregon. They are just ordinary family pictures such as anyone would snap on such an outing. Trent looked up and saw the UFO about two hundred feet away and snapped the picture which the artist used in the drawing. The photo appeared in LIFE magazine, but the U.S. Air Force or some other agency would not return the negative. Trent's photo cannot seem to be satisfactorily copied as there seems to be a slight difference in density between the UFO and its surroundings. But the author feels that this is due to the radiations which would be coming from such a highly charged body. After about 20 seconds, the very material UFO zipped off at high speed.

A close examination of the UFO photo shows that there are two rolls around the side whcih contain the acceleration chambers. These are also shown in the diagram under the VORTEX ATOM. The particles in the chambers are accellerated at a very high speed (even beyond the speed of light) and the UFO may dematerialize to ordinary vision, BUT appears at night as a very bright light of various colors, as the speed of the particles in the chamber is increased with an increase in acceleration. The lighted or glowing hull thus is seen to move through the visible spectrum from the red through the violet range and then to "disappear" from sight. In daylight, the UFO appears, disappears, and reappears as a silvery object.

BUT the fundamental "secret" of the saucers, electrical space flight and the UFO is the ETHER PUMP conception which does away with the conventional atom and substitutes a SPACE VOTEX atom which is in itself an ETHER PUMP.

The construction of the earth space vehicle then rests on the engineering problem of a power source for the maintenance of the particle (and wave) stream in the acceleration chambers of the space travel pod.

For those who would be interested in the understanding of the complete ETHER VORTEX conception of the universe's building blocks, the KRAFFT ETHER VORTEX THEORY explains this idea of the fundamentals of the cosmos.

Western science and USSR projects are vying with each other in building various plasma accelerations. The U. S. Atomic Energy commission and the Princeton SHERWOOD Project plus the British at Harwell are examples of attempts to produce some kind of thermal hydrogen reaction.

The BRITISH Z E T A (Zero Energy Thermonuclear Assembly) is trying to generate some fantastic heats by "pulsing" a stream of neutrons (particles) and leaving it to the magnetic "pinch effect" to squeeze this particle stream into a heat pulse of some 5 million C°. There is some element of success attached to these projects.

The ZETA "doughnut" is also diagramed for comparison and when the three fundamental theories from the NUTRINO doughnut to the UFO photograph showing acceleration chambers to the British ZETA, it can be seen that we are mighty close to the most fantastic "BREAKTHROUGH" of all recorded time -- true and pure electrical space flight, un-

*Ed. Note: The "hum" of a UFO as reported can well be the pulsing of the particles in the acceleration chamber at an audio frequency as the UFO hovers.

fettered by tankcars full of fuel in the crude rocket projects on which we now spend so much money, with so many failures.

If the ZETA were to be unchained and mounted in the manner of an ether pump we would hazard the speculation that it would be pretty hard to tie the laboratory down. Weight would not particularly be a problem, since the ether differential would cause this force field to work with the space machine and not hold it down.

SECONDLY...the problem is to provide power for our projected UFO-type-spacecraft. The drain on the conventional power system to provide a pulse current of 200,000 amperes is quite a jolt.

The "secret" of this is to use a resonated feedback system to use part of the pinch stream of neutrons to feedback and through resonance, lift the space-craft mostly by its own bootstraps. The reaction can be started by just a bit of radioactive material and through resonance, the velocity of the particles in the acceleration chambers built up to the point of the speed of light or to whatever speed pure radiation is obtained.

THUS the claim of the unit on conventional power could be eliminated. In the ZETA project and in the other projects the blasts of power fed into the machines are most wasteful. The next SECRET of the ZETA and SHERWOOD Project scientists to "discover" will be how to sustain their reactions through this type of resonance design. They can then lighten their equipment and through use of resonance multiplication of energy fed back into the circuit they can sustain the reaction.

RESONANCE ... it must be remembered... is used already

in radio engineering and is in reality the pulling of this energy from the space, or ether, of the universe. The great I^2R power fed into these great atom smahsers is NOT the power used to achieve results, at all. The phenomenon used is the vertical vector of I^2R known as the imaginary number (Operator J). It is interesting to note that in the Einstein equation the imaginary number $(-1)^{\frac{1}{2}}$ (square root of a minus one) is ued for "time". This little mathematical trick is used to convert multi-dimensional mathematics to the conventional level.

BUT the phenomenon of resonance, once it is understood by Western researchers, will do away with the inefficient use of great coils of magnetic wires to get effects that at the moment the gropers at Harwell and Princeton cannot even explain by any conventional theory.

Let's just examine for a nonce whether our statements are too hard on the billion-dollar projects. TIME says: "The most impressive U.S. thermonuclear work was done at the Los Alamos scientific laboratory with a machine called a PERHAPSatron(perhaps we may get something for the next billion?) Its doughnut is made of glass surrounded by copper as big as a scooter tire, with its minor diameter about 2 inches, compared to ZETA's 39 inches. The temperature of its pinch is greater than ZETA's (about $6,000,000°C$) BUT THE PINCH LASTS ONLY A FEW MILLIONTHS OF A SECOND, about one thousandth as long as ZETA's. Other thermonuclear machines at Los Alamos use short, straight tubes through which heavy currents are forced to flow and to pinch particles. All machines give off abundant neutrons.

The big question is whether these neutrons really come from the fusion of deuterium into Helium 3. Powerful electrical discharges give "false neutrons" (Nutrinos?-- Ed.) formed in other less important ways, but Sir J. Crockcroft is convinced at least 90 percent that some of ZETA's neutrons come from their project's goal of thermonuclear reaction. Dr. Thoneman of Harwell does not want to commit himself. U.S. scientists are not sure either. Sir John Crockhof says the trail may take ten or fifty years.

That's what the best rational thinkers have to say about the wave-particle paradox. It is our suggestion that a little more driginal thought be done along the lines of the ETHER PUMP theory of matter and a change of fundamentals to really understand what goes on in these great force field machines. After all, someone already has some UFO's in our atmosphere, so Harwell and Princeton are not the last word in the cosmos.

It is certain that the present dogmatism is going to cost the public nothing but more billions. Correct use of resonance and realistic understanding of matter's fundamentals can put these projects on the track of real space-flight and unlimited energy.

SHELL MATERIEL --- is of course the other part of the "secret" of pure electrical flight. In about 1926 a study was carried on in a small Ohio university's physics department. It showed that a charged condenser tended to move to the positively charged plate. This has been known for some time and is the second "proof" that in the electrical fields of the universe a highly charged body can indeed lift itself "by its own bootstraps". With the two doughnut-shaped acce-

TRENT UFO...artist sketch from actual photograph..... this is one of the most significant UFO photograph s in existence as it shows the two circular acceleration chambers which are used to obtain the "ETHER PUMP" type of gravitic device which is so necessary to true electrical flight rather than the reaction motor of the rocketeers.

leration chamber construction and the correct outer shell material, it can be seen how a UFO is ready for space flight. The ZETA type acceleration chamber (2) with the correct shell material is ready for this type of flight. However, the principle of resonance must be used to cut the prohibitive power consumption of this Harwell design.

GRAVITY... seems to be just a special case of proton attraction and not the fundamental field that Einstein assumed. A whirling body will cause the ETHER SINK FIELD of its outer surface to have a difference of ether (or spatial) pressure. This is demonstrated by the erratic and, to date, unexplainable deflections of the Sputnik orbit. Close to the earth the Sputnik keeps hitting the slight difference in pressure which causes the slight gravitational deflections and orbitual variations detected and heretofore unexplained.

Western science already knows the fundamentals of space flight by electrical means, but the interpretation of the fundamentals is so steeped in out-of-date dogma that the world will have to turn many more times before the space projects are back on the right track.

BUT (not being dogmatic) This is how saucers fly .

COPYRIGHT 1937
BY CARL F. KRAFFT

Box 687
Annandale, Va.

VORTEX THEORY
price $2.00

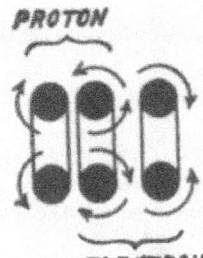

More Ether Vortex atoms showing how more complicated proton groups are built to form more complicated structures.

The fundamental vortex concept overcomes many many errors in concept in the conventional atomic theory which undermines our whole structure in physical science---but the dogmatists go stubbornly on.

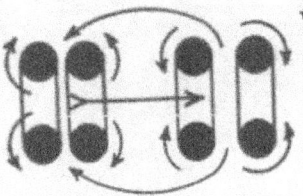

Figure 1.

The neutron and the hydrogen atom--two electrically neutral particles of mass 1, but with entirely different properties and incapable of being converted into each other. If any explanation for this were possible under the nuclear theory, then it would have been found long ago. As the diagrams clearly show, the vortex theory has the explanation ready.

In the days of hydrogen bombs, can we afford to be disinterested in the structure of the neutron?

Fig. 4

Atoms with periferal hydrogen groups which provide valence bonds. The chemical valence of an element is not always equal to the number of hydrogen groups because valence bonds may be branched or may be joined to other bonds in the same atom. Each hydrogen group adds 1 to the atomic number.

Since these atoms have an abundance of hydrogen groups by which they can become anchored to one another, they will resist fusion up to relatively high temperatures.

Unlike the inert gases, these atoms liberate free electrons and will therefore be conductors of electricity.

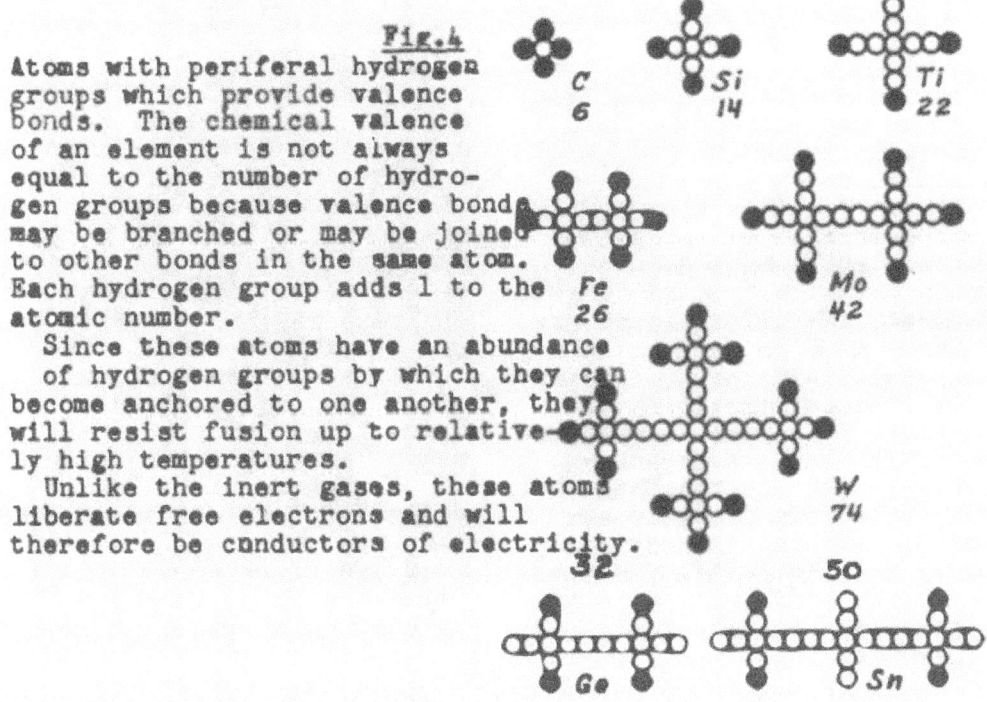

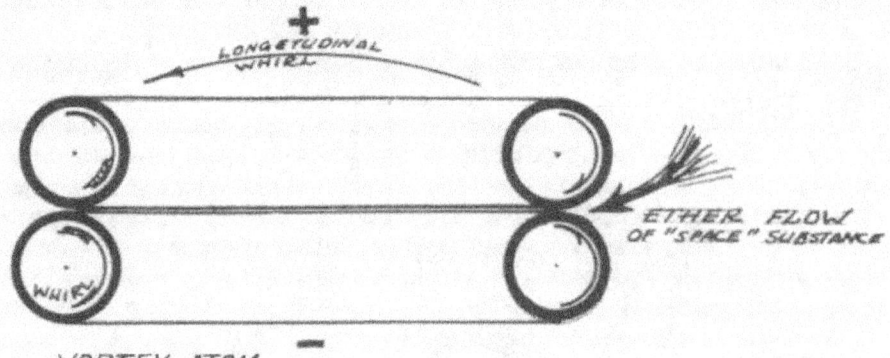

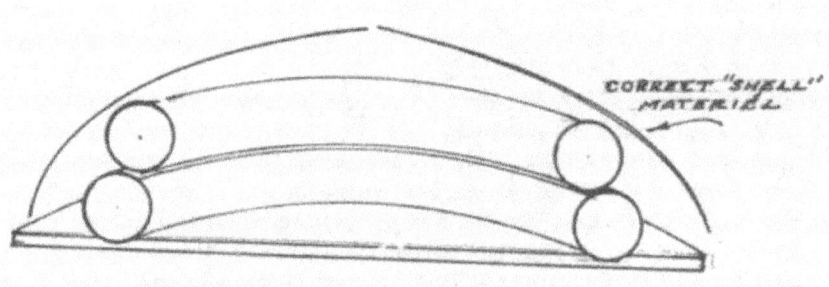

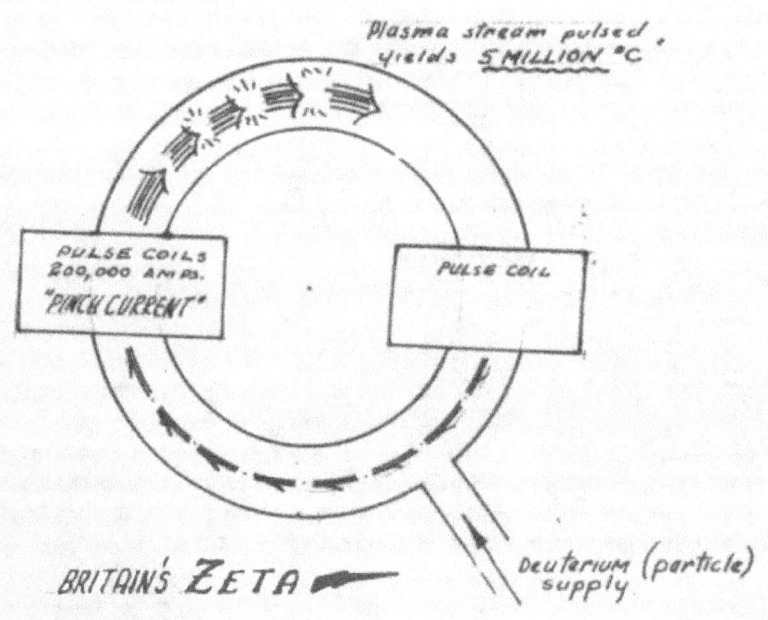

A New Vista of the Entirety

w. gordon allen

In December 1956 the BELL AIRCRAFT Co. published their bulletin #98-001. Its title was ORGANIZATIONS AND VISTAS OF THE ENTIRETY.

Dr. I Browning drew the final table of his conception of the ENTIRETY as shown in fig.6.

BELL AIRCRAFT is a lrge defense contractor and manufacturer of airframes who would like to propel one of these airframes at least to the moon and in that way insure its future in the "spaceframe' manufacturing business.

The offering of the SYSTASIS (study figure 6 closely) at first inspection seems to be a very fine compilation of the fields of organized learning and the progresssion of the universe as our Western Science believes it to exist as of this mid-20th century.

Western man brags that he is on the edge of the "space age" even tho he is already on a space vehicle--the earth. Another direction that scientific dogma has taken is that our poor knowledge of science has cataloged a few facts but as shown in the "Heisenberg principle" of UNCERTAINTY we are having to admit that "facts" are never consistantly taken to a conclusion and finalized. It indicates that scientific facts themselves are certainly NOT a "stable table" to operate our certainty of reality from.

An examination of the output of the BELL Research department which we quote should then be examined in this light.

It is our purpose to point out that Dr. Browning has done very well in his tabulation of the fields of learning that we have recognized in our highly departmentalized universities. These are the fields of knowledge that doctorates are given in and which are our Western scientific specialties.

But the U.S. finds that tho we have the tens of thousands of specialists we do not have the necessary all-encompassing minds capable of administrating these specialists. It has become a case of the blind leading the blind ---as each specialty views its limited conception of the entirety thru its own narrow slit.

The university traning of the rational mind has bogged down because it seems not to yet comprehend just what the human mind itselfis---and just exactly how it functions. The highly specialized mind pumped full of "facts" that are not facts--but UNCERTAINTIES-- is just a memory machine NOT a T H I N K I N G   M I N D!

Particular issue is taken with the right side of the BELL diagram that is fig.6.....which tabulates from:

MOLECULE
         to SIMPLE MACHINE
                  to COMPLEX MACHINE
                          Tc AUTOMATIC MACHINE
                               to CONTROL MACHINE

This is where the effort of the BELL offering seems to fall short in its attempted portrayal of the ENTIRETY--THE UNIVERSE!

THE MACHINE---control machines, memory machine (human or electtronic) or whatever certainly seem out of place in any fundamental scheme of the universe. Man-made machines have no more place in the fundamental cosmos than do insect machines (trap door of a spider) or animal machine etc.

THE MIND -- should certainly be substituted in this fundamental and primary conceptive effort , we believe. It is the BRAIN that is the many-leveled mind receiver. NOT only the human brain, but also the brain of the higher animals. Human brains have abilities that some animals do not and vice-versa. The many-leveled mind may be capable of fantastic development as a receiver of truth.

WE OFFER....in this scheme a different progression than does BELL.

A MENTAL ENTIRETY (probably in its own force field)

SINGLE NERVE CELL
    to INSTINCT CONTROLLED GANGLIA
        to RATIONAL SCIENTIFIC MIND
            to COSMIC MIND (receiver of fundamental truths)

This obviously leaves room for progression to higher mental understandings which now lie dormant in the man-animal brain.

We must continually remember that it is our bodily chemical factory that provides the electrical energy that runs our nerve cells and the "LIVING RECEIVER" that is our animal-brain. It could well be that a so-called thinking entity could exist in the cosmos under ANY condition that could supply this electrical energy and not necessarily need a "body" to supply its "mind" with chemically generated electrical energy.

So, let's eliminate machines completely from any concept of the ENTIRETY. The mind-receiver of the fundamental truths of the correct conceptions of the cosmos is certainly then to be substituted for MACHINES in any conception of the ENTIRETY.... if one doesn't work for a company that is in the machine manufacturing business.

FURTHER ..another important portion of the concept omitted by BELL is the truth of constant movement. EVERYTHING in the universe is moving. BELL uses the "link" of the molecule in the central portion of Fig.6. This perhaps should be the NEURINO (simplified to NUTRINO) the whirling doughnut shaped vortex of pure spacial electrcity which composes every material existence that we know. THE NUTRINO is the elemental building block of the cosmos. All of our highly classified "pinched plasma" research will one day show this and many of the "mysteries" of the sub-atom will then be solved. We'll find that at that time we'll achieve the "breakthru" that will enable space ships to drive up to and beyond the speed of light. (Explained in How the Saucers Fly). Now it must be noted that each nutrino particle (as built from the nutrino vortex fundamental proton) must exist in a continuum of fields. Einstein tried to have a fundamental three field continuum of electromagnetic, electrostatic and gravitic (gravity). His error was in the assumption that "gravity" was a fundamental field. He made a further error when he restricted his "Unified Field" theory to three----what of the LIFE forces that exist---and the MENTAL ACTIVITIES that exist? Even in the cold world of science it must be apparent that there are biological entities with brainboxes inhabiting the planet. Or would the scientists of the West ignore their own existence to promote their own narrowness?

GALLILEO was most observant when he said..." man is poorly equipped by his senses to guess the secrets of the universe".

WHAT OF LIFE FORCE?...If our Western scientific "facts" are correct then intelligent life does not exist---i.e. such as the machines of BELL.

THE ODIC field as promulgated by Reichenback and others is most fundamental as well as an INTELLIGENCE or "I" field. Simplified--- here's the conception:

Illustrating bonding of the different
states of matter from radiation thru the
states of fundamental hydrogen protons
thru to spacial galaxis

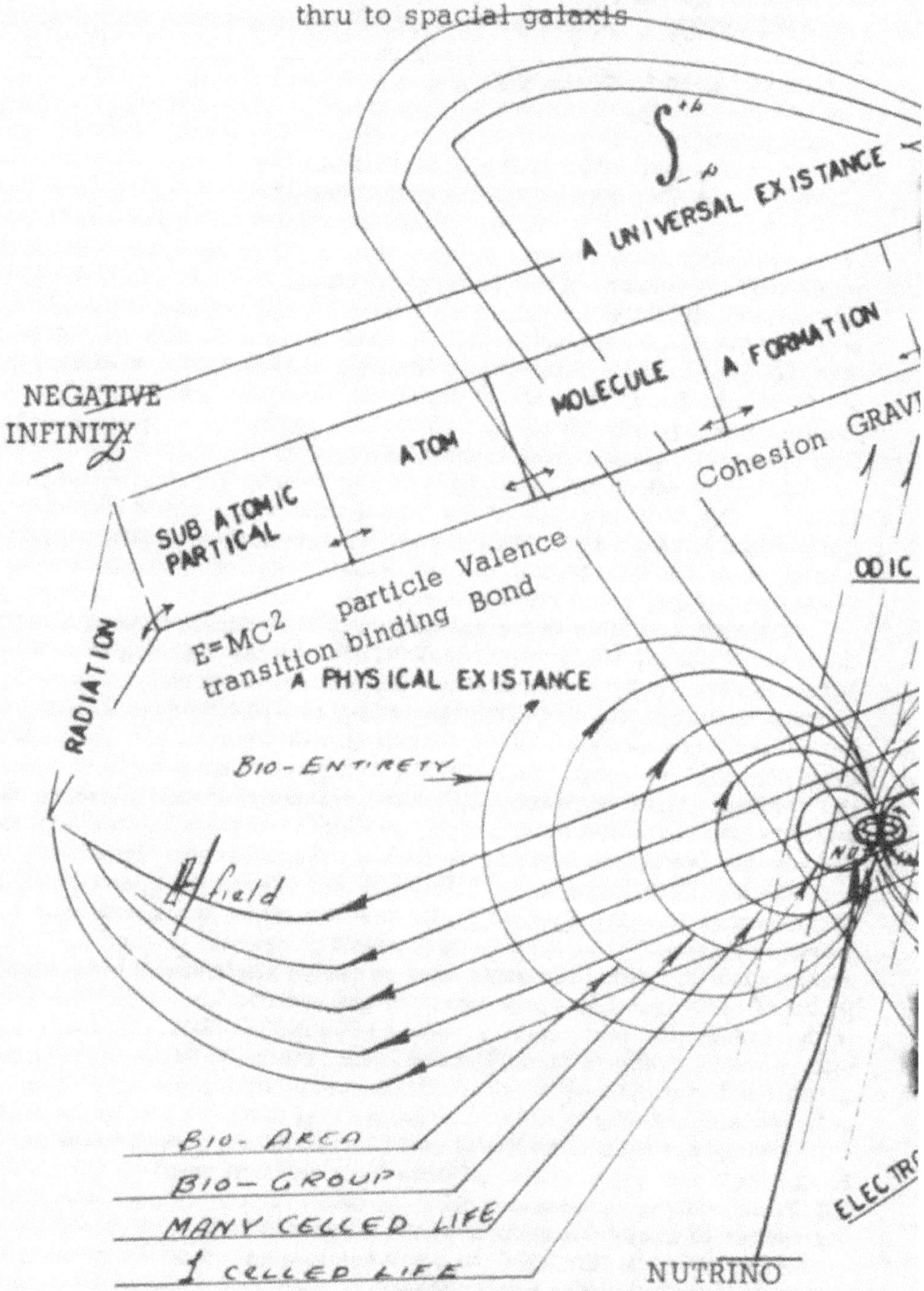

$\int_{-\infty}^{+\infty}$ A UNIVERSAL EXISTANCE

NEGATIVE INFINITY $-\infty$

MOLECULE — A FORMATION

ATOM

SUB ATOMIC PARTICAL

Cohesion GRAVI...

ODIC

RADIATION

$E=MC^2$ particle Valence
transition binding Bond

A PHYSICAL EXISTANCE

BIO-ENTIRETY

H field

BIO-AREA
BIO-GROUP
MANY CELLED LIFE
1 CELLED LIFE

NUTRINO

ELECTR...

(fundamental of ALL material exister...
"I" FIELD may well be universally fundame...
make the 'whole' a FOUR FIELD CONTINU...
an "N" number of dimensions and states...

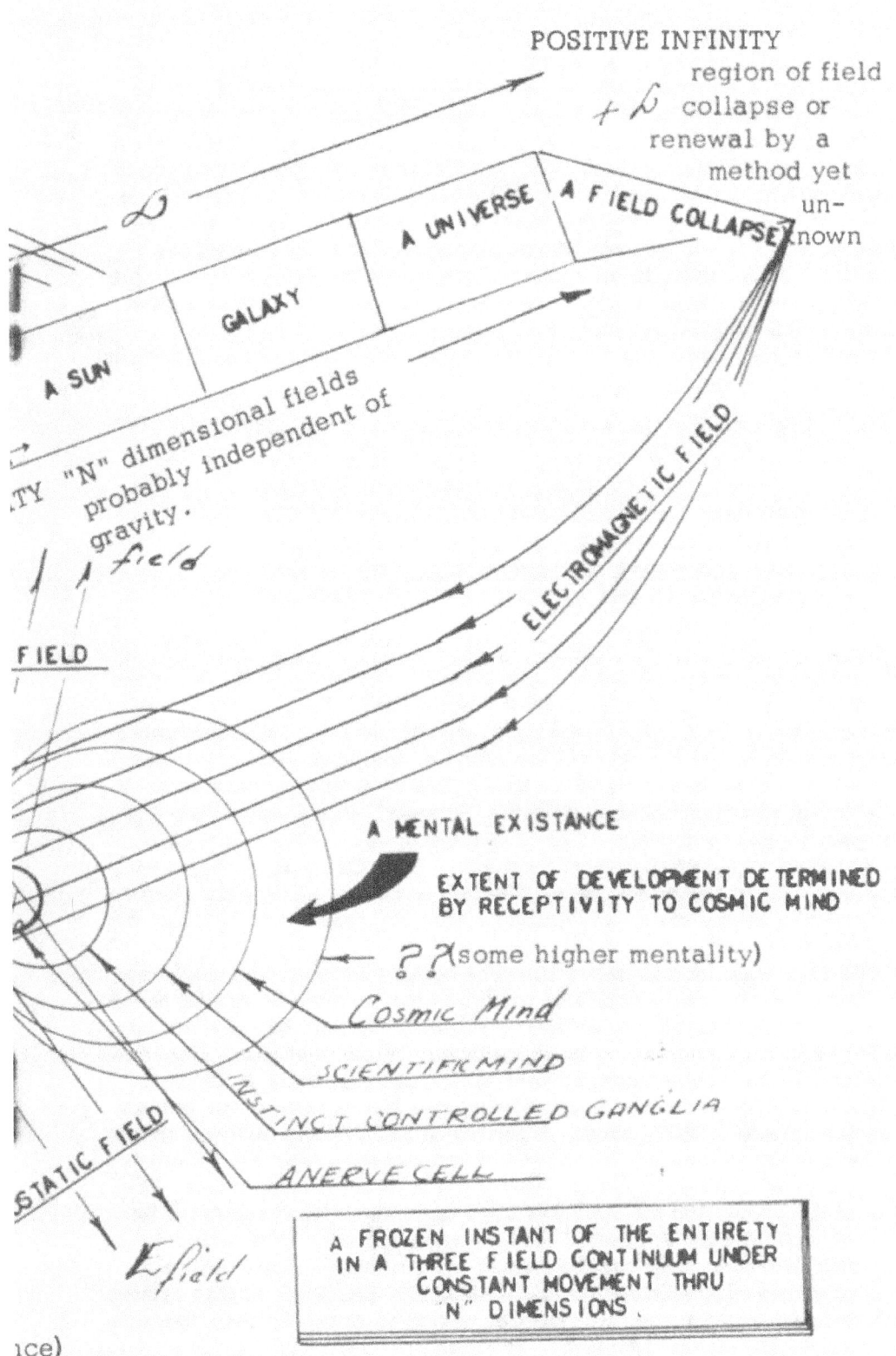

ntal and would then permiate the ENTIRETY to
UM under constant movement thru
of reality from waves thru to universes.

In any spacial gathering under stable conditions in a two-field continuum we may have bare elements combined from hydrogen vortex protons. If we have added to the two fields (electrostatic and electomagnetic) a third field THE ODIC which is the life force field...This would give the budding galxial entities life, but not intelligence. THE "I" FIELD or intelligence field which we can detect at this time only by our own mind (but not yet by instrumentation) seems most fundamental of the cosmos. It might well be an all pervading field. This is the conceptive development that is left out of the BELL offering. Nerve cells in an animal organism evolve until they are able to "tune into" the "I FIELD" of the cosmos just as "dead" elements evolve in an ODIC FIELD into living plants and animals.

Dr. Browning does make severl brilliant statements in his presentation and this one we have permission to quote:

> THIS SCHEME APPLIES EQUALLY WELL TO A HUMAN
> TECHNOLOGIST, A RACOON WHICH WASHES ITS
> FOOD, OR TO BEINGS WHOSE EXISTENCE WE CAN
> ONLY SURMISE CARRYING OUT PROCESSES WE CAN
> NOT IMAGINE. IN THIS UNIVERSE SUCH BEINGS
> COULD ONLY HAVE CERTAIN TYPES OF UNITS AND
> PHENOMENA TO USE AS TOOLS ---AND THESE ARE
> OUR TOOLS AS WELL!

For the last hundred years Western Science in its pre-occupation with gadgets has been in possession of the fundamental truths which should have been unified into an over-all conception of the ENTIRETY. Our universities in their ignorance of the many-level functions of the human mind jammed their students in their formative years into a "mold" which prostituted their minds. Those who didn't comply with the "system" were ejected from the memory machine degree factory. Only a few escaped. These minds still had the political andsocial dogmas to escape. From this prison only a very few escaped. These few minds in the Western world are at this time carrying the burden of producing a conception of what the real composition of the universe might be.

EINSTEIN was the first to try to mathematicly develop a unified field theory. Because our mathematics of today insists on transfer of ALL phenomena to a three dimensional reference ---Einstein failed, but at least he tried. At the present state of our mathematics it seems that if a 3 field con tinuum might not be handled that a four-field concept might be hopeless. INTUATIVE development then seems the only possible answer at our present stage of development. BUT, as Dr. Browning of BELL points out---if these are the tools of other thinking beings--they are our tools as well. There is "proof" in our own existence that at least a 4 FIELD continuum exists. The students of the occult and metaphysics have been shouting these facts for years. Why should they be ignored? The mathematciians have failed-- but RADIONICS---at a distance; the mental systemsof the higher animals all point to a more complete ENTIRETY. THE ALLEN ENTIRETY is this attempt to gather this information in a simple relationship to convey a very complex multi-dimensional thought-concept.

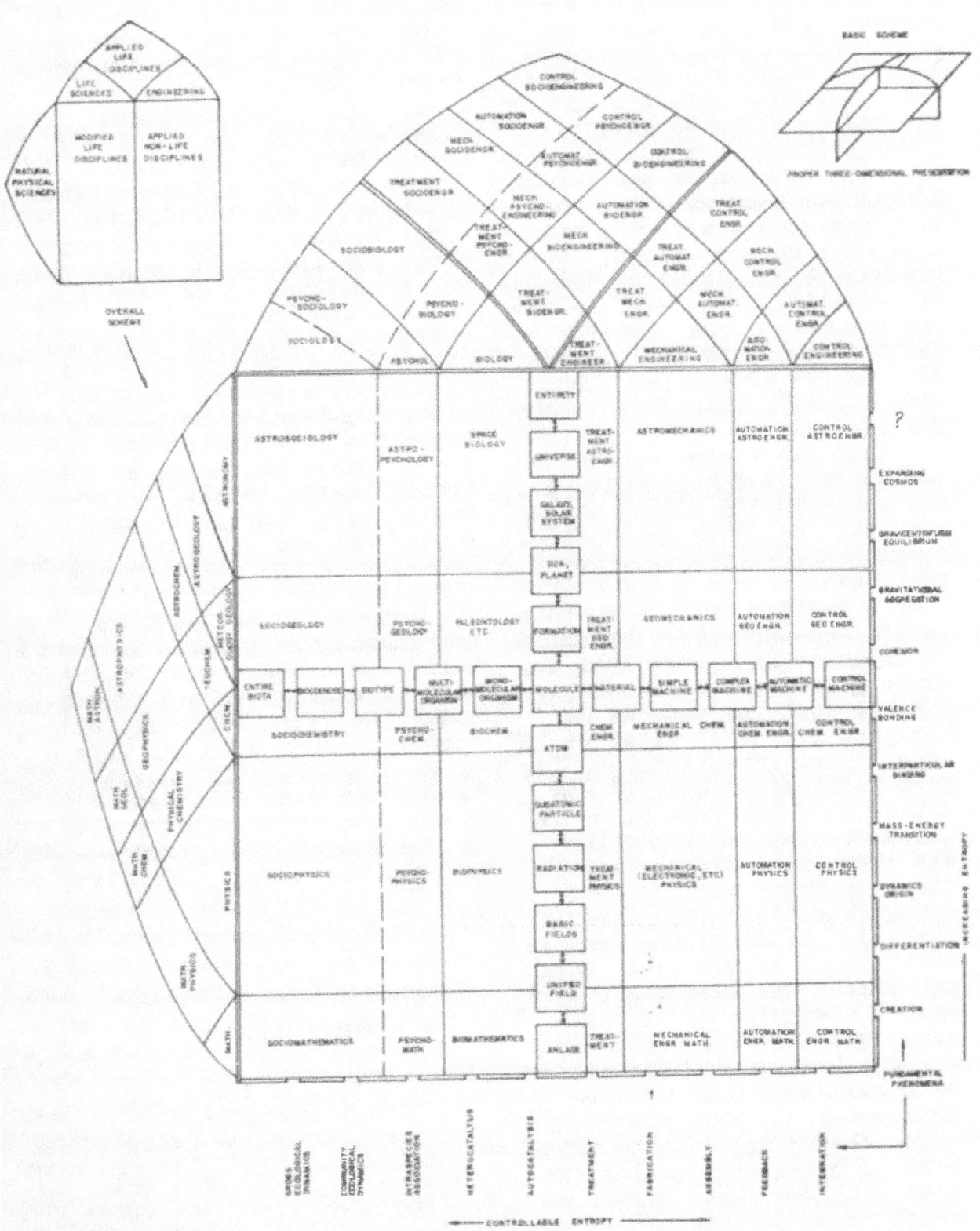

Figure 6. The Systasis

Physicist Believes Universe Probably Has Doughnut Shape

Our universe is most likely shaped like a doughnut reports Dr. Winston H. Bostic of the Steven's Inst. of Technology at Hoboken, N.J...."and quite possibly there are at least several universes rather than just the one in which we live....."

The doughnut shape could be expected because of the way hydrogen gas behaves. All the billions of stars in the universe make up only about one thousandth (or less) of the total material. The rest is the fundamental of the universe -- the hydrogen atom(gas). All of this gas is charged (ions) thru the far reaches of interstellar space.

Such gas seems to have an uncanny knack for generating its own magnetic fields and under this influence we have the doughnut or ring shape, Dr. B continues.

Dr. Bostick has proven this in his own laboratory by build in galaxies in a test tube ... these photograph and look to the eye just the same as do the photographs of galaxies in outer space taken thru our largest telescopes. Some of the shapes took the form of spiral galaxies like our own milky way when the hydrogen ions in the laboratory were exposed to a magnetic field and properly charged. Galaxies are familie of billions of stars. A dough nut shaped universe might well have a companion or twin, he said, one universe could have a right-handed spin and another opposite spin to balance this out.

One theory is that the universe is being continually created with new basic atomic material being created out of energy (radiation into the fundamental hydrogen proton) and by this process there could be several universes.

We humans are ourselves literally made of stardust, he continues, and are kind of a cosmic collectors item. The sun is much over 90% hydrogen but our bodies contain other trace minerals...but all of these minerals are of course made by various combinations of the hydrogen fundamental. (See the Kraft ETHER VORTEX explanation)

The editor believes that Dr. Bostick is as close to a really new fundamental physical conception as is any Dr. of physics in the world. The doughnut shape of the universe is also the shape of the fundamental building unit of the universe the NUTRINO. Also, Dr. Bostic, is bordering close upon the possibility of other universes at differing energy levels interlacing each other. Our poor senses are not yet able to conceive of the infinite possibilites and realities of the cosmos but at least as our human mind evolves we can build our conceptions. Dr.B's test tube galaxies are formed under the right magnetic field conditions and with the glow of an electrostatic charge. Two of the same fundamental field conditions exist right to the end of the universe-- and the beginning. See also (A NEW VISTA OF THE ENTIRETY) ....30.............

Borderland Science Research Associates

3524 Adams Avenue
San Diego, California

Meade Layne's ROUND ROBIN and CLIPS AND QUOTES tell a great deal about the possibility of other energy level situations that should not be ignored by any serios investigator.
We recommend his work very highly........ed.

De La Warr's "THOUGHT RESONATOR"
.....a clue to a new force field?

De La Warr is a graduate civil engineer but since 1942 he has with his wife, been developing the "Odic" or "life-force" field evidences mentioned by Reichenbach thru research in his laboratory at Oxford, England.

De La Warr follows a long line of those who felt that the theory of mitogenic radiation (Columbia U.) (Abrams, Dr. Ruth Drown and others) was a fundamental force field of the cosmos. The theory stated simply is that each living cell vibrates just a tiny radio transmitter---but only on one frequency at a time--but thru the whole electromagnetic spectrum. Also, the intensity of the radiation reveals the state of health of the cell!

The whole human and animal nervous system is just activated by the chemical battery of the body and the blood is the carrier of the vital chemical energy. The TWO HUNDRED QUINTILLION cells in the body are like little units of a giant battery which emit frequencies that are detectable and which indicate the strength (health) of the cell thru the intensity of its radiation. Under this principle the health of the blood then, is MOST VITAL.

In the view of De La Warr the whole cosmos is knit together by a UNIVERSAL PLEXUS OF COSMIC RAYS (force field) and all forms of material from solid rock to the rarest gas is just varying degrees of denseness of this matter. Or, as Einstein has said "something material is just "frozen matter". De La Warr first found that sonic vibrations and magnetic orientation made startling differences in the rate of growth of plants. He reasoned ("like Tesla) that in the correct magnetic field orientation and with the correct (resonant) frequency he could stimulate the life processes of plants. He then tried to transfer his theory to the more complicated animal world. Finally, of course, to the area of the human mind.

Could actual thought photographs be made? Could disease be diagnosed by tuning into the resonant frequencies emited by the radiating cells of the diseased organ? IT COULD!

By the use of a sensitive operator, a blood or spitum specimin correctly oriented in a magnetic field, resonant cavity (tuned by a series of tuning stubs) the laboratory was able to tune to a specific disease frequency. This was done by tabulating over 4,000 rates of radiations of bacteria from the pure cultures supplied the laboratory by a friendly bacteriologist.

The machine was then tested in various hospitals and the diagnosis checked and time after time the De La Warr machine came thru with the confirmed correct diagnosis.

Actual "thought resonance" was obtained and excellent photographs were made. (See foto of diseased tibial artery) This brought about the fantastic principle that to THINK of an Object is to tune to that object in the person's mind! This is the resonance that is necessary. These diagnoses were made from samples submitted from all over the world. Distance is no barrier to thought! It is not the purpose of the SPACECRAFT DIGEST to go into the science of Radionics, but rather, it is our purpose just to point out that such a science is in its amazing infancy and that we use it to provide support to our contention in the presentation of our NEW VISTA OF THE ENTIRETY of the existance of another field of force and that this is the "O" field of the cosmos. There is doubtless an "I" (intelligence) field also which operates at extremely high frequencies.

One of the buildings of the De La Warr Laboratory—Oxford, England

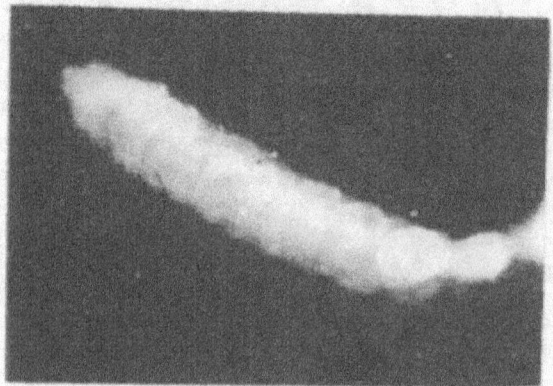

THOUGHT PHOTO from the De La Warr Laboratory at Oxford, England

GEORGE De La WARR

(above) "THOUGHT PHOTOGRAPH" of a diseased tibial artery taken in a typical diagnosis of a development of a disease thru resonance with operator's mind (plus the cavity resonator tuning) with the blood specimin of the patient. The white (intense area) is the evidence of the strong radiation of the disease bacteria radiating at their characteristic frequency. The tuning stubs of the De La Warr resonator are set for this specific frequency and then by resonance by the operator's mind to the 'thought' of the tibial artery this picture is obtained.

MIND AND MATTER is the quarterly journal which provides some of the funds for this amazing research and SPACE-CRAFT DIGEST recommends a subscription to members of the Lemurian Society. The Fee is $4.50 per year and the address is De La Warr Laboratories, Raleigh Park Road., Oxford, England.

The combination of the 'O' field and the 'I" field along with the more widely used electrostatic and electromagnetic seem to be also a necessity for the understanding of the UFO. The suspension of "gravity"...thought control..... the level (or multi levels) of the possible existance of life and the materiality of the cosmos are all important...for the UFO touches all fields of human knowledge.

Karmology - -movement thru TIME!
by W.W.Wood
Tacoma, Wash.

The secrets of the Pineal have long fascinated students and its control of mental functions is most revealing.

Great doctors of the past and even today have tried to isolate the secretion of this gland. The animal glands used were from dead animals. It follows that an extract from a source like this could not really be a true reflection of the "magic" of this action on the human mental processes. The effect of a DEAD extract on a living brain may by its very lifeless nature preclude any real stimulation of the human mind. According to Carey P. Mc Cord,M.D. the author of <u>Endocrinology and Metabolism</u> about 3200 dead sheep are needed to get about 2 oz. of the Pineal extract. Many experimenters have used a similar product and the results are contradictory. The only stable conclusion seems to be that the extract stimulates genital growth of males more than that of females.

But, it has been postulated that the brain may not be the seat of thinking but may just be a "receiver" thru which certain mental processes are initiated. The yogi's "third eye" is thought to be the pineal. It may well be then that the thinking process is conducted in the aura or ODIC force field surrounding the body. Thought is brought in thru pyramid cells located in an area just below the gray matter in the brain which are able to detect "thought" and that an essential in this process is copper and other trace element oxides. These along with the pineal secretions (not existant in dead animals) REACT TO TUNE sections of the brain in th.se pyramid cells so that under NORMAL conditioning thinking processes are limited to rational levels.

BUT--what of the known ability of human perceptions to operate on other psychic and intuative levels?

If and when the pineal gland is caused to reduce the controlling material by a condition of only slight pressure on the outside of the head at two nerve points, one directly over the olfactory bulb and the other at the central area of the "H" suture, a reaction results that causes this Pineal control to be lessened to a degree that the NORMAL LEVEL OF CONSCIOUSNESS IS BROADENED to encompass the realm of the subconscious!!! More than a hundred cases of this condition have been observed or controlled by the writer while under the tutorship of Dr. Strath-Gordon and since his death.

The procedure for this observation of the action of the Pineal in a "live" human body was brought to this country after long years of study under the training of JAYNE practioners in India. Dr. Strath Gordon graduated from one of Europe's best known medical schools (Edinburgh) before he studied for some six years in the esoteric schools of the East.

Thru this method of Pineal control, many people experienced memory from the "other" conscious realms of the mind while still in the conscious state. This is called in the East the study of KARMOSIS. The person remembers not only his present rational life,but also incidents that have been known to have happened in former lives. Languages formerly spoken are recalled. Under the practise of KARMOSIS the person lives in both the present and the "other" period. The most amazing characteristic of KARMOSIS is that the person may also go into the future and predict future events that have their pre-conditions known to the person under treatment!

The Principle of Uncertainty

(or) Is "Reality" an Illusion?

The Jan. 1958 Edition of the SCIENTIFIC AMERICAN contains an article which we should like to digest (with comment) which has profound relation to the subject of reality and the UFO.

Materialists and Metaphysicists have long debated the subject of a conception' of reality. The question of whether UFO's are 'fireballs' or saucers seemingly under intelligent control is a problem in "reality". Are these "real" or just vapor clouds with a very high electrical charge? May they just be ignored as "unreal" phenomena? The military seems to seek the latter refuge every time UFO's are sighted. It is not too important WHY such a refuge is sought be minds in responsible positions. Never-the-less such a haven is used each time they cannot explain fundamental "truths" of the universe. Yet, as these minds spend billions of dollars of tax money immediately the question is raised as to their competancy to spend this money.

Following is a digest of the problem if REALITY and the PRINCIPLE of UNCERTAINTY as seen by George Gamow:

It may seem a paradox (he says) that one of the cornerstones of modern physics is something called the PRINCIPLE OF UNCERTAINTY. The idea of indeterminancy as a RULE of science does certainly disturb many 20th century philosophers. But the uncertainty principle has proved a powerful answer so far, the most fruitful--to important questions in present day phsyics.

At the break of the 20th Century a fundamental revolution occurred in physics. (just as it has done recently in the middle of the century with the re-discovery of the UFO phenomena--ed.) Men, at that time, suddenly discovered that of the classical laws, one, (Newton's compilations) of mechanics and energy did not work very well, either for the atom or the universe. Einstein took another look at the cosmos, time, and 'motion'--while the explorers of the atom produced the quantom theory. These new ideas (in the early 1900's) we so strange that they contradicted common sense!

Just as the earlier notion that the earth was round was against common sense, because any one could plainly SEE it was FLAT!

In the atomic realm, two discoveries especially confounded common sense and common experience. One was the behavior of light. As the result of the work of Max Planc, Einstein, and others it was developed that light seemed to be made up of packets of pure energy--PHOTONS. The energy of these photons varied with the frequency (proportional to wavelength) and is equal to the frequency (v) times planc's constant (h) giving the energy contained in a "photon" of light.

Matter emitted and absorbed light only in certain definite quanta (PHOTONS) and because even dim light contained billions of photons we cannot well detect these packets of "graininess". BUT Einstein and Compton did a fine job with their contributions....."COMPTON EFFECT" was one such (the change in frequency of X-rays when they lose energy in collisions with electrons).

This was awkward, for these researchers had just illustrated that light behaved BOTH as waves and as material particles!

This was not supposed to be, for particles can be measured with a three dimentional ruler of length, width, and depth while "waves of energy" are not three dimentional in nature--not REAL by the materialist standard. The tough mental problem was to accept that here was a phenomena in the universe that behaved both in a real and unreal manner--both as a beam of radiation and as a material particle! Waves to particles to waves...

So, with continued argument and more research the distinction be-*tween waves* and partcles had all but vanished. Light waves behaved in the manner of the "real" and material...or like unreal "waves---common sense reeled.

In the good old classical physics such a paradox could not exist. It was Heisenburg and his pinciple of UNCERTAINTY who laid down the idea that FACTS ARE NEVER STABLE.

Now, we leave our paraphrase of the SCIENTIFIC AMERICAN and rpoceed with our own comments as "ye ed.".

".....it seems that when driven into a corner the materialists who are mere statisticians had to come up with some "principle" which would explain the phenomena that appeared and dis-appeared (dematerialized) into light and then back again into "real" particles. A great physicist gave a name to this bastard child, but did he solve the problem?

It is interesting to observe that the Hindus might be more correct than mistaken when they say that "REALITY, as the human senses conceive it, may in itself be ONLY AN ILLUSION!

--- ----------30----------------

UFO AUTHORS---Mc Coy ("The shall be Gathered Together) and George Hunt Williamson (Other Tongues Other Flesh) shown in Portland Oregon with Jim Ewart founder of the Portland UFO Research group tell of their visit to the lost cities of the high Andes.

Williamson and Mc Coy are currently back in this area of the plateau of the Wizzards and other 2 1/2 mile high areas. Williamson maintains that he has determined that these people must have built these cities well over 100,000 years ago. This would indicate that in the South American areas the colonists of Lemuria left a mark much older than science admits.

UFO PHOTOGRAPHS .... the scarcest and most precious items of a UFO-ologist......mail your photographs plus stories to SPACE-CRAFT DIGEST Also, we welcome your comments and contributions. Even if you might differ with the basic theories of electrical space-flight as we have developed them in this issue----we still would welcome your comments......
Mail to: SPACE-CRAFT DIGEST..po Box 768--Salem, Oregon, USA

SPACE SHIP LANDING REPORT

WAS IT SAUCER?

Fireball Seen Over Longview

2·Hurt as Plane Dips to Dodge 'Object' in Air

AMARILLO, Tex., July 23.—(AP)—Two women were injured last night when a Trans-World air liner dipped suddenly in what its pilot said was an attempt to dodge an unidentified object.

Mrs. Mary Clark, 68, of North Adams, Mass., suffered head cuts and a bruised back. The hostess, Miss Dorothy Rekow, suffered a bruised hip and back injuries.

The pilot, identified as a Captain Schamel, said he dropped the four-engined craft about 500 feet when he sighted the running lights of "an approaching object" flying a collision course.

Mystery Ship Over London

LONDON, Wednesday, Sept. 18 (AP)—An unidentified luminous object, shaped like a cigar and traveling at a high speed, was seen by north London residents early today, the Air Ministry said.

A Ministry official said callers reported the object blue-green, cigar-shaped and traveling very fast.

SPEED OF LIGHT

Professor Cyrill Stanukovich, the Russian satellite expert, said their scientists are now working on "photonic rockets which will develop super-cosmic speeds approximating the speed of light."

ASTRONOMERS SEE PINK UFO

The London *Times*, of November 7, reported that hundreds of people in Bathurst, near Sydney, Australia, saw a metallic object over the town on the previous day. Police, press and radio were deluged, the *Times* reported, with reports of a flying saucer. Two R.A.A.F. Sabre jets circled over Bathurst for an hour without seeing anything. Finally Sydney Observatory stated that it was usual for Venus to be visible during daylight at that time of the year.

However, on the same day, four astronomers at the Commonwealth Observatory at Mt. Stromlo, near Canberra, Australia, on "Sputnik watch" reported a strange object moving across the sky, which was neither a meteorite nor one of the Soviet space satellites! The object was a vivid pink and unlike anything seen before, it was stated. It remained in view for about two minutes, and disappeared under the moon.

"The strange thing is that it should disappear after passing under the moon as it was a perfectly cloudless sky," said Dr. Przybylski, who saw the object *just after having completed observations of the passage of the two Russian satellites!*

CIGAR-SHAPED OBJECT OVER JAPAN

This photograph was taken by Mr. Shinichi Takeda, of Fujisaw City, Japan, near Enoshima Miami Beach, at 11.28 a.m. on August 20, 1957. His sister saw the object first and indicated it to him. It was silvery in colour and gave off a brilliant glow. The space-ship was flying at about 4,000 ft. in a southerly direction. When it was directly overhead the cigar made a 90° left turn and increased its speed. Subsequently, 15 bathers at Enoshima Miami Beach spotted a similar object passing over them at high speed. There was no sound heard with either sighting (Photo: courtesy Mr. Yusuke Matsumura.)

SAUCER VIEWS DANISH ARMY MANOEUVRES

From: FLYING SAUCER REVIEW
plus various newspapers

Did Christ Visit India?

By B. J. Bhandari

(From *Blitz Newsmagazine*, Bombay, India—August 31, 1957 issue)

The Place of the Esoteric Schools and Groups

Most highly trained rational scientific minds of the Western world seem to have a mental block whenever other less tangible fields of perception are mentioned.

When metaphysics, occultism and for many years even hynotism were mentioned these "mentalities" would eye the ceiling and refuse to admit reality on these other mental levels.

What is the place of the little-known esoteric schools of the world in the understand of the secrets of the cosmos? Were (and is) there various schools of knowledge that the Western society builders did not wish to admit the existance of?

Without doubt, there is in this very digest, resumes of this very type of learning in our various concepts. Much of this learning has been, we are certain handed down thru these various little-known schools and groups every since the time of the mother-land of MU's existance some two hundred and fifty thousand years ago.

Many of the "discoveries" so laboriously "proven" by the expenditures today of the billions of taxpayers dollars have been available thru this type of thinking for thousands of years.

Dr. Strass-Gordon (who you will hear much more of in later issues) was a pupil in modern days of one such group so was Ouspenski and about 2,000 years ago so was Jesus Christ. Here is an interesting account of Christ that is not told about in the Christian bible.

Mr. Nicolas Notovitch in his book THE UNKNOWN LIFE OF JESUS CHRIST....has brought out certain facts that compel attention. He says that when Jesus attained the age of 13 he left his father's house, went out of Jerusalem and, in company with some merchants stayed in India visiting many important places of learning in Nepal and India.

In the course of travels in the Himalayan regions the author (1877) learned from the head of a Lamasary that there did exist some very old writings of the history of Ladakh Monastery dealing with the visits of Jesus to their group some 1850 years before. Other monastic groups also had copies of the visits of Christ and the copy at the monastery of Himis. They were in the Pali language and certain Lamas were able to make translations. The versions, Mr. Notovich explains, were written three or four years after the death of the Christ from the testimony of eye witnesses and is more likely to bear the stamp of truth than the narratives of evangelists who wrote at diverse epochs and so long a time after these real events took place.

Without preliminary details or explanation the manuscript begins by announcing that in the year of the very death of Jesus Christ a few merchants who had returned from Judea brought back the information that a just man named Issa in Israel, after having been twice aquitted by his judges, was finaly put to death by the Roman gov., Pilate who felt that Jesus would take advantage of his popularity to re-establish the kingdom of Israel.

Jesus began in India by frequenting the temples of the JAINS (or Jaynes) who were amazed at the wonderful and brilliant intellect and asked Jesus to remain with them. But he left them to settle at Puri which was a great spiritual center. Puri then had a great Sanskrit library. Jesus spent some six years there and at Rajgir, Benaries and other holy cities. He delved deeply into medicine, mathematics philosophy and religion.....
Jesus found much to condemn in the Brahman laws and customs and even entered into public debates with them. Among the things that Jesus much condemned was the humiliation of the laborer (caste) and Jesus preached to the Shudras reminding them that God was One according to their own laws, that all exists thru Him, that all are equal in HIS sight and that the Brahmins had obscured the great principle of monotheism in perverting the words of Brahma Himself and insisting to excess on the exterior cerimonies of the religion.

Seeing that the people were beginning to embrace the doctrines of Jesus Christ whom they had hoped to gain on their sideand who was now their adversary the Brahmins resolved to assassinate him. But being warned in time by his devoted servanthe left Puri and took refuge in the mts. of Nepal.

There he spent six years among the Buddists where be found the principle of monothism in its purity. He then mastered the sacred writings of the Sutras. After being in India some 16 years Jesus bethought himself of his native country. At this time he sent the following letter to his mother:

Beloved mother: Be not grieved, for all is well for father as with you. He has completed his present work here on earth, and has done so nobly. None in any walk of life can charge him with deceit, dishonesty, nor wrong intention.

In his period of life here he has completed many great tasks and is gone from our midst truly prepared to solve the problems that await him the future. Our God, the Father of all of us, is with him now as He was with him heretofore; but even now the Heavenly Hosts guard his footsteps and protect him on his way.

Therefore, why should you weep and suffer? Tears will not conquer your grief and your sorrow cannot be vanquished by any emotion of your heart or mind. Let your soul be busy in meditation and contact with him who is gone, and if thou art not idle, there will be no time for grief.

When grief throbs through the heart, and anguish causes you pain, permit yourself to rise to higher planes and indulge in the ministry of love. Your ministry has always been that of love, and in the Brotherhood thou canst find many opportunities to answer the call of the world for more love.

Therefore, let the past remain the past. Rise above the cares of earthly things and give your life to those who still live with us here on earth. When your life is done, you will find it again in the morning sun, or even in the evening dew, as in the song of birds, the perfume of flowers, and the mystic lights of the stars at night.

For it will not be long before your problems and toils here on earth will be solved also, and when all is counted and arranged, you will be ready for greater fields of effort and prepared to solve the greater problems of the soul.

Try, then, to be content until I come to you soon and bring to you richer gifts than any that you have ever seen, and greater than ele made of gold or precious stones. I am sure that my brothers will care for you and supply your needs, and I am always with you in mind and spirit. Your son, Joseph.

Strong Case for Investigation

The editor of the SPACE - CRAFT DIGEST believes that all cases of the "cosmic mind" should be investigated in the light of the possible existance of a universal "I" field existing as a fund amental force of the cosmos. The narrow tree limb of the learning of the Western peoples is not adequate to explain the wonders of the Universe. The dogmatists in science and religion have for ages concealed this know ledge to keep their little domains which they consider-threatened just as did Pilate and those who drove Jesus from their midst. The different church grmups seem to have done their share in the prostitution of learning.

Man - - - On His Blindness

The inability of the senses of man to detect the many actualities of the cosmos is most confusing. For how can man make instruments to extend his senses unless he is aware of what he wants his instruments to detect?

If one were to have operated a radio transmitter a hundred years ago ... no scientist of that period could have built a receiving set because he did not know that an instrument could be made to detect messages from the "air".

TODAY ... we are in the same position when we talk about the higher energy levels of the universie. Man is still "blind".

THE EYE ... detects just a very narrow sliver of the "so called" electromagnetic spectrum. The red, orange, yellow, green, blue, indigo and violet. Let us imagine that the ability of the eye to detect the light spectrum were to be narrowed to just the red portion of the spectrum. His would then be only a RED universe in the daytime and an even blacker night. An even more narrow slit of the actuality of the spectrum... the light spectrum being just a small slit of the whole electromagnetic, of course.

THIS ILLUSTRATES how close to being blind man now is, even though on a bright sunny day he thinks he sees ALL of the magnificence of creation.

FIELDS beyond the electromagnetic exist. Man at the moment gropes for these great fields of force which are fundamental in the universe.

These are the fields of the many-leveled mind !

The ancients of Lemuria had an "eye" called the Third-Eye which could detect this field of the cosmos. Since the time of the catastrophe that destroyed the motherland of MU, man has lost his "third eye", just as he would have lost the sight of his "light" eyes if he had not used them through the hundreds of generations since MU.

THE MIND EYE (the pineal) is more developed in some parts of the world's inhabitants than it is in the "blind" Western Man.

WE WHO cannot understand this must nevertheless not deride those who have the ability which we lack. For just as our eyes detect the electromagnetic field of force, so the mind's "eye" operates in the area of another great force field of the cosmos where today we are only groping at the edges.

There have been men who have conversed with Lemurians and left notes of their conversations. They have moved thru the "curtain" by means of the MIND'S EYE which can penetrate to intercept the radiations of this higher level of universal radiation -- -- The UNIVERSAL MIND. These writings shall be made available to members of the PACIFIC LEMURIAN SOCIETY as they become ready for publication.

BUT, today, the great frontier seems to be the area of the understanding of the many-leveled mind. This is the frontier that Lemurians had solved nearly two hundred thousand years ago. Strangely enough, they also had solved the problem of pure electrical space flight using the natural forces of the cosmos.. using their own multi-leveled minds.

Emerald Tablets of Hermes Trismegistius

have left us " AS ABOVE-- SO BELOW".... the simple four-word formula that is the "Secret of the UFO"... all of the laws of the cosmos can be found in an atom (and its formation and behavior) or in any other phenomena that exists as some thing created or completed according to certain natural laws. These are the fundamental laws of the universe and the metaphysical laws of triads and octaves penetrate everything.

It is certainly amazing to find one of the fundamental esoteric laws explaining the way that one can better understand the UFO---or is it?

Study the space-vortex atom and you'll find that a vortex coneption answers the reality of the atom. It follows that a ZETA-type atom-plasma accelerator (with modifications) works particles into heat pulses in pure wave form (this is pure energy form) and is accomplished due to the constriction effect of a great magnetic field concentration. The acceleration is done by tremendous voltage differentials. TWO Zeta machines can result in an ETHER or SPACE-PUMP to give a required gravity differential. Then, the power problem is licked by the use of resonance and we have the UFO-type space vehicle that can travel at unlimited speeds. For the faster it travels it begins to resemble the pure energy of space itself (electrically) As the UNITY of the space fields and electricity is now beginning to be understood it follows that free converson of the "frozen matter" of the material into pure radiation energy becomes the "secret" of space travel.

BUT--in the so-called plasma concept which has been contracted to ROCKET*DYN the expelled plasma is going to be used as a THRUST FUEL reaction practical rocket.

Again we must emphasize that reaction motors are crude. The SPACE VORTEX THEORY forces upon us the ETHER PUMP concept which provides a gravity shield that reaction vehicles never will provide. As man is subject to gravity he will not become a successful space animal.

MAN, to travel in space, must therefore be an integral electrical part of his machine No reaction-type craft can accomplish this for he will always be the "load".

To make the space-craft a complete planetoid is the objective. To do this it must be _independent_ or shielded from the force fields of the objects in the cosmos. Upon landing man must then adjust electrically to his destination.

----------30--------

DR. I.M.LEVITT director of the Fels Planetarium mentions how valuable a space-platform with an astrophysical setup would be. He says such an observatory could learn more in one week than all of the observations made thru the atmosphere of the earth to date. He emphasizes that a new distribution pattern of the white dwarf stars (incredibly dense some millions of times as heavy per cubic inch as lead) might show them to be much more numerous than hitherto suspected. This would make the universe much more material than hither-to postulated.

Dr. Levitt indicates that slowly but surely the dogmatists are taking a licking and we are having to revise our theories of the cosmos almost by the day. When we get rid of the dogmatic in our Universities we will be on the track to reality much faster for then the new minds will not be so cluttered with claptrap needed to get as degree as they are today.

"... the roads of the Incas were the most useful and stupendous works ever executed by man."
— ALEXANDER VON HUMBOLDT

HIGHWAY OF THE SUN

By Victor von Hagen
(Little-Brown) publishers

The amazing story of the re-discovery of the centuries old road system which extended throughout the fabulous Inca empire for 10,000 miles!

These descendents of the LEMURIANS built this fabulous system from sea level to 15,000 feet. Suspension bridges that rival any of the world today. Only a trace of this fantastic civilization remains today....whathappenedto this knowledge?

George Hunt Williamson author of OTHER TONGUES-OTHER FLESH told the editor of the SPACE-CRAFT DIGEST that in the Fall of 1958 he is to return from some of the areas of these ancient cities with some of the answers to this fascinating riddle. He has traversed the plateau of the wizards on which there are carved in granit figures of giant animals such as elephants, cougars and camels which can ONLY BE SEEN FROM THE AIR! What people did this? There are no camels and elephants in So. America! The chambers of rejuvenation of these ancients show that the angle of the early mornings sun's rays seem to be the secret of health and long life.

BELOW.... is a "compass rose" showing true North and which only can be seen from the air. It also carries the message of the "tree of life". These "secrets" of a people that lived up to a HUNDRED THOUSAND years ago give us a new conception of the time-table of man in this hemisphere. Man has been on this planet much longer than our school system admits. These "fables" that have been Taught as truths have done our understanding of the path of man on the planet great harm. SPACE-CRAFT DIGEST and the PACIFIC LEMURIAN SOCIETY feels that when we know the real story of these peoples that built monuments and indicators to be seen by their own space-craft perhaps as long as a 1,000,000 years ago we will know more about the real story of man. these explorers have now found indications that these ancients may have been on the earth as intelligent inhabitants for much longer than just one to two hundred thousand years. WHAT HAPPENED? WE are not immune from that type of catastrophe. We must have the answer if weare to be ready for any contingency.

The Tres Cruces or Tree of Life at Paracas. Its direction is true north-south.

Finale ------20 March 1958

The year 1960 sees the approximate completion of a basic 7,000 year cosmic cycle. Whether one is a student of the esoteric or whether he is a hard-headed business tycoon who is a member of the FOUNDATION FOR THE STUDY OF CYCLES it is apparent that the early 1960's are a very critical period.

The cyclists state that in their study of wars for the last 2550 years that the early portion of the next decade is to be a time of extreme crisis.

The occultists have some of the following predictions from the publication PSYCHIC OBSERVER:

The master teacher Agasha is quoted:

1965 is painted as the target date for the start of the "Golden Age of Peace". The "other world" is definitely going to be brought nearer and its exploration will be further stimulated more completely by "strange things" observed in the skys....more lights, mysterious objects, and material falling from space.

TOKYO.....Japanese scientists are now studying a metal object that "appeared" from outer space it is reliably reported by INS (March 13, 1958)

Agasha says further...." one great discovery, already suspected if not actually postulated by atomic physicists in the forefront of atomic research will be the 'ghost' of the atom...what Agasha calls the "anim" or the etheric counterpart of the atom! It is to the physical atom what the Astral body is to the physical body.

FATE MAGAZINE in its April issue has the following UFO reports:

LOUISIANA...near Natchitoches Hestel Rayford, 32, employee of the Rothchild Tank and Boiler Works of Shreveport .."came over the hill and saw this object shaped like a football about 15 feet long and 10 feet high in the middle of the road. I drove to within 100 feet of it and it emitted sharp bright rays of light. I felt the car get hot and immediately stopped. The car kept getting hotter and I got out and took cover in a ditch. In a matter of seconds the car burst into flames. The light rays came from the top of the object. It then made a sound like a deisel and roared away." He went on to say IT LEFT A PECULIAR SMELL IN THE AREA and that he was within 15 feet of the object at one time and that it was army green in color. IN MEXICO...... near Tampico technicians Camarillo and Silva of Radio-Atlas saw a UFO 20 feet in diameter which " PASSED THRU ALL HUES UNTIL IT BECAME INTENSE WHITISH BLUE AND THEN DISAPPEARED!!!!

COMMENT...... these reports seem to the editor to be very important. The "Heat Ray" of the UFO indicates that such a thing actually exists. The moving thru the hues of the visible spectrum and then "disappearing" indicates that radiation propulsion is being used. The importance of this type of concept of the reality of the ufo cannot be over emphasized.

Two UFO's Over San Francisco

LEMURIA

The Lost Continent of the Pacific

The PACIFIC LEMURIAN SOCIETY is dedicated to the accumulation and preservation of the lost knowledge of the "Motherland of MU" from which descended our planet's present inhabitants through the rocky road from ancient Lemurian civilization, through flood and cataclysm, low savagery and finally to today's gadget-packed civilization living from the brink of one war to the brink of the next. For a hundred thousand years no Lemurian fought in a conflict of nations.

If we analyze what we have today as representing our advancement in civilization, we will find that we have gained nothing that the ancients did not have, and that they enjoyed immensely long lives and a natural happiness that is beyond our dreams of today. The Lemurians devoted themselves earnestly to the establishment of communities in distant lands and to the education and advancement of the peoples of these colonies. The Eastern Boundary of this ancient continent was the present West Coast of the United States.

The Lemurians have left their traces in Washington, Alaska, Oregon (see below), Mt. Shasta, Santa Barbara and Baja California, as well as in the ancient buildings in Peru and Yucatan. The Lemurians colonized China and India and inspired the great Pyramid of Egypt. This knowledge of the ancients is still with us today. We shall search it out and publish it for all members.

KLAMATH FALLS, OREGON, LEMURIAN WRITING

A MEMBERSHIP APPLICATION

Name _____

Address _____

_____

I am enclosing five dollars (2 £ in sterling areas) for a yearly subscription to **SPACE CRAFT DIGEST** published by the PACIFIC LEMURIAN SOCIETY which will also enable me to be included in the future releases of this society for a period of six months.

Mail to: **PACIFIC LEMURIAN SOCIETY**
P.O. Box 768
Salem, Oregon, U.S.A.

ENROLL A FRIEND

SPACE CRAFT Digest

SUMMER ISSUE 1958

Theories of Electrical Flight

published by the PACIFIC LEMURIAN SOCIETY

W. Gordon Allen in the Pacific Ocean areas where the thin wisp of the legend of the LEMURIANS still hovers today.

In his compilation of the background of the items that appear in the DIGEST he calls upon his background in electrical engineering and the reports of the UFO sightings from all parts of the world which come to his radio stations on the 24-hour news services. The tips are checked and brought into focus in time for each issue. Another actual source of a lot of material is through his hobby of the study of history. The UFO has appeared in all recorded history. At the present time he is checking the reports of the Cortes Mexican conquest to digest them for the DIGEST. Cortes took a UFO sighting as a "sign" that his conquest had divine sanction. Montezuma took the same sign as a meaning that Quetzacotl, the god from the sky, had at last returned to the area. It was a sign, but it was a sign of space-traffic even in those times. Cortes even found bones of GIANTS in Mexico!

DITORIAL

Three distinguished civilian scientists have warned Congress against letting the armed services dominate space research or spend vast sums for such "useless projects" as a weapons base on the moon. The warnings came from Drs. C. C. Furnas, chancellor of the U. of Buffalo; Lee A. Dubridge, president of Cal Tech; and W. H. Pickering, director of the Jet Lab. They testified before the House Outer Space Committee. Contrast this with the testimony of a general that appears elsewhere in the DIGEST. The three scoffed at the Pentagon's claims that the moon or planets would provide military bases for the future.

"Some people," Dr. Dubridge said, "seem to feel that the term 'conquest' means military conquest . . ." He derided that concept.

The whole testimony of these competent men stated that the military should not be allowed to waste vast sums of money and that the space program should be on a "continuing" basis.

Now from all kinds of sources the DIGEST points to more and more knowledge developing the thought that man's knowledge of the universe calls for a great amount of revision and new concepts which cannot be ignored.

PURE ELECTRICAL FLIGHT seems the only real space-travel possibility. And secondly, it appears that the space program must be taken from the hands of the military before they bankrupt the country. Our battles of the future may well be of a propaganda and psychological nature and the military under the present methods cannot deal with these concepts. Their inept handling of the public that sights UFO's is an example. The use of "SECRET" to cover their boondoggles is another. We feel they must be stopped and that the civilian control should step in and make them behave.

They are no longer playing with childish popguns but with a large percentage of the national budget of the largest nation on the planet. IT WAS THE MILITARY DECISION to drop the atom bomb on the Japanese that was a propaganda mistake that shall live in infamy even longer than the attack on Pearl Harbor. The military cannot be forever permitted to operate in the zone of irresponsibility as they have in the past . . . NOW is the time to make them behave and the removal of the space program from their bungling hands is a "must" in the opinion of the SPACE-CRAFT DIGEST! Write your congressman NOW!

Birmingham Woman Meets Spacemen

digested from British FLYING SAUCER REVIEW

The time of the appearence of an extra-terrestial was about three in the afternoon on the 18th of Nov. 1957. And here is the account of Mrs. Cynthis Appleton of Fentham Rd. Aston, Birmingham, England:

Suddenly, there appeared the figure of a man standing on her left by the fireplace. She said he appeared "just like a TV picture on a screen, a very blurred image and then suddenly everything is clear". She was, of course, very frightened. At the same time she was conscious that he was trying to calm her by some influence which he exerted upon her mind. She then felt calm and collected.

Mrs. Appleton noted too, that at the moment of his appearance a "whistle" exactly like that of the old wireless sets used to make when tuning a station. The man was tall and fair. He was wearing a tight fitting garment in a color like a silvery plastic mackintosh. The sleeves reached to his wrist. The collar part of his garment rose up like an "Elizabethan" collar. The man's lips were moving as if in speech, but she heard no audible words. He seemed to be able to read her mind and altho she used no speech her questions were read and answered mentally. On the floor there was some newspaper and the man was standing on this. After he left she noticed that it appeared to be scorched.

WHERE DO YOU COME FROM?
" another world--<u>he did not say which one</u>"---like yours it is governed by the sun ("a" sun?..ed?) We have to visit your world to obtain something of which we are running short. It is at the bottom of the sea".

(later the English lady in conversation with her husband who was a metal worker determined that he might well have met titanium)

LATER COMMENTS by the extra-terrestial: "..... you are concentrating on the wrong power. You are trying to go UP.......we go like this: (he made a lateral movement with his hands.) At this time there appeared between his outstretched fingers what she could only discribe as a TV screen. On the screen she could see clearly a space ship. It was circular with a half top like a transparent dome. Within this space ship she could see several observers looking at her. The visitor said that this ship was the "MASTER CRAFT". There were two of these on the screen and several smaller circular craft were attached to the underside of the "master craft". The visitor went on to say that they never fought but lived in peace and harmony. He also told her that they would return to her in January. Suddenly he "was not there any more".

TUESDAY JAN. 7 1958..... The evening before she had a complete blackout. The next day at 2:15 she again became aware of the "whistle" and suddenly there appeared TWO figures this second time. They appeared exactly as before---a blurred image and then everything came into sharp focus. They were both tall and slim and over six feet in heighth. The hair of one was cut similar to what we call "page boy" and the second had a "ballerina" cut. On this occasion they both addressed her not by telepathy as before, but in ENGLISH! They told her that her blackout of the previous evening was due to their preparing to make contact with her again. This time she was told that they came from Ghanas Vahn on VENUS! She was told that she was one of the few that were able to receive such communications thru her brain. She was told that to touch them would be dangerous to her bodily health. What she was seeing, he said, was a projection of himself and his companion. She asked why they did not seek wider contact with the human race. She was told that such an immediate action would produce panic. Who could provide an explanation of what would happen in a world so divided as ours? She asked if it were possible for her husband to see them. She was told that his brain was not capable to receive such a transmission. He then said:

The BEARERS OF THE HAMMER AND SICKLE WERE ON THE POINT OF PERFECTING A RAY GUN..... this could disintegrate matter. He told her that in the near future there would be much bloodshed and suffering. He said she would be paid no further visits because of the effect on her health. There was a smell left after the men left like the smell of an electrical dicharge.

-------------30-----------------

COMMENT BY EDITOR---- it is the feeling of the editor that this contact must be taken at face value for we cannot take the risk of overlooking the amazing information given to the woman.

FIRST....his discription of the correct method of overcoming the space-travel problem is that of pure electrical flight which is the feeling of the editorial policy of THE SPACE CRAFT DIGEST. A BLAST UP with a tank car full of fuel is childish. The method of communication is that of the advanced studentof YOGI or the account given of the method of the Lemurians according to those who have spoken with them while in their astral travels....be they yogi--or Swedenborg.

SECONDLY.....the RAY GUN....sounds like ultra-sonic disintegration, does it not? we know that "sound bullets" can kill at thousands of yards and that a thin beam can slice an extremely hard quartz crystal. Why would an ultra-sonic disintegrater be out of the realm of possible for the USSR to develop?

THIRDLY.....the FOUNDATION FOR THE STUDY OF CYLCES .... which has charted every major war for some 2575 years (frequency of small battles over the planet) states that the early 1960's will be a very very critical period. TRUTHFULLY', their figures almost P R O M I S E a world war by that time! Thisis for those that must be hard headed and have no truck with the occultists. The fact that the occultists are extremely alarmed we will not go into at this time.

FOURTHLY: This whole thing is not so particularily fantstic from a scientific stand point, either. All we have to do is admit that a group more advanced than we are could well have mastered the method of a projection of their electrical entitities. Whether one recreates an image on a TV master mosaic or in a person's brain which receives images by various methods is not too far beyond even our present comprehension. AT LEAST....that could be one method, however, it seems to be a little more material than that because the images must have been highly charged "realites" because of the fact they left some scorched newspapers on which they had stood.

We pretty much believe this "contact" because some of the same characteristics of highly developed "M E N" appear elsewhere in very scholarly accounts of Tibetan adepts as well as those of Swedenborg, Brahma etc. From the standpoint of even our Western Scientific knowledge of today an open mind must admit of such possibilities. Certainly it must admit that our study of matter's fundamentals is not at this time giving us many of the answers. Mrs. Appleton did not have any of this knowledge as she said that she had not been previously interested in flying saucers nor had she read any literature on the subject. Under clever questioning it is very doubtful if this housewi'e could have fenced successfully with any well educated indivdual well enough to dupe. It is so straightforeward that we must in every way state that we feel that the story is one of the best of the late year accounts of a meeting with a Venusian........Ed.

Fiery Sky Object Seen Across NW

By THE ASSOCIATED PRESS

A greenish-blue object showering a trail of sparks streaked across Pacific Northwest skies Tuesday night. Radio and police switchboards were swamped with telephone calls.

First report came from Everett, Wash., at 9:07 p.m. and one Everett man, Dennis Lundberg, reported it was bright enough to light up the roof of his home.

Another report, two minutes later, came from Aberdeen, Wash., and witnesses said it was traveling south to north. It also was sighted at nearby Hoquiam and Westport.

The object also was seen at Rainier, Ore., where Ira Mitchell said it moved across the sky from east to west.

Officers at Paine Air Force Base near Everett said the object was not sighted there and declined further comment.

The object was sighted at Albany by Mr. and Mrs. Fred Potter, at about the same time it was seen at Everett. The Potters said it looked to them as about one-quarter the size of the moon.

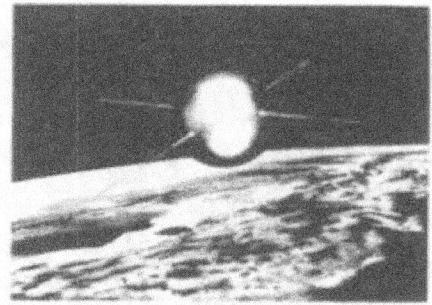

"SPUTNIK I," world's first artificial satellite, was rocket-propelled into outer space by the Russians in Oct., 1957. Epoch-making "moon" travelled 18,000 mph, circled earth every 96 minutes.

25 April 1958 BOMARK fails at "CAPE" LAUNCHING

WELL!!!!!.....the airforce disposed of that one real fast, did they not? from the Salem,Oregon, CAPITOL JOURNAL 21 April'58.

From SAUCERS.......The logging crew (in Oregon near Coos Bay in August 1957) told that a gigantic spinning object had hovered 30' above one of their spar trees for about 15 minutes. The top half spun one way and the bottom half another and around the middle was a row of portholes out of which came flames. The crew of 8 men sat down on logs so they could see the UFO some 150 feet from them..............On this report we hear from the Oregon Forest Service that it is very true, but the "spinning" we do not reconcile as we doubt if UFO's are in any way mechanical. Perhaps the highly charged body of the UFO was spinning vapor which gave it an appearance of a solid body spinning. This is certainly a very fine siting by some very hard-headed (and hard muscled) fellows, is it not?

VERTICAL LAUNCHING makes the Boeing IM-99 *Bomark* a more effective interceptor. After the boost rocket burns out, missile is propelled by two ram-jet engines mounted on its explosive body.

GREEN BALL OVER SCOTLAND

Two men driving back to Easdale, near Oban, Scotland, early on the morning of January 9, saw a large fiery ball appear in the sky.

Mr. Jack Campbell, who was with a farmer, Mr. William Ferguson, said: "We had almost completed the run to Easdale at 1 a.m. when we noticed the headlights of the car I was driving had changed to a greenish colour. On looking round we saw the green light, which seemed to reflect over the whole district.

"It was then that we noticed the ball of fire resembling a moon high above us. It was travelling over the sea in an easterly direction, sending sparks flying all round in the heavens."

Our "truthfull" Airforces who couldn't "see" a UFO that many taxpaying civilians saw has told the public for years that the BO-Mark was operational.....Is it reliable? "SECRET" is used many times to cover expensive miliatry boondoggles. Is this another case? The public should have truthful, candid answers.

British Can't Handle Rock As Druids Did

SALISBURY, England — A colossal engineering feat pulled off by ancient Britons 3,800 years ago gave British government engineers a headache Friday.

With a powerful derrick, they have been trying for two days to put back into place one of the giant stones of Stonehenge—a job done originally without benefit of modern gadgets.

This 24-ton piece of roc is part of the famous Stonehenge monument, a 320-foot ring of giant stones used for magic rites by the ancient Druids. The stone fell out of place in 1900.

The British recently decided to put it back up and on the basis of modern engineering plans, it was supposed to be done last Wednesday.

"Getting an absolutely level platform is proving difficult," said a harassed official on the job. "The weight of the stone and the crane and equipment immediately makes everything unlevel as soon as it's put on the ground."

Reds Develop Scope

MOSCOW — The newspaper Evening Moscow says the Soviet Union is developing radio telescopes which will enable scientists to see 10 times farther into outer space than at present.

14 SCOTS HAVE BRUSH WITH UFO

A Scottish National Sunday newspaper, the *Sunday Mail*, devoted the whole of its front page on November 10 to an account of how fourteen Edinburgh people saw a green-glowing flying saucer humming along less than 60 ft. behind the lorry taking them home from work on Friday night, November 8. The 14 "tattie-howkers" or potato pickers, were singing and joking in the back of the vehicle when the object swept in from over the North Sea. FLYING SAUCER REVIEW's special investigator in the area, Mr. John M. Spark, interviewed Mrs. Mary Horne, of 20 Hay Road, Edinburgh, one of the passengers in the lorry.

"I swear on the bible it was no balloon," she said. "It swooped down and kept behind us until it suddenly stopped. It then flew away leaving two vapour trails."

An Air Ministry official in London told the Press, "whatever it was, it was not a plane or a met. balloon. We have tried hard to get an explanation for this strange business, but so far we have been unsuccessful. It is quite baffling...."

Edinburgh police have been treating the sighting very seriously, and have interviewed all the potato pickers.

FROM THE NICAP

LIFE ON MOON POSSIBILITY CANCELS H-BOMBING PLAN

NICAP's public warning against bombing the moon, a warning seconded by several space travel planners, is believed to have influenced White House advisers in banning an H-bomb shot.

NICAP stressed in the October issue of UFO INVESTIGATOR the possible dangers of a bomb hit — if the moon were occupied.

On March 27 the President's Scientific Advisory Committee made a cautious reference to this in their official "Introduction to Outer Space." The paragraph follows:

"While the moon is believed to be devoid of life, even the simplest and most primitive, this cannot be taken for granted. Some scientists have suggested that small particles with the properties of life—germs or spores—could exist in space and have drifted on to the moon. If we are to test this intriguing hypothesis, we must be careful not to contaminate the moon's surface, in the biological sense, beforehand."

In another possible hint at a moon base, the President's Committee stated:

"Photographs of the back or hidden side of the moon may prove quite unexciting, or they may reveal some spectacular feature now unguessed."

Behind the announced "lunar probes," not to include bombing, is a serious official concern. Defense Department references to the "hidden side of the moon" are rapidly increasing. On March 19 Dr. James B. Edson, Army's Assistant research and development director, stated the future danger of "an opponent whose main base may be shielded on the back side of the moon."

Though he probably meant the Soviet, other officials have shown intense interest in present moon conditions. One was Maj. Gen. Donald N. Yates, C. O., Missile Test Center, Cape Canaveral in Florida. Discussing camera-equipped rockets for moon "probes", General Yates stated that such a rocket could collect "good information" if it passed within 1000 miles of the lunar sphere. Several

SCIENTIST SAYS SHIPS IN SPACE

Dr. H. Faust, a research meteorologist, of Frankfurt, Germany, said on October 27, in an address to the Society for Space Research, that the Russian satellite was not unique, because it could be taken for granted that space ships built by intelligent creatures were cruising peacefully through space.

He said that it could be accepted that a trillion earthlike planets were populated by living creatures, of which a billion at present supported intelligent beings.

ROCKET ENGINEERS SIGHT UFOs

Four veteran engineers of a well known rocket company recently signed and sent to NICAP one of the most convincing UFO reports on record.

In mid-afternoon in a fairly clear sky a large flying object—shaped like a thick cigar—was sighted at approximately 10,000 feet, accompanied by two smaller disc shaped objects flying precise formation. The cigar shaped UFO—at least as large as a four engined airliner—shone like stainless steel, as did the smaller objects. Flying a southwest course the UFOs swiftly climbed to an estimated 30,000 feet. The speed, by concensus of opinion, was at least 5000 mph. There was no sound nor exhaust.

One engineer, a former skeptic, states: "I am now firmly convinced. What are these UFOs and where do they come from?"

—Sources verified by NICAP are now confidential; names may be given later.

--------30----------

rockets will be sent, he added, to get pictures of "what is on the moon."

Pictures of what? Lunar craters? The moon's terrain?

In general, these are well known. Only one vital question remains unanswered:

Do living creatures occupy the moon—perhaps on the hidden side?

If White House and Defense officials now suspect this is true, it would explain the canceled H-bomb shot and the sudden drive for careful "probes".

Convincing UFO evidence—much of it kept secret—may have led to the lunar probe policy. The first camera rocket may bring us the answer, perhaps in months.

Tell your friends about

FLYING SAUCER REVIEW

1 DOUGHTY STREET, LONDON

REPEAL OF THE LAW OF CONSERVATION OF ENERGY?

> Those who hold to the letter of Newtonian science will be hard-pressed to explain this statement by Dr. Ruark.

Dr. Ruark told newsmen at a weekend conference of the American Physical society in Washington D.C. the first part of May that the AEC is proceeding mainly with four different laboratory approaches to producing thermo-nuclear reactions----the fusing together of heavy hydrogen atoms by heating themto extemely high temperatures. (Remember the two different approaches to the atom bomb that the US used in the second World War?....ed.) The Sherwood project as it is called, is GEARED TO GET EVENTUALLY MORE ENERGY THAN IS PUT INTO THE FUSION DEVICE!

In january the commission described only one of the research title roles it was following in this field. This is the so-called "pinch effect" process involving the use of electro-magnetic currents to confine heavy hydrogen gas in a narrow line, thus heating it and also keeping it away from the wals of the container.

Scientists at A.E.C. laboratories handling three other approaches said research work on them thus far hasn't resulted in producing fusion re-action. They explained the complex concepts involved in these mthods but withheld experimental details.

Research results on these and other aspects of the Sherwood Project will be disclosed in papers to be presented at the second international conference on the peaceful uses of atomic energy to be held in Geneva in September.

Major progress in one of the approaches ....which uses a device called a -----
S.TELLARATOR (star maker ?) is expected to be made in a few years when the A.S.C.'s laboratory at Princeton Univeristy starts starts operation of a new unit that, it is hoped, will heat hydrogen gas up to 100 million degrees. The big Model "C" Stellerator is scheduled for operation in 1960.

In the Stellerator, the hydrogen gas (hydrogen is used because that is the most simple fundamental atom) is first heated to around a million degrees, then a "magnetic pumping" process is used to "pinch pump" it to even higher temperature. Scientists describe these two other laboratory approaches to fusion as : FIRST, a "magnetic mirror" from which extremely hot gas bounces back and forth without touching the walls of the container; the SECOND injects high energy hydrogen ions into a steady magnetic field.

The US this Summer will disclose "substantial" new laboratory progress toward converting H-Bomb energy to peacetime power, according to Dr. Ruark. New research achievements to be revealed, he goes on to say, will go considerably beyond the laboratory feats announced jointly by the US and Great Britain last January. That announcement said each nation apparently had succeeded in producing thermo-nuclear reactions in laboratory devices that were heated up to 6 million degrees centigrade. (Surface of the sun about 6,000 degrees Centigrade....ed.)

It is very interesting to conjecture on the basis of this information that in this research work with molecules pinched, pressured, and prodded far above their ability to remain matter as we know it that there is hope, according to Dr. Ruark, of tapping the fundamental electrical energy of thecosmos.

OUR MILITARY BUNGLES ON-----

> Elsewhere in our editorial we have pointed out that the space program should be taken from the hands of the military. These two United Press news stories are ample reason to give us a case in point.

HERE'S WHAT THE GENERALS TELL THE HOUSE------

(from UP) John Hagen, chief of the Vanguard satellite project told congressmen that the U.S. could launch a manned satellite within two or three years if it started an all-out program.

Hagen also said that such a crash program would permit launching of a half ton satellite in "another year or two".

During his testimony before the house space committee Hagen also said that putting too many satellites in the sky could jeopardize peace. He said a satellite could be mistaken for an enemy missile.
****

Brig. Gen H.A. Boushay said the US could put a man on the moon in 8 years.
****

Scientist Krafft Ehricke said a missle already under development could be converted into a manned space station in 5 years.
****

NOW THAT'S WHAT THE PEOPLE WHO SPEND OUR MONEY SAID. They love "crash" programs because they can waste tremendous amounts of tax payers dollars and then if they fail they can have a handy excuse by saying "what else can you expect" it was a 'crash' program, wasn't it?

****

NOW HERE'S A PRETTY COMPETENT FELLOW WHO HAS ANOTHER STORY.......
This is from UP too,

Dr. James van Allen who designed the cosmic ray instruments for the Explorer revealed that MAN MAY RUN INTO SOME DEADLY RADIATION if he goes more than 1,000 miles into space. Van Allen said the rays are 100 times more than expected. He reported the radiation intense enough to "overwhelm cosmic ray counters." Van Allen said this could mean that it would not be safe for man to remain more than one-thousand miles out in space for more than five hours unless he could be shielded with lead or other materials which would block the deadly radiations. This would of course be impossible in rocket ships already over-loaded with fuel.
****

The military doesn't care as long as they get CRASH PROGRAMS at deadly cost to our tax-paying economy. They get up in front of congressmen and scream about "national defense" and point the finger of treason at anyone who would criticize them. BUT-- it would certainly be the end of our freedom as we know it if we continue to give a blank check to our bungling military. THE SPACE PROGRAM'S problem can never be solved in the haste of a "crash" program, but can only be mastered thru long years, and careful planning, and a re-shuffle of our whole scientific fund of knowledge as we know it today. No "General" will accomplish that by a "crash" program. The public is losing confidence by just this kind of contradictory statements. The military would like to cover their bungling by use of "SECRET" to keep the tax payers from knowing the truth. The minute that is successful we will no longer have a free nation but the kind of dictatorship that certain military groups would like to have right now in the United States!

| THE STATE INTENTIONALLY DECEIVES......
| from AUTOBIOGRAPHICHES.....Albert Einstein |

The citizen of today is intentionally deceived about a great many facts of life by "the powers that be" ---be they military, university, or bureaucratic. The concealment of the true facts behind the UFO from the American taxpayer is certainly in this category. THE SPACE-CRAFT DIGEST hopes to operate in area as free from dogma as it is possible to find in our world today. In EINSTEIN'S auto-bio graphy he too stated how he found that the state deceives.....and here are his own words as he set them down in German.

"...... thru the reading of popular scientific books I soon reached the conclusion that much in the stories of the bible could not be true. The consequence was a fantastic orgy of free thinking...coupled with the impression THAT YOUTH IS BEING INTENTIONALLY DECEIVED BY THE STATE THRU LIES(!) It was a crushing impression. Suspicion against every kind of authority grew out of this experience --a skeptical attitude towards the convictions which were alive in any specific social environment ---an attitude which has never left me, even tho later on because of a better insight into its causal conditions, it lost none of its original poignrancy.

It was clear to me that the religious paradise of youth, which was thus lost, was the first attempt to free myself from the "merely personal" from an existance which is governed by wishes hopes and primitive feelings. Out yonder there is this hugh world, which exists independly of man and which stands before us like a great eternal riddleis at least partially accessible to our inspec tion and thinking.........."

That's what the little man with the deep brown eyes found at the end of the last century and it is interesting, tho tragic, to see that things have not changed. Today we have a memory-machine degree-factory university and school system that prositutues the students thinking abilities; a military that madly stamps "secret" on fundamental universal truths; a dogmatic religious schism which makes mental and physical wars upon each other. Into this maelstrom of evil and ill-will a young mind is thrust to find the truth--if it can!

Only a few adult minds in the world today operate in any way free of these deceptive factors. That is the main reason why the road to the real cosmic truth is so hard to find. But as the great Buddha has stated...." .... when man is ready to find the real secret of the universe; he'll find it very close at hand--because it has been in his own mind all of the time...."

Now lest it be thought that timesare diffcerent... Friday April 18,1958....from the editorial pages of the PORTLAND OREGONIAN.....If a "catastrophic accident" caused the Soviet Union to halt its recent nulcear tests, as reported by the Berlingske Tidene of Copenhagen, the United States government would know about it. Our detection system is able to pick up ordinary atomic ex pl0sions in Russia.

One presumes that Senator Hubert Humphry of Minnesota has reliable information that the Soviet nuclear tests were the "dirtiest" the world has ever known...etc. ....it goes on to say......The world and the American people are entitled to know the truth of the matter....etc.

SPACE-CRAFT DIGEST....asks just one question. WHO is the U.S. keeping this a secret from....THE RUSSIANS?

THE LIST IS LONG AND DAMNING..........here's another story of about the same date. It has to do with ....cancer! Certain that is one field in which the public has a right to know---NOT SO!

HOUSE PROBERS CHECK SUPPRESSION OF SCIENTIST'S CANCER HAZARD PAPER
Washington (AP) House investigators are checking to determine whether a government scientist's paper on cancer hazards in consumer goods was suppressed for non-scientific reasons.

Rep. Moss (D-Cal.) chairman of the government information sub-committee wrote secretary of Health, Education and Welfare, Folsom, about " a restriction on medcal information" which Moss said was imposed against cancer specialist William C. Heuper. The paper went into a long list of chemical and physical agents found in fodd and elsewhere. Hueper said many create cancer hazards to the general population...."

------------30------------

LOOK TO YOUR SOURCES, GENTLEMEN:

$E = MC^2$ ..an equation that every scientist, newspaper-man and nearly everyone who wishes to sound learned on the subject of the atomic nucleus like to bandy about. We are going to try to demonstrate that in the use of this equation as "Einsteinian" we have a cardinal example of how US science-writers operate. They seem to be prone to group together a number of references and then proceed to draw conclusions depending completely on the accuracies of the work done by those who wrote the reference sources--which in some cases was in itself not original work, but likewise borrowed. For Instance, in the May issue of <u>SKY AND TELESCOPE</u> Otto Struve of the Leuchner Observatory of the U. of Cal. discussed a simple derivation of "...Einstein's Equation E equals MC^2...." <u>NUCLEAR STRUCTURE</u> by Leonard Eisenbud and Eugene P. Wigner Princeton U. Press are two other examples of men who were told that this equation was of Einstein derivation and thru their many years of graduate study never thought to check.....Most everyone in US physics says that is so...so it must be so. page 4, "....the binding energy is related through Einstein's mass-energy equation....."etc.   SPACE-CRAFT DIGEST DOES NOT BELIEVE THESE STATEMENTS ARE CORRECT AND HERE'S WHY: If the last two gentlemen had looked in their own wonderful Firestone Library at Princeton they would have found this reference. HANSENOHRL, <u>Annalen der Physik,</u> 15, 363 (1904) his publication of the equation in July 1904 and Einsteins publication was over a year later in September 1905.

Certainly if anyone must admit that the U.S. school of physical thought has gone far to champion their adopted son, Einstein. However, there are some fine thinkers in Germany who take a great deal of issue in many of his fundamental philosophical postulates. The SPACE CRAFT DIGEST certain feels he was in error in assuming "gravity" as a fundamental field of the universe. But the US in many ways as close minded as were the Nazis who drove Dr. Einstein out of Germany. Always it seems political thought permiates pure science---this is just as much in error either way if it ignores cosmic fundamentals.

PSYCHIC PHYSICS   EXCLUSIVE!!!********************

A NEW FORCE FIELD?.... a whole field of force whose study is neglected in Western Universities? It seems fantastic that once again our dogmatism finds it so easy to neglect a set of principles whose correct understanding could well determine whether man is to ever become a space-born animal in his physical body.

Nowhere in the literature on space travel prospects has any of the so-called authorities touched on the problem of how the delicate electrical system of the human body might react out of its native force field situation of the home planet.

The development of new cells, the operationof the brain and nervous system, all are effected by the electro-magnetic and electrostatic fields of a certain specific magnetude. If the human organism is taken out of its accustomed set of field conditions will it still remain the normal organism we started with?

Cosmic ray bombardment (intense tho Dr. van Allen says it is) is certainly not the only problem. Will the brain of man react differently than the brain of a mouse or monkey? Chances are that it certainly will and some mighty addle-pated spacemen are likely to come back to us if we are foolish enough to try a space-capsule design without allowance for a stable force-field situation in the space-capsule design so that the human passenger may function in force-fields of the strength that he is used to.

ACTUALLY....instruments would be much more reliable and it is quite possible that instrumentation would give us better returns than trying to fool with space craft passengers at least at our stage of knowledge. Further, we are not even certain just what force fields make up the universe as yet and so perhaps the cries of our military aboutwhat they can do with space-manned vehicles are a bit pre-mature.

A great amount of work has been done in Germany and England on the radiations around a human body. Much of this has been ignored by our medical researchers because they do not believe in RADIONICS. BUT, some years later we find that John's Hopkins has been forced to take another look at RADIONICS. There is certainly some hope left even tho the public handling of the story is ridiculous.

Our human body cells (and other animal cells too) are delicately balanced electrical organisms with natures very sensitivewith electrical charges and potential changes both of an electro-static nature and electro-magnetic. It is quite possible that an all-encompassing "I" field or intelligence field also permiates the cosmos. This might also be a determining factor in the functioning of an electrical entity also. Witness the fact that medicine now admits that most ilnress is fundamentally psychosamatic in nature ... electrical in nature controlled in some manner by the person's own mind, or intelligence, or whatever.

So, we pose the question --is man's body suited electrically to travel in space? We have already pointed out that rockets are childlike solutions of the movement problem and now we offer a medical problem that might be even larger and harder to solve than pure electrical flight that we believe is the practical solution.

SO, WHAT IS PSYCHIC PHYSICS?

It is the study of the true nature of man's electrical system and its orientation in the force fields fundamental to the universe. The SPACE-CRAFT DIGEST in the evolvement of the thought of the fundamental four-field continuum postulates the fundamental fields as :

    Electro-static (E)

              electro-magnetic (H)

                      ODIC (life force)   (O)

                          INTELLIGENCE FIELD or (I)

S.W. Tromp of the faculty of geology of Fouad the 1st. University in Cairo gives us a very good summation of this amazing situation in his PSYCHIC PHYSICS published by the Elsevier Book Co. in Amsterdam. A scientific analysis of dowsing radiesthesia and kindred diving phenomena. He has a very interesting preface.

He says that these people with this knowledge are "undeterred by public ridicule and the belief has been upheld for some 7,000 years of recorded history.(a hold over even from ancient Lemurian knowledge?)....and even to the most critical scientist it should be indicated that there must be some possibility of truth in the art. Too often, he reminds, scientists willing believe that facts that cannot be explained by current theories do not exist. Even among the most broad visioned scientists it is difficult to find one who is willing to make a careful study of the phenomenas (of radionics and like manifestations.).

For those of sufficient professional and scientific background we recommend a close study of the book. However, to show just how sensitive the animal cell structure and nervous system is to the home planet's force field we will just list a few observed results of a change in magnetic intensity and then pose the question of what will happen in a completely strange field situation in which the human body may be thrust as it first ventures into space.

From the Zoological laboratory of Leiden, Holland, using constant magnetic fields: Growing speed of mice (cell development).... was definitely retarded .... testicles and mammary glands increased in size...."they suggest even weak but constant magnetic fields hamper the development under normal conditions...." further quoting".... the growth experiments in both a pulsating and interrupted constant fields are of particular interest as they indicate the influence of disturbances (gradients) of the magnetic field of the earth on organisms that spend a considerable part of their time in zones of magnetic disturbance..."

Another problem pointed out is the development of cancers of various natures.

Now of course this is just one facet of the problem and we. aren't just indicating that spacemen will come back with large testicles or that space women will return all Jane Mansfields. We certainly are saying that the field problem is at present far beyond our knowledge. We cannot cover the great number of bio-electrostatic effects, of course, but thousands of effects on animals have been noted by Europe's workers in this field. If spaceman moves out of his native force field and ventures into others more or less powerful ----can he come back a"normal," human being? Might it not be best to send instrumentation? Further, are many saucers or UFO's now flitting about the earth-moon system inhabited, operating on instrumentation...or are they thought controlled? We must develop the understanding of more of the universe's force-field reality before we go far into the galaxies......or even leave the gravity-held earthly frog-pond of our birth.

THE SAUCERS FLY----part two

> In the Spring issue of the SPACE-CRAFT DIGEST we developed a portion of the theory of pure electrical flight in space as used by the UFO. The SPACE VORTEX THEORY first mentioned as a fundamental of the atom by Lord Kelvin and later refined by C.F Krafft as essential to an understanding of space-craft propulsion. Here is a letter:

Annandale, Va.
April, 8, 1958

Dear Mr. Allen:

Your SPACE CRAFT DIGEST has arrived and I thank you for the valuable publicity you have given to the ETHER VORTEX THEORY. I thoroughly agree with you that rocket propulsion using chemical fuels is destined to become obsolete, at least for space flight purposes. I cannot share the prevailing optimism as to our ability to go to Mars or Venus on clumsy rocket devices which sometimes work and sometimes don't.

According to present day science, the only other method by which large amounts of power can be released suddenly upon demand is by the use of atomic energy, but this must first be converted into heat before it can be used for propulsion, and that requires large and heavy apparatus, very unsuitable for space ship propulsion.

Reguardless of whether chemical fuels or atomic reactants are used as a source of energy, the material that produces the thrust of the rocket motor consists of thermally hot but electrical neutral molecules. Even if ionic propulsion by alkali metal vapor were used, it would still be necessary to draw upon some source of energy to accelerate the ions, and the same energy could be used more efficiently by the conventional methods of rocket propulsion.

Under the prevailing nuclear concept of the atom, we are indeed limited to either chemical energy or atomic energy, but according to MY EITHER VORTEX THEORY it should be possible to produce a totally new kind of energy by use of what I have been calling "SUPER MATTER". This is a material in which adjacent atoms are joined thru their negative charges functioning as valence bonds.

Upon DISINTEGRATION, "SUPER MATTER" would produce positive ions and not electrically neutral molecules. It is therefore not any form of chemical energy. NEITHER is it atomic energy (in the usual sense....ed.) because in all known procedures for obtaining atomic energy there is always a transmutation of one element, whereas in supermatter one would end up with the same elements. This does not involve any violation of the principle of the law of conservation of energy because the energy was put into the material in the power plant where it was made.

It will readily be seen that a material which suddenly liberates large amount of positive electrcity is exactly the kind of material that will be needed for space craft propulsion, and the observed characteristics of the UFO's are strongly indicative of the use of such material. At first glance the entire super-matter scheme may seem too speculative for serious scientific study, but the UFO's leave us no other alternative. THE EXISTENCE OF THE UFO's can be NO LONGER SERIOUSLY QUESTIONED, and as they do exist they require an explanation of their methods of propulsion. Rocket propulsion using chemical fuels is wholly inadequate for that purpose. Even if we assume that some new fuel will be discovered in the future which will be ten times more powerful than anything known today, still it will not explain the FREQUENT LUMINOSITY of the UFO's, their ability to stop automobile engines from a distance, or the ability of living pilots to survive the terrfic accelerations (...and abrupt change of directions, ed..)

As I see the situation, the only real question that confronts us today is whether the propulsive force of the UFO's is produced simply by some new electric or magnetic contrivance or whether it also involves the use of a "new" material as the propellant. Undoubtedly the UFO's do use some special electrical or magnetic contrivance, but I think they also use a new propellant----some material that liberates electrcity rather than heat. This possibility of producing electrcity de novo where there was no electrcity before, is of course at present unknwon to science, but my vortex clearly shows that this should be possible (see Spring issue of the SPACE CRAFT DIGEST ...ed.) Physicists will probably tell us that it is impossible but everything is impossible until somebody does it. The UFO's are physical objects, therefore they require a physical explanation. Shoving them off into the realm of metaphysics will not bring us any closer to an understanding of them.

Your correlation of the structure of the ether-vortex proton with the antigravity problem seems very logical, but should have been set forth in more detail. I think you should have pointed out that in the di-polar proton there will be a tendency for all the polar flux to come out from one pole only, and not equally from both poles. Such a behavior is often encountered in electonics when we attempt to operate two devices in parallel. They will not always share the load equally. This is especially pronounced in a structure like the hydrogen atom which is in effect a minature electrical condenser, and because of the BIEFIELD-BROWN effect will move the ENTIRE ATOM IN THE DIRECTION OF THE PROTON. This effect can be explained by a diminuation of ether pressure on the outer side of the prpton and an increase of ether pressure on the outer side of the electron. It can also be explained by the theory that when the proton send its polar flux to the electron, the proton will experience a recoil, and thus tend to move the entire atom in the direction of the positive charge. Both of these explanations might be true. They might be just different versions of the same phenomenas. I am convinced that this is essentially the method used by the UFO's to overcome gravity (so is the S-D....ed) but they probably use some kind of super-matter for positive electrification, rather than the cumbersome static machines which in turn would have to be driven by the prime mover on baord the space ship (as some have proposed--ed) The weight of all such aparatus would make it very unsuitable for spaceship propulsion, not to mention the weight of fuel that would have to be carried.

The problem of spaceship propulsion cannot be solved by conventional methods, and yet under prevailing ideas of atomic structure, only conventional methods are possible. It is for this reason that our first step in solving the space ship problem should be to acquire a correct understanding of the atom. If rocket propulsion is really the best method for that purpose , then why are not the UFO's using rocket propulsion???

                Very truly yours,
                C.F. Krafft
                Rt.2, Annandale, Va.

We are indebted to Dr. Krafft for his explanation of his "super-matter" theory. It is essentially similar to the medthods outlined in this publication previously. We would like to add that to his theory Dr. Krafft should add the necessity of resonating the resulting field so that by feedback excitation the field could be maintined on long travels without the great amounts of fuel that any actual consumption would require during long operations. Photos of these slowly pulsating UFO's have been seen by the editor and this pulsation and form-change of the electrical field surrounding the UFO must have some significant explanation.

BOOKS TO READ

THE DRAMATIC UNIVERSE
By J. G. BENNETT
Hodder and Stoughton. Price 2 gns.

A review by G.W.Langston Day from MIND AND MATTER a publication of the De La Warr Laboratories, Raleigh Park Rd. Oxford, England. We present the review because we feel that the time has come when even our universities must admit the "truths" they teach of the universe are but sugar-coated fables.

Since the time of the babylonians many attempts have been made to define the universe and man"s place in it; but as scientific knowledge has advanced each set of ideas has had to be scrapped. Evidently the mental background was quite different in the Ptolemaic age when our earth was thought to be the center of the universe from today when we KNOW the earth to be an infinitesimal particle in creation. So, too, the new physics has profoundly modified our ideas about matter and energy. Science has now come against so many cul-de-sacs and dichotomies that the suspicion is now gaining ground that the 4 dimensional continuum is too narrow a framework into which the universe canbe fitted.

The SCIENTIFIC method is also coming under criticism. As professor white head has pointed out, ANY SYSTEM CAN BE MADE TO APPEAR PLAUSIBLE AS LONG AS THOSE ELEMENTS WHICH HAVE NO PLACE IN IT ARE IGNORED!

Instead of the "scientific" method, the author if this book adopts what he calls the method of progressive approximation. This is the concept of WHOLES instead of abstract fragments (or isolated "facts"....ed) These concepts are necessarily vague and faulty to begin with, but they can certainly be corrected as one goes along. From this point he defines what he calls a progression of categories in which the WHOLES evolve in accordance with the law of octaves. They are given specific characteristics according to their position in the octave. On this foundation a large part of the book is based.

Other foundation stones are the postulation of a sub-stratum of existence which, after Aristotle --he calls HYLE; also additional laws of framework besides those of space and time.

Hyle -- is neither spirit or matter, but something that is able to receive form and character. As to the additional laws of framework, the first is ETERNITY The condition of potentiality, the dimension in which are found the different style or levels of organization, the "jacob's ladder" of BEING. The second is HYPARXIS (corresponding internally to the dimension of space) which reconciles the actual (time) to the potential (eternity). It is "ABLENESS TO BE in this sense. Just as values are related to eternity--meanings are related to HYPARXIS. BUT, meanings imply recognition and recognition is impossible without meanings thru recognition. So HYPARXIS is characterized by recurrence.

once these foundations have been laid, a great many of the problems which baffle present day thought begin to find solutions. For we are now viewing WHOLES instead of fragments, and more-over not thru the totally inadequate peep hole of space-time but thru the greatly enlarged apertures of ETERNITY and HYPARXIS. We also have the help of the categories which guide our footsteps stage by stage from the formless HYLE to the totality of creation.

Man, as the author points out, being eternity-blind recognizes the 3-dimensionality of his outer world but treats his inner world as tho it were one dimensional (or even non-dimensional?....ed.) . Many things such as a magnetic field or the force of gravitation , appear to him inexplicable. But the enlarged framework offer satisfying explanations.

For example, the line of eternity must orthogonal to the space-time continuum. But the space-time continuum for the universe as a whole is one thing--- BUT FOR SEPARATE REGIONS it is another! This means that eternity lines might not coincide. NOR MAY TWO POINTS COINCIDE WITH EACH OTHER IN TIME!

It is this non-coincident which gives rise to gravitational and electro-magnetic and electro-static fields. Combined with non-coincidence of the Time-axis, we have the origin of the electro-magnetic forces.

Before the appearance of matter, Hyle is a finite but limitless reservoir of existence, with time, eternity and hyparxis as the shores, bottom and surface of the ocean. Occasionally the surface is stirred into ripples by the winds of experience --momentary concentrations of ABLE-NESS TO BE. In this way TIME and eternity are brought together for an instant and droplets (matter ?) are formed.

THIS, says Mr. Bennett ' is the process sometimes referred to as the continuous creation of matter'.......but the word 'creation' is here quite misleading, for what occurs is a re-cycling of matter thru the action of entities that are capable of passing thru the threshold of existence. The threshold of existence is a barrier that is not strictly potential--that is eternal--but rather hyparchic.'

The primary entities to emerge are corpuscles, after which we ascend to the world (or level) of particles. And here by virtue of the extended framework we find the keys to many of the puzzles of the sub-microscopic world. For instance the mechanics of quantum action and the principle of indeterminancy (uncertainty of Heisenberg.....ed.) and the true nature of static charges. One of these keys is rotation, a property of hyparxis, or re-currence, which is found not only inplanets and galaxies, but also in atomic nuclei.

Higher up in the scale he defines LIFE as the reconciling power that stands between the active world of creativity and the passive world of mechanism regulating the universal processes of involution and evolution by submitting itself to both at the point where they meet. THE BIOSPHERE, or thin film of organic life on Earth, therefore stands at a critical point in the cosmic scheme. It corresponds, the author believes, to the colloidal surface of a living cell. It has all the charcteristics of a living entity of which the human race composes the brain cells and the metazoan animals the ordinary cells. Notonly this, every fully formed planet must have a bio-sphere (!) in which some sort of creature corresponds to man. he points out that the prescence of life on earth would be inconceivable if we did not know it for a fact, and that the elasticity of chemistry is so enormous that life could exist under conditions very different from our own. He takes the seven inner planets from Venus to Neptune, as a seven-fold structure in which the position of each planet gives some indication of the kind of life that we might expect to find upon it.

In guessing the kind of life that might exist on VENUS we are handicapped by our knowledge (lack of) of low-temperature reactions that are possible in the absence of water. With a far greater intensity of solar radiation and an atmosphere composed mainly of carbon-dioxide, there would be no end of immense biochemical actvity, photosynthesis and production of bacteria--but no stability. (this assumes that are earthy spectroscopic analysis can be relied upon..ed) The highest type of beings would probably live short but intense lives, which agrees with the nature of the first note on the active.

Earth, which occupies the second position in the Octave is characterized by strife. It creates a demand for harmony without providing the conditions under which harmony is possible. Here-in lies the clue to terrestrial existence, the stern rule of the SURVIVAL OF THE FITTEST.

On Mars the atmosphere is thin, there is little water, and at a distance of 34 million miles we can only observe fairly gross features, such as seasonal variations in color over immense areas, suggesting vegetation and the 'canals' which are possibly a gigantic system of irrigation.

The conditions suitable for very large, slow moving creatures subsisting on simple forms of vegetation. They would be heavily protected against temperature and be able to use directly the ultra-violet light which would not be absorbed by their atmosphere. They could be very long lived and could develop forms of consciousness unknown to us.

Standing on the third note of the octave, at which help is needed from outside the planetary system to bridge the interval in the evolutionary ascent, Matians would be more aware of the sense and meaning of their existence and the nature of the extra-planetary force on which they depend. The point at which this force enters is occupied by the asteroids.

Beyond this is the great planet Jupiter which with its many satellites SEEMS TO CONSITUTE A SOLAR SYSTEM IN THE MAKING. Opaque clouds several thousand miles thick exert a pressure sufficient to liquify all of Jupiter's gasses. The planet must generate large quantities of heat. The "RED SPOT" and other phenomena point to high concentrations of energy.

The Jovian atmosphere is virtually three dimensional so that living creatures corresponding to man can probably move freely upo and down as well as horizontal. Methane and ammonia seem to predominate which favors photosynthesis at lowtemperatures. We know very little about low temperature, high pressure systems because we have had no incentive to study them. Nevertheless there is evidence that Jupiter is suitable for creatures of very complex energy transformations in their nervous systems. They could have perceptions embracing the entire range of the electromagnetic spectrum and hence knowledge and apprehension far surpassing our own.

The reamining planets are so remote and with conditions so far removed from those on Earth that, the author says their forms of life are hard even to imagine. According to the principles of 7-fold structure, their inhabitants should be nearer to self perfection and more concerned with the life of the solar system itself. The remainder of the book deals briefly with higher forms of being, the galaxies and the Universe as awhole. The author points out that the higher we ascend the scale of creation the more incomplete our view becomes, becomes Creation is receding into the inner worlds to which we are blind.

One additional idea is that the extreme relative distances between suns is a factor which enables them to fulfil their role as independent creators. Another factor is the apparent waste of solar radiation only aninsignificant fraction of which falls on solid bodies. But actually, he says, all this radiation passes into the 'reservoir' from which future worlds will arise. In the word of today the scientific method is worshiped and this book will not be proclaimed by the Royal Society, but in 50 years time it may be regarded very differently.

by G.W. Langston Day.

from MIND AND MATTER
    De La Warr Laboratories
        Oxford, England

TWO RINGED PLANETS IN THE SOLAR SYSTEM ..Eart
(Saturn by the 100" telescope)

The Internationa
over a hundred
around the earth
cation----

:h and Saturn?

l Geophysical Year scientists and other observers for
years have known about a very strong electrical girdle
l.........following page summarizes this amazing indi-

IS THE EARTH RINGED—like Saturn?

A SPACE-CRAFT DIGEST EXCLUSIVE
by w. gordon allen

Previously reported in 1953 by two scientists of the USSR and again re-emphasized by IGY scientists it now appears that the earth is also a ringed planet--like Saturn?

The most clearly defined of the "rivers" of electricity is the EQUATORIAL ELECTROJET, which girdles the earth at the magnetic equator. Its intensity is thought to equal several hundred thousand amperes. It is thought also to be generated by tidal movements of the earth's atmosphere and to be part of the globe circling system of electric currents.

The currents apparently flow thru the ionosphere and their patterns seem to follow the path of sunlight around the earth. This causes the ELECTROJET's flow TO REVERSE ITSELF TWICE DAILY. In the daylight it flows in one direction and at night it flows in the opposite direction.

These rivers of electricity are thought to be continuous. THE CONCENTRATION SEEMS TO BE IN A NARROW EQUATORIAL BAND.

Other currents of a somewhat different nature are believed to circle the earth in both polar regions, in the zones where the Northern lights appear.

GEGENSHEIN was first reported about 100 years ago in 1855. Since that time until the present IGY it has been largely ignored. In the tropics this is known as the "Zodiacle" light visible both in the morning and in the evening. In very clear skies at night it is visible from horizon to horizon in a very narrow strip.

This is alluded to in the holy writings as the "arch of the firament".

This ring maintains the balanced interchange of power thru the crust and atmosphere of the earth. It is the prime cause of vortices truning clockwise in the Northern hemisphere and counter-clockwise in the Southern......as do whirl pools and the worn side of river-banks (turn).

The RESONATING ELECTRO-MAGNETIC FIELD of BOTH the Earth and Saturn is very intense......this is evidenced by the flattening of the poles of both---Saturn more so in proportion than earth (only 27 or so miles).

Now as far as the editor of the SPACE-CRAFT DIGEST is concerned we'd like to pose this question?

> WHY WERE THESE FACTS OR TRUTHS TOLD TO CERTAIN "SENSITIVES" ON EARTH (by so-called 'spacial entities") AND SO KNOWN BEFORE THEY WERE DISCOVERED BY CONVENTIONAL AND RATIONAL SCIENTISTS?

The more the IGY seems to "discover" the more it seems to only CONFIRM what has already been known and revealed some years ago by those who claim communion with the space people.

That's why we feel that the account (elsewhere) of the Birmingham woman's conversation with the extra-terrestial from Venus is to be taken seriously.

SHIFT OF THE POLES? ....

Some years ago a man named Brown who was an engineer tried to interest various governmental "athorities" in his hypothesis that the earth was in danger of a shift of its poles due to accumulation of ice deposits in the polar regions. He was not taken seriously----but now from SKY AND TELESCOPE we offer a digest of an article by T. Gold of the Harvard Observatory. Again we can't help but emphasize that a new (or old) idea has a tough struggle unless it is endorsed by the dogmatist group of our scientists. We can't help but point out that Dr. Menzel who hates UFO's and saucers worse than poison is also associated with the observatory. Remember his very bad appearance with Major Keyhoe on Armstrong TV Theater?

These schematic maps, after K. A. Pauly, show the drastic changes in climate produced by shifts in the pole position with respect to the continents (modern outlines). With the North Pole in the Pacific Ocean (see chart at top of page 286), Greenland and Scandinavia were in the tropics.

How much have the poles moved? There has always been a little wobble. The big question is can it ever grow to a sudden catrostrophic "pole switch"? T. Gold estimates that it might take millions of years. There are some who would dis-agree by stating that the "quick freezing" of the Siberian mammoths points to even a switch taking place in a matter of days or hours is possible. This could occur if the "wobble" was the result of a major deposit of ice that was at the point of major instability.

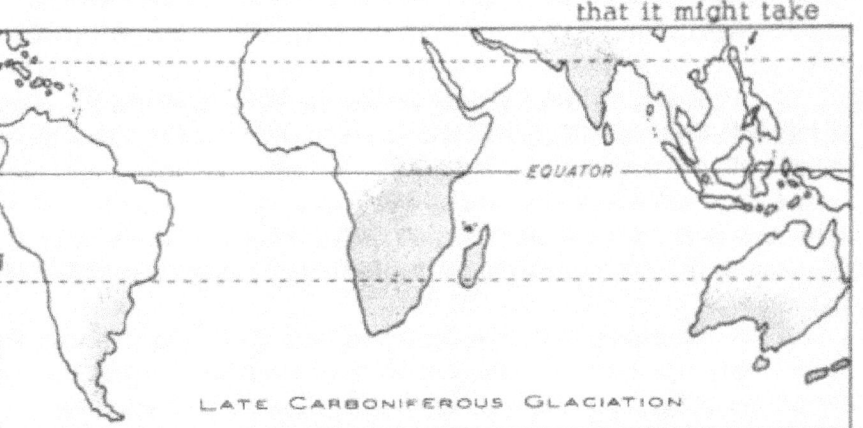

During late Carboniferous times, some 200 million years ago, the dotted areas of South America, South Africa, India, and Australia, were covered by great ice sheets. The coastlines on this map are modern — not those of the Carboniferous period. Adapted from "Lectures on Rock Magnetism," by P. M. S. Blackett, published in Jerusalem in 1956.

These effects cannot be explained in the same way as the minor general climatic variations that account for the growth and shrinkage of the polar ice caps. In the last million years or so. Clearly (Gold says) no growth of the ice caps could account for the glaciation of India, if that country were where it is now........ especially since we know that other areas were not glaciated at that time.
LET ME MAKE IT CLEAR THAT THERE IS NO GENERAL PHYSICAL LAW THAT PREVENTS A BODY FROM TURNING OVER WITH THE AID OF INTERNAL FORCES ONLY.
There might be an unbalance (also) arising from processes in the interior of the earth, but we do not have much information on that.

Walter Munk's calculations confirmed by gold's former work who that a time from 10 million to a 100 million years would be required for the earth to turn 90 degrees. Would a large polar drift therefore help explain this geological record?

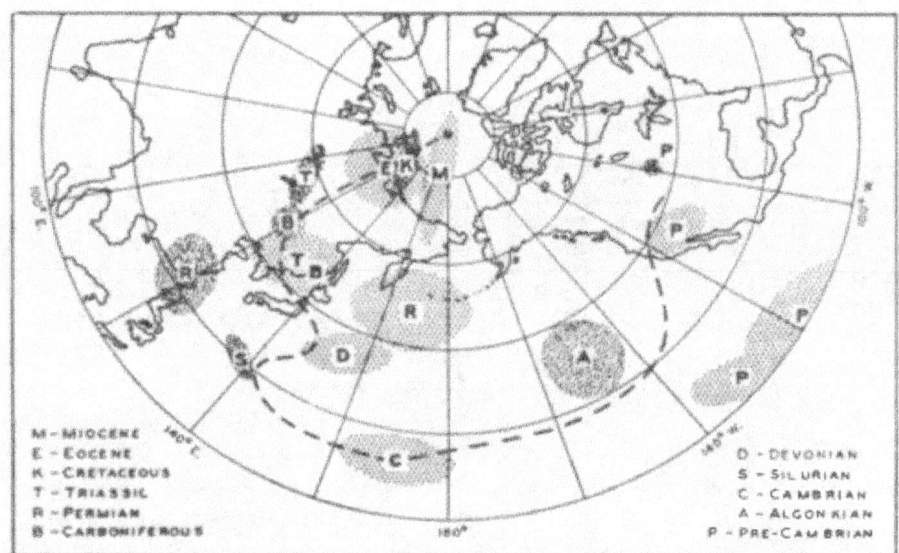

Migration of the north geographical pole since Pre-Cambrian time, after S. K. Runcorn. Dark ovals represent probable pole positions from North American rocks, dotted ovals from British. The dashed line is the inferred track of the pole.

Many geologists have formed a theory of continental drift, thinking that the main masses of the continents have shifted their relative positions by large amounts.

There is no doubt that ancient rocks show very different directions of manetism than recent ones. ------end of quote--- TOKYO(Reuters).... The Geophysical Survey Institute here has reported that the various land masses of Japan " are moving in different directions at the rate of seven to 10 feet a year". The survey said the shifting was thought to be due to the UNSTABLE POSITION of Japan, sandwiched between a continent and a large ocean....end.

    Now, at the rate of 10 feet a year that would result in a change of about a million feet in a hundred thousand years. Since the days of LEMURIA that would see a shift of about 200 miles ... or two thousand in a million years even at this rate. Of course it could have been much faster or much slower. But these two indications from widely scattered sources show that it was indeed more than just possible for the earth to have had a missing continent .. or two (Mu and Atlantis).

    The only other thought we'd like to mention at this time is that in the last 12,000 to 20,000 years since man had been able to record even a bit of his actions on this planet we have seen him grow from a savage to one having just a thin vineer of civilization. WHAT.....was the great catastrophe that almost wiped him from the planet at that time? Was it flood, a pole switch, radiation that killed the genes, or what? TODAY....it is the editorial feeling of the SPACE CRAFT DIGEST that one of man's most needed projects is to answer this question and certainly 18 months of the International Geophysical Year is not enough to solve this vital mystery. However, the IGY has done a great deal to "scientificly confirm" much of the meta-physical knowledge that man has had for centuries. Now, it would appear that man must expand and continue the wonderful work of the IGY groups. It is amazing that man thinks great secrets of the universe can be solved out of year to year appropriations. This should be a 1,000 year project. Just as SHOULD OUR SPACE PROGRAM! We must raise our sights!

CHANGES IN THE EARTH'S ROTATION

Time Span Years	Wobble of Axis		Length of Day	
	Amount	Causes	Amount	Causes
1	Up to 12 meters	Shifts of air masses.	0.001 second	Winds.
10	About 3 meters	Sea-level changes? Changes in core?	0.001 second	Changes in core.
1,000	(Unrecognized, but could be 80 meters)		0.01 second	Sea-level changes. Tidal friction. Separation of materials inside earth.
10⁹ (Geological times)	90 degrees	Shifts of masses on crust. Possibly interior changes.	Unknown	Gravitational sorting of material. Oceanic tides. Atmospheric tides.

THE HINDU CONCEPTION OF REALITY   as handed to them by the LEMURIANS

> The importance of the understanding of the reality of what our senses perceive is always with us in the problem of the perception of the reality of the U.F.O.

The LEMURIAN SYSTEM assumes that the individual is part and parcel of the universal substance, but so involved in the matter of TIME and SPACE as to have lost all recognition of his or her true identity...or reality; therefore the LEMURIANS set forth to the YOGI a means and a way of life to bring the individual back to his true and original position, to absolve him from the clutches of matter, to return him to the essence from which he came, to abstract him from every aspect of his relation (as he might think it to be) to 'space' and 'time'.

Yogis now hold that all in the manifest (to his senses) and the unmanifest world come from one source, the divine and primordial intelligence; that man is but a spark of this intelligence and, by the process of Yogi is able to get a view of this great intelligence which bestows all knowledge, all wisdom, all power and all there is in the seen and the UNSEEN universe. (meaning unperveived even thru our most sensitive instrumentation).

The best proof of the nature of YOGA and the entirety and extent of its influence is the fact that every system of religion in India and every school of philosophy has recognized Yoga as the most scientfic means of realizing philosophical truths. (Even Western Christian Science brings much from Yoga). Men of marvelous mental powers and intense heroism in ancient India, Tibet, and China (All colonized by Lemurians) were the outcomes of the teachings of Yoga. It is said that all mthods of human culture other than Yoga are like beating about a hole to kill a snake. What would require many lives by methods known to the world at large, is done in a remarkably short time by the art of Yoga.

Yoga gives its devotees a tangible knowledge of the future and the unseen world; it enables man to appreciate the life around him and gives him the power to make that life worth appreciating. What the intellectual, moral, and spiritual hopes for, whatever he loves, wishes, or wills is to be found in the teachings of Yoga. The practice of Yoga enhances the sensibilities and the powers of man; therefore Yogas claim far-reaching knowledge of secrets of nature and extensive control over natural phenomena.

The systematic study of the Yoga has now been stopped for hundreds of years, having gone into a state of decay on account of idleness, ignorance, and the unscrupulousness of the generality of its latter-day followers. The cancer of laziness, selfishness, canity and delusion commenced to work its destruction at the beginning of this age (KALI YUGA). Corrupted rites, false ideas, dogmatic tennets, which human selfishness begot in the course of ages, led man to practice social abuses and crimes, evils so common and rampant that YOGA was perforce compelled to retire to secret abodes....the ultimate was reached about 100 years ago in the British RAPE OF INDIA. Until this day only mere remnants are available to the most diligent deliberate seeker. THE PACIFIC LEMURIAN SOCIETY hopes to lay much of this learning before its members from time to time. BUT, even in India, the only remaining home of Yoga, supreme ignorance prevails about Yoga in general, especially in the educated circles. Yet it is not thought to be lost by those those who are well practiced in some of its arts, and who may be presumed to know.

However, very few persons are really competent in the higher forms of Yoga. They seem not to have the determination to devote the time to Yoga necessary for this accomplishment; but it is non-the-less for him who has the capacity.

The LEMURIAN YOGA SYSTEM assumes the same cosmological doctrines as set forth in the SAMKHYA system. The only difference between the two is that the latter pertains to the universal system of nature....the Yoga to the individual condition of nature. The process of evolution and involution is both the same. Both are based on the fundamental logical principle that something cannot come out of nothing...that every shadow must have its substance. Therefore, the Yoga system MAINTAINS THAT THE GROSS INDIVIDUAL MUST HAVE A SUBTLE ASPECT FROM WHICH IT MANIFESTS ITSELF AND TO WHICH IT WILL RETURN. THIS SUBTLE ASPECT IS BUT A SPARK OF THE DIVINE, AND IS THE SOLE CONCERN OF Y O G A.

Before it is possible to understand man fully, it is necessary to examine first what the forces that sustain him and cause him to be what he is. The energies of nature operate in him according to the necessities of survival, yet man has the inherent quality of dissolution, for he is a compound being. He is constituted of both the gross and the subtle. The gross can be known by perception but the subtle can be known (for the want of better phraseology) ONLY by the power of spiritual perception. The subtle aspect consists of the abstract energies of nature; they are always invisible, for they are beyond the mind, beyond the senses never to be seen, but they are to be known only thru the practice of Yoga.

The Yoga system is based upon the principle that there is but one law that governs a single force which operates in all conditions of nature, manifest and unmanifiest. THAT FORCE IS CALLED LIFE. It is the invisible force that unites the spirit and matter and brings all things into being. It is not the result of the chemical stimulation of protoplasm, yet protoplasm is the carrier of life. DEATH does take an inexorable grasp of the manifest individual, but the continuance of life is not effected ......LIFE is actually the sensibility that precedes the senses.

LIFE is not the creation of something new; it is only an expansion of what IS; therefore it is not linked to the unseen realities which constitute the essence of man before he becomes manifest in the gross form. WE SEE ONLY THE MIDDLE LINK IN THIS CHAIN OF EXISTENCE AND CALL IT L I F E !! We utterly fail to take note of the preceding and succeeding invisible stages. Inasmuch as nothing can exist without being attached to its antecedents, the material manifestation called "life" must be then linked to a finer and immaterial form; therefore man is said to be the off spring of the invisible aspect of nature, appearing ONLY when a condition for his manifestation has been created. Since the effect must always be manifest with the cause (uniform with the cause) LIFE must procede from life as light proceeds from light (radiation) and not from darkness (lack of radiation).

Each conception is the influx of a new self, for the lifeless constituents of the human body cannot create a man, no matter how many chemicals or physiological actions are postulated. The manifestation of an individual aspect of univers versal consciousness. Therefore, the soul can operate in both the visible and invisible world.

Those "scientific" individuals who observe ONLY the superficial appearances of nature confound the eternal order of things, and fail to perceive the true nature of man. Man is a combination of self-conscious self and five kinds of matter formed into an organic body.

He possesses infinite consciousness and is ever subjected to the process of being evolved into a finite organic individual through the dynamics of the combined sperm and ovum. The soul is not corporeally and dimensionally present, but is spiritually present as one's voice is present in a room. It has no inside or outside, but is only a mass of intelligence, just as a mass of sweetness has no inside or outside but is still a mass of taste.

The manifestation of an individual is the reduction of the universal force to an individual principle caused by a stress raised in the universal consciousness. Man as a genus is the result of the differentiation of the whole into an infinite multiplicity of correlated centers called individuals; effects of nature. In order to produce the differentiation, energy must become concentrated so as to create a "field" in which stress can take place.

SEE....A New Vista of the Entirety in the Spring SPACE-CRAFT DIGEST.......

Here's an International New Service report of a plane crash in Michigan.

We feel that it is most amazing from the connection with UFO's and the fact that the pilot at first scoffed at the reality of the UFO...then he saw for himself.....here is the story:

R0l159ACS

NEW YORK, APRIL &, (INS) RUTH DENECKE, THE 27 YEAR OLD STEWARDESS WHO WAS KILLED IN THE FREELAND MICHIGAN, AIRPLANE CRASH, WAS DISCLOSED TODAY TO HAVE BEEN MARRIED SECRETLY FOR MORE THAN A YEAR.
    THE STEWARDESS WAS ONE OF THE 47 OCCUPANTS OF THE CAPITAL AIRLINES PLANE THAT CRASHED AND BURNED LAST NIGHT, ALL ABOARD WERE KILLED.
    SHE WAS MARRIED TO GEORGE BARDOWSKY, 29, A FLIGHT ENGINEER FOR EASTERN AIRLINES. HE DID NOT LEARN OF HIS WIFE,S DEATH UNTIL THIS MORNING. THE COUPLE LIVED IN JACKSON HEIGHTS LONG ISLAND.
    ANOTHER VICTIM WAS THE PILOT, CAPTAIN WILLIAM J. HULL, 44, WHO LIVED WITH HIS WIFE AND TWO YOUNG CHILDREN IN WESTWOOD, N.J.
    HULL, A COMMERCIAL PILOT SINCE 1941, WAS ONE OF CAPITAL's MILLION MILE PILOTS. HE WAS WELL KNOWN IN AVIATION CIRCLES BECAUSE OF HIS INTEREST IN FLYING SAUCERS.
    IN 1953 HULL WROTE AN ARTICLE FOR A PILOT'S MAGAZINE DISCOUNTING FLYING SAUCER REPORTS. THREE YEARS LATER HE WROTE ANOTHER ARTICLE FOR UFO INVESTIGATORS, A MAGAZINE FOR THE UNOFFICIAL NATIONAL INVESTIGATIONS COMMITTEE ON AERIAL PHENOMENA, DISCRIBING AN UNIDENTIFIED FLYING OBJECT THAT BUZZED HIS AIRLINER NEAR MOBILE ALABAMA.
----------30----------

He was just another of the now hundreds of hard-headed "you have to show me" pilots who were certainly convinced once they had seen their first UFO. That he was open-mided enough to completely reverse his outlook once he was "shown" was certainly to his credit. This man had a million miles in the air- he certainly was a man of strong convictions. He then chose to go on record correcting his former thought once he knew himself to be wrong.

SCRIBE'S REPORT --from the LEARNING OF THE MOST ANCIENT ONES

Immanuel Swedenborg (Born 29 Jan.1688) A very great mind both scientific and "ecclesiastical" (like Newton) seems to have been a re-incarnated Lemurian. At Least his writings are the only modern Western writings telling of the mode of life and beliefs of the MOST ANCIENT ONES
If we believe his other writings have merit--should these have less?

****

"....... I have conversed with those of the MOST ANCIENT LEARNING---those called man or adam (HU-mans were the "man" of earth.....but man himself was the space colonizer of this planet) ...I now relate: eating the flesh of animals was considered somewhat profane; for the ANCIENT ONES ate not the flesh of dead animal or fowl but fed solely on grain, especially bread made of wheat; on the fruit of trees, herbs, milk, and what is prdouced from milk such as butter and cheese etc. To kill animals and devour their flesh was to them unlawful, being regarded as somewhat bestial. But in the course of time when mankind became as cruel as wild beasts, yea even more cruel, he first began to slay animals and eat them. And as men acquired such nature he killed other men and so killing is now permitted by the state even to this day..."

".......They lived in the highest degreeof light (radiation or vibration level) in which the light of this world would scarcely admit of any comparison....."

"....the nature of their speech, such as it was when they lived in the world, was shown to me by a "KIND OF INFLUX" which I cannot discribe (telepathic?) It appeared that it was not articulate (vocal) like that of our time, but that it was tacit being produced not by externalrespiration, but by internal. It was further shown me, that by such speechthey were enabled to express more fully the real sentiments of the mind, and the ideas of thought, than can possibly be done by articulate sounds or sonorous words. IN THEIR DAYS DECEIT WAS A CRIME OF THE GREATEST ENORMITY,

LEMURIAN CELESTIAL SOCIETY..... The TRUTH of the MOST ANCIENT ONES before the flood was not a written truth, but was felt, perceived or revealed to everyone of this learning for they were CELESTRIAL MEN (not HU-men) thus in perception of good and truth. In this they had revelations from infancy so that they knew the TRUTH when perceived. THESE SAME COSMIC TRUTHS IN THE PRESENT DAY MUST BE LEARNED TO BE KNOWN. It is scarcely possible now to acquire by learning a 1,000 th part of the knowledge they possessed. Nay, to-day man is even impressed by falsehood and believes it to be true!"

"......their body auras were brilliant, pearly, and even of a diamond-like luster...."

FOLLOWING ARE THE LAST EIGHT OF THE LOTUS PRINCIPLES OF LEMURIA

The first eight are in everyone of the HU-man racethis day.....but the last eight are those which have to be acquired.···

> We shall contue these excerpts of the most amazing accounts of the first celestial man on this planet...THE LEMURIANS.... the anti-deluvians (man before the flood) before the great cataclysms drove him to the hills to descend a low savage. For HU-man apparently did not originate on this planet. MAN in LEMURIA was a spaceman!

1. **HOW TO ACQUIRE IDEAS AND CONCEPTIONS**.......people usually allow themselves to be led by chance alone. They see or hear one thing or another and form their ideas accordingly. While this is the case the 16 fundamentals of the celestial man remain ineffective. It is only when the student takes his self education in hand in this respect that his real self becomes effective. His ideas and conceptions must be guarded; each single idea should acquire significance for him; he should see in it a definite message concerning things of the outer world. He should derive no satisfaction from ideas devoid of such significance. He must govern his mental life so that it BECOMES A TRUE MIRROR of the outer world (reality) and direct his efforts to the exclusion of the incorrect ideas (conceptions) from his soul (the mirror of his "mind").

2. **CONTROL OF RESOLUTIONS** .....The student must not resolve upon even the most trifling act, without well founded and thorough consideration. <u>Thoughtless and meaningless acts should be foreign to his nature.</u> He should have well con sidered grounds for everything he does and abstain from everything for which no significant motive is forthcoming.

3. **CONTROL OF SPEECH** The student should utter no word that is devoid of sense and meaning. All talking for the sake of talking draws him away from the path. He must avoid the usual kind of conversation with its promiscious discuss ion of indiscriminately varied topics. This does not imply his preclusion from intercourse with his fellows. It is precisely in such intercourse that his conversation should develop significance. He is ready to converse with anyone, but he does so thoughtfully and thru deliberation. He NEVER speaks without grounds for what he says. He seeks to use neither too few or too many words.

4. **REGULATION OF OUTWARD ACTION**...The student tries to regulate his actions in such a manner that they harmonize with those of his fellow men. .... with events and with his environment. He refrains from actions that are disturbing to others and antagonistic to his surroundings.. When an external motive causes him to act he considers how he can best respond. When the impulse proceeds from himself he weighs with minute care the possible effects of his activity.

5. **MANAGEMENT OF HIS LIFE** The Student tries live in conformity with both nature and spirit. Never over-hasty he is never indolent. Excessive activity and laziness are equally alien to him. He looks upon life as a means for work and so lives it. He regulates his health and habits in such a manner to become one and harmonius with the whole.

6. **HIS ATTEMPT AT ACHIEVEMENT ARE WITHIN HIS POWERS**. He tries nothing beyond his powers and omits nothing within their scope. He so knows his capacities. His aims coencide with the GREAT DUTIES OF A HUMAN BEING. He does not not mechanically regard himself as a great cog in the wheel of mankind, but seeks to comprehend the tasks of life and seeks to look out beyond the limits of the daily and the trivial. He seeks to fulfill his obligations ever better and more perfectly.

7. **AN EFFORT TO LEARN FROM LIFE**. ... He seeks to accumulate life experience from his careful observation of everyday events. He learns from his wrong and harmful actions. He observes those acts of others that are not harmonious and learns from them in the same manner.

8. TAKE TIME FOR INTROSPECTION.. this is perhaps the most difficult of all. His wrong acts must be self-analyzed free from self justifications! His actions toward his fellows must not be judged right thru excuse. His treatment of his body must be always such that it is worthy of being the home of his divine spirit. His thoughts then become the sum total of his life...HE BECOMES THEN... WHAT HE THINKS!!!!

Thus did the LEMURIANS develop the 16 lotus petals of life. When they did this on this earth they were said to have become a true celestial being. THUS TOO, did they develop the power of clairvoyance and thru this true knowledge of the reality of the cosmos and they were then not deceived by the apparent reality of the truths they thought they perceived thru their senses. The constructive forces of their lives were TRUTHFULLNESS, UPRIGHTFULNESS AND HONEST. Their crimes were the distructive forces of mendacity, deceitfulness and dishonesty. The student also realized that actual good deeds were needed and were not merely good intentions. "If I say or even think something that does not conform with cosmic reality --I kill something in my spiritual organs, even tho I believe my intentions to be ever so good..." The true faculties of the knowledge of the cosmos thru clairvoyance cannot be attained until the student truly regulates his life as outlined....it must be natural, if he believes it irksome he has not achieved the true way---and is not yet fit.

NOW.....did these celestial beings attain the ability of true physical space travel? Here is a very interesting passage from Churchward's CHILDREN OF MU. "......Maha Bharata (1,000 B.C.) mentions the gift of a space (or flying) machine by a king to a brother monarch as a token of affection. These were the stories of a Hindu space-craft of about 20,000 years ago. It says".....except one which is a drawing and instructions for the construction of an (airship or spacecraft) and her machinery, power or engine etc. THE POWER IS TAKEN FROM THE ATMOSPHERE (space?) in a very simple manner. The engine is somewhat like our present day turbine in that it works from one chamber to another. When the engine is once started it can run until its metal parts wear out. (of other fuels elsewhere is mentioned mercury...ed.) The power is limited only by what metals will stand. ...flights from 1,000 to 3,000 miles are mentioned.... All records relating to these craft state that they were self propelled. There are many Chinese records of about the same date that tell of these machines. While modern Hindu hisorians look upon the RAMAYANA and someother Hindu writings as myths, the Hindus, themselves, do not; they know better and so do I (Churchward.) I now the origins and from whence they were taken......"

AND IT WAS THE LEMURIANS WHO GAVE THIS KNOWLEDGE TO THE HINDUS AND IT IS THE HINDUS WHO RECORDED IT (AND CHINESE) FOR ITS TRUE LIGHT INTERPRETATION SOME DAY. These records were recorded in stone tablets which seems to be the only semi-permanent way to record the knowledge of a civilization. TODAY...our whole vital civilization would crumble to dust leaving no records in about two hundred years! Our records are the most impermanent of ALL!
It seems most remarkable then that these most ancient ones were able to forsee that even to their celestial knowledge there must even to them come a day of reconing and that they, too, must find some way to leave permanent records. One such repository was in the city of SHAMBHELLA on the river oxus in central ASIA. Another is supposed to be in certain Lamasaries in Tibet. In later issues we shall bring to our members some amazing facts from these writings gathered in the 1930's/

FIRE WALKING ... another remnant of Lemurian mastery

> Conventional science has no explanation for the ability of the Yoga or the fire-walkers. Their abilities have been derided, but accounts like the following are again beyond Western Science. The only explanation seems to be that it is a remnant of lost Lemurian knowledge out of the dim, distant past handed down to the peoples of the Pacific.

"....I have an idea, white brother", exclaimed Taurae, looking searchingly at me. "You are an uneasy soul just now, and do not know where you will lay your head tonight. Far up in the valley here, where the liana thickets cluster densest you can, if you will, see something this evening that will give you peace. For a short while at any rate. Have you ever seen a FIRE WALKING ceremony? Perhaps you have, since you have been so long in the islands here."

I went with Tuarae. I liked him. As to fire walking, that was neither here nor there. It was his companionship and sympathy that I needed.

Before we went, we bathed in the deep dark stream close by, and massaged our bodies with flower scented coco-nut oil. We took clean, red pareu and bound them about our wastes, and we were ready to start. Tuarae led the way in silence. His walk was gliding and rythmical. We followed a winding path that led through the floor of the valley, lighting our way ahead through the wooded darkness with a long bamboo torch. The district was quite unknown to me, and I searched in vain for familiar landmarks.

Without the ti plant no Polynesian would venture upon fire-walking

No stars were to be seen, for the jungle hung to densely above our heads. Knotty forest giants stretched their grotesque arms in every direction, and in the fantastically flickering light they almost looked to be moving. It was as though they threatened us and shook with anger at our temerity in intruding among them with this fire spurting torch that scorched them. Soon we became aware of the hollow sound of the sharkskin drum.

That comes from the clearing where the UMUTI, the fire walking is to be held. Now the UMATI, the pit of fire, is ready and the people are waiting for me. I am the Tahua, the leader of this ceremony **THAT CLEANSES PEOPLES SOULS**
(note: that this is the phrase that appears so often in esoteric literature. It is often said to be just symbolic. But this REAL event was certainly NOT to be just symbolic in nature----these people were REALLY going to walk thru a furnace!)

I could not believe that these people were actually going to expose themselves to that great burning pit!

I was the only white man in the large crowd that stood about 20 feet from the enormous oven, whose volcanic stones shown mauvish-red and white with heat! It was on these stones that they proposed to walk barefoot this night. I tried to move foreward toward the fire, but I could not because it began to feel intolerable and burn my skin.

Tuarae told me that the guava wood and mape logs had been burning here for two days and nights. All the time the stones had been drawing up the heat. The white priests had told him, he reminded, that Hell was like this oven. " I do not myslef, believe that there is any Hell, but if there is I should not be afraid of it. You will see very soon yourself with the aid of the varua, the good spirits, that we can walk over the glowing umu."

A young girl asked me if we had UMUITI the same as they did.

"no, walking barefoot over white-hot stones would seem as impossible and extraordinary to my countrymen as it is easy and natural to you polynesians," I said.

The UMU pit was about six feet wide, six feet deep and 12 feet long. On the bottom they had laid dry faggots and over this logs of Tahitian Chestnut. Large volcanic stones were laid on top, and over these again a layer of small stones about the size of a human head. Tuarae had set light to the fire through a tunnel on the Western side of the UMU 48 hours before the ceremony. Fire was made in the natural way by the friction of two pices of wood rubbed together. Matches would never be used on such a high occasion because it would have been taking too great a risk with tradition. South of the oven they had built an upraised platform a walled structure of plaited aplm leaves.

On the edge of the dark forest stood a banana plant, quivering in the wind. I could not resist the temptation to test it in the heat of the oven. I cut down a large, dew dripping leaf and held it towards the UMU without touching the stones. When it was about 6 feet away the juicy leaf began to crackle and glow and I drew back hastily for I could not stand the heat on my outstretched hand.

A murmur of amusement ran through the crowd. Yes, now the white man could see for himself that the UMU was hot!

Just as I had convinced myself of the heat of the oven, Tuarae stepped out of the darkness. He was adorned with green TI leaves, and in his right hand he held a spray of the same plant. Straight and calm he moved forward and stopped three steps from the UMU. To me it was a marvel that his half naked body could withstand the heat even at that distance. We spectators were so silent that not a sound was to be heard save for the rustling of the mysterious jungle about us. Tuarae raised the TI-branch and looked into the deep night sky. For a moment he stood quite motionless, and in the light of the glowing pile of stones he looked like some fantastic heathen memorial to a vanished world. Yes, so like he was to a figure of moulded bronze that for a moment I caught myself wondering how it had ever found its way into this remote jungle spot in the middle of the great area of the Pacific. Now he began with a powerful voice to intone an ancient hymn from no one knows how many years out of the distant past calling on the ancients to protect the firewalkers. Three times he struck the TI-branch against the edge of the UMU. Then he stepped barefoot, with deliberate resolution on the white hot stones. He was dimmed by the heat radiation from the pyre. His gaze was high and his face showed not a trace of fear or pain.

Slowly and with great dignity the TAHUA moved over the oven. When he had come to the other side he raised his TI branch and returned as he came!!!! Now, he made a sign to the others to follow him. Most of the spectators passed in line after Tuarae over the still white-hot UMU. All moved calmly and held to their high gaze into the darkness of the remote heavens. All carried TI-branches. From a long way back in the dark dim reaches of the Polynesian mind dated the knowledge that this ceremony to cleanse the soul was possible and normal. BUT, they knew too, that without the TI-plant there would be no UMU.....or ceremony of UMUTI.

BUT AS IF THIS WERE NOT ENOUGH-------

"White Brother, come with me over the UMU"-- I was to be invited!

For a second I felt in a quandry. Suppose it needed "faith" to succeed in the strange progress over the UMU? In that case I would burn myself to pieces for all my Tahitian sandals. This great marvel of the UMUTI was surely not to be possible for a very skeptical white man? What could I say? There stood the gentle Taurae waiting for me and the eyes of the group were on my questioningly. What was their white brother going to do? Had he enough trust in his brown friend to go over the UMU as they ?

I rose. I had hoped that no one had noticed my short hesitation. I certainly could not let these good and friendly people feel that I was afraid.

Someone thrust a TI-branch in my hand. Tuarae told me to follow right behind him. "Remember not to look down or back! Many years ago there was a white man who turned about when half way over the UMU and his white shoes turned as black as coals and his feet and legs were very badly burned. He began his chant that at this time even I had trust in. E haere tatou i teie nei............

It was a fascinatingly gruesome moment and it felt fantasticly queer to take the first step. To be truthful, I expected to smell the sharp odor of burning flesh, my own. I looked fareward and upward at the deep dark twisted silhouette of a pandanus tree. One had to move slowly and feel his own way over the stones. Strange of the strangest---it did not burn, but my head felt hot and ready to burst from a strange inward pressure.

It was as though we had been for hours on this strange journey and when I at last reached the other side of the oven, it was as iff it were strange to be on the solid earth again.

I stopped and ran my fingers over the soles of my sandals...very cautiously, only to find that they were still cool to the touch.

Once more there came a murmur of amusement from the closely observing Tahitians.

I was happy that I had come through unbroiled, but I found there was still more to come!

"Come with me once more over the UMU, but this time without the sandals because it is 'airier' that way," he said with a sly twinkle.

This time I did not hesitate and I knew that the Sandals meant nothing either one way or another against that terrible heat.

So, I stepped barefoot on to the UMU. The unpleasant sensations I had expected to experience in my head the time before, had completely disappeared, and I passed across to the other side without discomfort of any description. At the terminal point I quickly examined my feet. THEY SEEMED OF ---NORMAL BODY HEAT------ not even the small blond hairs on my legs were singed.

Tauae looked down on my and said solemnly:

"Now you have seen for yourself that the SPIRIT of man is superior to the strongest fire. Varua, the good spirits help us. They lived here (in the Pacific?) once like you and me and ordinary people. Now they still live here, but in another "world". Sometimes we can even see and hear them for a little while. Many people are with only "course" understanding and they can never see them or apprehend them at all. People ears and eyes are different. One man can see a ship far off, but another can't see. One man will hear a wild dove in the hills, while another less sensitive hears nothing. I, for one, see many VARUA (spirits) here this evening, but there must be many around this UMU who have tonight seen or heard nothing from the world of the spirits."

Tuarae then climbed cat-like on the platform that was erected South of the oven and made a sign to the Tahitians to light the dry leaf walls. They flared with flame violently and the flames began to lick at his feet. He stood there absolutely still, his arms upraised and his gaze held high. The flames leaped higher and higher, until the bronz-like figure was swallowed up in the roaring seas of fire.

By now I had such utter confidence in Tuarae that I certainly never doubted for a second that he would come safely through. It was clear that the intense flash heat was not effecting him.

The raging fire and the thousands of sparks forced us spectators very soon to draw back.

In a short while the flames subsided and there stood Tuarae as before with glistening body and outstretched arms. Even the TI-leaves shown as fresh and green as at the outset of the ceremony.

The platform itself was now in flames, and it looked as though the Tahua were standing in an enormous tray of fire. Just as I was expecting this to crash to the ground at any moment, Tuarae jumped up into the air and landed with his bare feet on the UMU, knocking the stones together with such violence that white and fine greenish sparks flew out. How could a jelly-like human stand such treatment in fire and not be hurt?

Immediately after the jump, Tuarae flung himself headlong down and ran on his hands and feet over the still red-hot UMU. He came over to me, and asked if I wished to look at him even closer. Not a hair of his head or body was even singed, his feet and hands were quite unhurt!

AS soon as I convinced myself of this, I took a twig of tree and thru it into the UMU. It started to smoke and burn almost as soon as it touched the oven.

Now the most important part of the ceremony of fire was over, and we all sat down on smooth green mats of plaited coco-leaves. They struck up an ancient Tahitian himene. It sounded like ordinary singing of choirs, but with a deep sound like a gigantic organ played by some musical genius. One heard A T I the cyclone sound, the roar of the waterfall down mountain steeps and the rythmic rumbling base of their good friend, the ocean--and their enenmy too.

It was breath taking and dramatic. Suddenly the sound of tumutlt and storm died' down and the gentle sound of the trade-wind sang.

A magnificent chieftain rose and started to speak.

Tamarii Tahiti nui! The atmosphere is good this evening. It is the atmostphere of the olden days. What we had always on these islands until diseases and poisonous weeds came to us on the ships of the white man. We have shrunk and now we are a little people. In valleys where once thousands lived there are now but hundreds. But let us be grateful that we still have Tahua such as our good and gentle Tuarae and Raiatea among us. Through this firewalking we have we have gained more faith in our selves and in our "spirits". Man lives beyond' the grave....we are few, but we are deathless.

After such an umuti as we have had tonight we know that the spirit of man is deathless, but what is the body? Nothing but a house of leaves that is fresh and green at first, but does it not wither and turn to dust like flesh and bones, the temporary dwelling place of the spirit?

The old chief was a great orator as so many of these people are. He told of the greatest of the spirits of the old days that were still with his people, waiting for those that were there that night to join them.

-------------30----------

Certainly those of us who are interested in what happened to the cosmic men of Lemuria this story is worth keeping in our archives. Western Science today can conceive of no method that many can so control the force-field around his body that it can turn aside the great heat radiations from a fiery pit such as was done this night on Tahiti. However, even for us today it does seem that proper radiation shielding might not be tons of lead as we use, but just might not it be radiations which counter the harmful radiations just as was done in this instance. The use of the TI-plant may have been nothing more than a symbol, but it might have been more than that. It may have been the kind of fundamental oscillator which the . circuit of the body tuned to to get the correct radiation component with which to turn aside the heat radiations on the trips thru the oven . What the answer is---we don't know. AL WE DO KNOW is that it was done and that it was done effectively and in the manner of the knowledge of the most ancient ones.

THE SPACE CRAFT DIGEST rests its case, but in co-operation with the Pacific Lemurian Society makes this offering of another example of knowledge from the "other limb of the tree" and challenges Western Science to duplicate the feat!

WHY DON"T THE 200"TELESCOPE OPERATORS TELL US WHAT'S REALLY TAKING PLACE ON THE MOON why is it left to the smallter instruments in private observatories?-----

Mapping the Floor of Plato

LAST August I started systematic observations of features on the floor of the lunar crater Plato, using the 8-inch reflector belonging to my high school science club. The drawing on page 22 of the November, 1957, *Sky and Telescope* shows many of the tiny craterlets and bright spots visible in this telescope under favorable conditions. Because these markings have long been suspected of year-to-year changes in visibility, I decided to make a careful chart of them as they appeared in 1957.

The accompanying map is based upon 15 sketches made between August and December last year. Next to each feature on the map is its "visibility index number," which is the percentage of observing nights on which it was recorded. These numbers provide a rough scale of the relative conspicuousness of the different features, and hence should be useful in any comparison with the work of other observers to detect changes. Italic numbers on the chart indicate doubtful objects, glimpsed faintly only once or twice; some of these could have been confused with neighboring markings.

The total number of spots charted was 64, five of which could be recognized as small craterlets by their interior shadows. The most seen on a single night was 39 on October 11th, but over 30 were counted on five nights, and in all but four of my sketches there were 18 or more. After the map had been completed, on one night of exceptionally steady seeing, January 2, 1958, I saw 38 interior spots, and made the pencil sketch reproduced above.

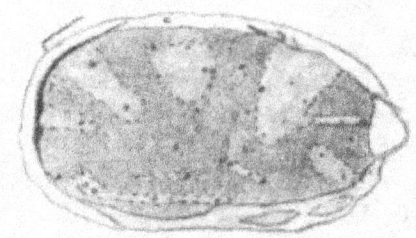

A sketch of Plato at 200x, made January 2, 1958, 0:40 to 2:15 Universal time, with an 8-inch telescope.

All but a few of the spots are invisible at sunrise on this portion of the moon, when the moon's age is between eight and nine days. At no time did any part of the floor appear to be obscured, as some observers have reported.

One problem of Plato is whether its floor follows the curve of the moon's surface, or has some low relief. Sketches made on two nights when it was near sunrise on Plato seem to me to indicate that the floor is rolling. On September 3rd there was a low place just east of the prominent central craterlet; west of this same crater there was an area slightly brighter than the rest of the floor, apparently the eastern slope of another depression. On October 3rd, both these areas appeared dark.

PATRICK McINTOSH
R. R. 2, Box 231
Robinson, Ill.

This veryfine observation work by an amateur shows that there is a real mystery on PLATO on the moon, our closest space neighbor. Why do the domes, lights, spots come and go? WHY is the true story of the moon kept a secret from the public while actually many people are pretty certain that events are happening on the moon that certainly should be explained immediately to the taxpaying public. "SECRET" seems to be forever a refuge behind which to hide actual incompetance and worse in our military. GOOD REASON to remove the space program from the hands of the military. (SEE EDITORIAL) This must be done before their bureaucratic madness bankrupts the greatest nation on this planet while in pursuit of the way to military dictatorship clothed under the guise of national defense! CIVILIAN CONTROL of the military must again be exercised! Must be why it's written into our constitution//?//

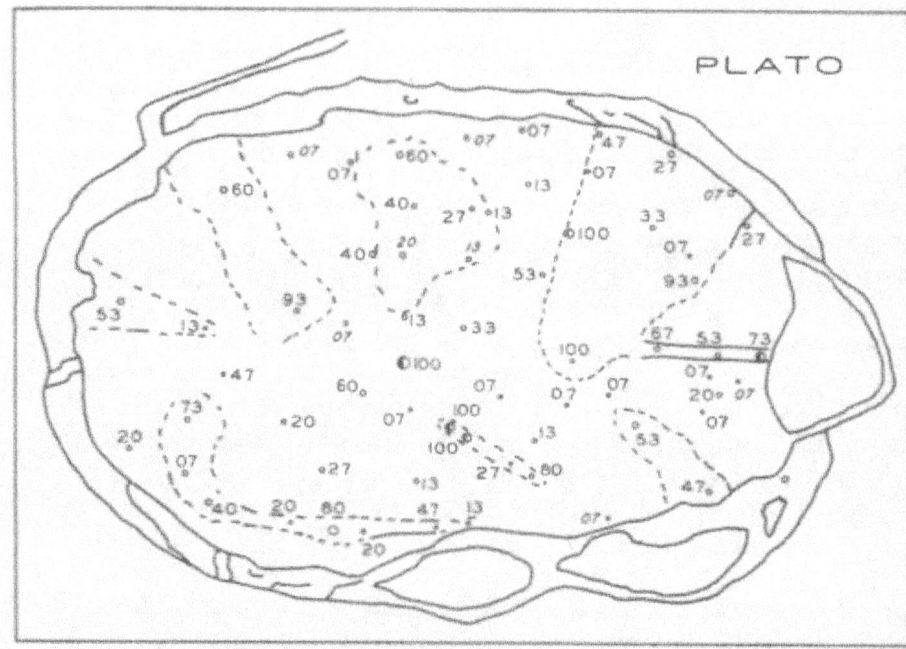

In this Patrick McIntosh chart, compiled from observations at 200x to 400x, dashed lines depict lighter patches on the dark floor of Plato.

UFO over KOREA caught in the act of "dematerialization"!!!!

THIS SPACE CRAFT DIGEST EXCLUSIVE obtained from an Oregon City, Oregon, Architect. The UFO seems in the initial stages of transparentcy!

LEMURIA

The Lost Continent of the Pacific

ENROLL A FRIEND . . . THE SPACE-CRAFT DIGEST now is mailed to subscribers and members of the PACIFIC LEMURIAN SOCIETY all over the world. Members have been most complimentary about the clearness of our U.F.O. pictures. We have more for our next issues. BUT we wish to DOUBLE our circulation and there is only ONE quick way to do this . . . EACH MEMBER right NOW makes a pledge to quickly ENROLL A FRIEND!!! We feel that each issue can see an improvement but our presentation costs more. Actually our mailing cost to some of our more remote members is quite high.

Many U.F.O. publications have fallen by the wayside, but the PACIFIC LEMURIAN SOCIETY will expand its revelation of the LEARNING OF THE MOST ANCIENT ONE from little-known archives and sources all over the world. This knowledge of the everyday life of CELESTIAL MAN can **only** be yours today through the greatly expanded activities of the PACIFIC LEMURIAN SOCIETY.

That's why we ask you to enroll a friend to aid in development of our group.

PLEDGE TO ENROLL A FRIEND

DO SO NOW

DO SO TODAY

WITHOUT FAIL!!

MAIL THE MEMBERSHIP BELOW TODAY — BY AIR MAIL!

A MEMBERSHIP APPLICATION

Name _____

Address _____

I am enclosing five dollars (2 £ in sterling areas) for a yearly subscription to **SPACE CRAFT DIGEST** published by the PACIFIC LEMURIAN SOCIETY which will also enable me to be included in the future releases of this society for a period of six months.

Mail to: **PACIFIC LEMURIAN SOCIETY**
P.O. Box 768
Salem, Oregon, U.S.A.

ENROLL A FRIEND

SPACE CRAFT Digest

FALL ISSUE 1958

Theories of Electrical Flight

published by the PACIFIC LEMURIAN SOCIETY

EDITORIAL . . . . In this issue, the subject of the Unidentified Flying Object, space-life and other phenomena that are unexplained by conventional science is presented in such a manner that it seems incredible that the US Air Forces can continue any longer to permit their obtuse prevarications to further harass the over-loaded US tax-payer.

Our rocket propelled "space" program has failed! Our DEW line radar is far from adequate protection against any type of USSR Missles from the North! Our SAC planes and their costly vapor trails are a very expensive, impressive, tragic JOKE! But still, in the "battle of the budget" in our "government by press release" still greater military budgets are proposed with the awful spectre of Communism used as the whip.

It will profit "our way of life" little if we are so over-loaded with incompetent, tax hungry, military and civil bureaucracy that we spend ourselves into bankruptcy even before the dreaded Communist-inspired war breaks upon us.

Let our government accept the obvious fact that force of arms never solved a political question short of "death to the enemy" and that "our system" is on trial over the world in a **political** arena. This is a **political** battle over the world, and armed force in Lebanon, Quemoy or Little-Rock will never solve a political question.

Conventional flight must one day succumb to the electrically propelled space vehicle which in itself is a complete planetoid capable of occupying its force-field-determined niche in the universe. Until this method of looking at the problem becomes our national scientific policy we can bankrupt our nation building obsolete, impractical rockets and jets.

Let the Air Force publicly ADMIT that "some one" is violating the airspace over our nation at will. They have thus failed doubly in their lawful task. Let them admit failure NOW. Let them now re-assess their blundering before the "dreaded Communists" actually do control the planet thru their electrical flight vehicles.

For the nation that correctly solves the "flying saucer" enigma will in that one stroke vault 10,000 years in the **real** space-age.

OREGON'S OCTOBER SPACE-CRAFT VISITOR

Oregon, without much doubt, had a persistant space-visitor, and the AM paper in Oregon, the Oregonian, carried the "sonic-boom" ACCOUNT of the arrival in the usual manner that distorts such stories:

VOL. XCVIII— NO. 80,563

Jet Plane Suspected Of 'Boom'

Morning Blast Rattles Windows Throughout City

"A heavy blast, apparently caused by a Portland based F 102 jet airplane breaking the sound barrier, shook houses, rattled windows and dishes and startled residents all over Portland Monday.

Calls about the blast swamped the Oregonian switchboard. It was first believed to have come from construction on the Baldock Freeway. But the contractor said there was no blasting on the project Monday and City Hall reported no permits for blasting Monday had been issued.

The Portland Air Base information office reported later one of the supersonic F 102 fighter planes based there had been flying on a routine mission at some 40,000 feet some 25 miles South of Portland around 11:15 AM and had cracked the sound barrier.

The information officer said the plane, breaking beyond the speed of sound, probably had created a sonic boom, somewhat akin to thunder produced by an electrical storm.

He said however, that while the jet's flight was the PROBABLE cause of the blast, there was no absolute certainty of it........"

COMMENT---again it seems that the story is ambiguous and misleading in such cases and a "handy" explanation is used by an Air Force officer who belatedly issues a cover-up release. Let's go on and quote the news stories the rest of the month from the Salem, Oregon, Statesman and the Oregonian and see if we can at least put forth an explanation which has as much basis as did the one quoted.

Here is the second headline and the story:

Blinking Flying Object Sighted Over Salem

".. A strange unidentified flying object with red and white blinking lights was seen by some Salem residents Monday night.

Thomas Warren, Leslie Jr. High Mathematics instructor, and Beverly Shriver, 14 year old daughter of Mr. and Mrs. William Shriver 3856 Seneca Avenue, S., reported they both saw a rectangular shaped object hovering in the Western skies................the object flying slow

---
SPACE-CRAFT DIGEST   P.O. BOX 768   SALEM, OREGON--U.S.A.---1

THEN increased speed and flew toward Portland, Warren said. A Portlander also reported seeing the object, a radio station reported."

Two Hunters See Eerie Sky Lights

BUT THE OBJECT STILL REMAINED IN OREGON in OCT.

Two Salem deer hunters were home from Eastern Oregon Tuesday with a story of sighting strange sky lights. Bab and Jack Brant 450 Beck Avenue, S. E. arrived at the Pine Mt. Area near Millican about 3 a.m. Tuesday morning. For about 20 minutes, as they were hunting for a camping site, a white and red light seemed to keep pace with their car at a distance. At first they believed it was either car lights on a distant mountain or a camp fire.

Then the light, alternately bright and dim, sped toward the car, suddenly halting and nearing the ground to the right and slightly ahead of them. As the ground became illuminated the lights went out.

Both men said the white light was the most brilliant with the red light beneath it.

They refused to remain in the area and returned to Sisters. There, they said, a waitress reported two other groups of persons had like-wise reported sighting the same type of light recently in the same general area. Bob Brant is employed by Southern Pacific R.R. and his brother is home on leave from the AIR FORCE ! !)

Both said that they considered reporting the event to the state police, but did not because they thought that the police would not believe them...."

On Friday night the 24th of Oct. others saw similar performances."..... Strange sky objects were apparently hovering in Marion County skies Friday night, judging from reports of two valley police chiefs.

Police Chiefs at Stayton, Mill City See 'Sky Light'

Statesman News Service

Stayton Police Chief, Everette Norfleet, Sgt. Ronald Frey and another Stayton man reported seeing an object in the Northeast sky traveling Southwest at 7:30 PM while they were on a routine police patrol.

"It looked like an evening star with a tail below it", Norfleet said. "I've watched for flying saucers ever since they were mentioned and I never saw anything like this," he added.

The object was reported to have been a light "star" color gradually changing to a ruddy glow and swinging like a pendulum. It was watched for some 15 minutes and still in view when the men resumed their police duties.

SPACE-CRAFT DIGEST p.o. BOX 768 SALEM, OREGON U.S.A.----2

At the same time, Mill City Chief of Police, Clarence Meader reported seeing an object moving East from where he was watching, North of Mill City.

I am not saying what it was, Meader said, reporting that it was a clear bright blue point of light. The object was seen later in the evening from a point west of Mill City. This time it was moving West, Meader said.

Although there were jet planes reported in the area Friday night, both men said they were familiar with jets, and that the object was something else.

****

Big Fiery Object Seen In Early Morning Sky

By The Associated Press

On the 18th of the month--- A big fiery object flashed across the sky in Eastern Washington early Friday and a weather observer at Spokane said, "it was as bright as lighting, too bright for a shooting star". It was reported to have been seen from Spokane to Pasco and Prosser (Near the secret US Plutonium works at Hanford, Wn. Ed)

Deputy sheriff William H. Miller of Spokane County said the object lit up the ground around the patrol car in the Spokane Valley for from 15 to 20 seconds and the object cast shadows from nearby objects. Spokane city police said they also saw it. Other reports came in from Othello.

****

COMMENT BY EDITOR: Now it seems that all of these people see these sky happenings. But what does the Air Force say: IN OCTOBER-----
FROM UPI...

WASHINGTON---THE AIR FORCE SAYS IT HAS BEEN UNABLE TO EXPLAIN 21 REPORTS OF UNIDENTIFIED FLYING OBJECTS (UFO's) DURING THE 13 MONTHS ENDED JULY 31st.

IT LISTED 84 PER CENT OF ALL SUCH REPORTED SIGHTINGS AS BALLOONS, PLANES, BIRDS, HOAXES OR NATURAL PHENOMENA. IN ITS REPORT THE AIR FORCE SAID IT HAD CHECKED 12 HUNDRED UFO REPORTS SINCE JUNE 1957.

OF THESE, IT REPORTS THAT ONLY 21 CASES OR FEWER THAN TWO PER CENT, ARE STILL REGARDED AS "UNKNOWN". AN OBJECT SIGHTED IS CONSIDERED UNKNOWN WHEN AT LEAST ONE VALID CONCLUSION CAN NOT BE DRAWN FROM THE FACTS AVAILABLE.... AND WHEN THE DISCRIPTION OF IT CANNOT BE RELATED TO NATURAL PHENOMENA IN THE SKIES.

BUT THE REPORT SAYS THERE " ARE NO AIR FORCE DOCUMENTS WHICH PROVE THE EIXISTENCE OF FLYING SAUCERS OR SHOW THAT THE EARTH IS BEING OBSERVED, VISITED, OR THREATENED BY MACHINES FROM OTHER PLANETS".

THE AIR FORCE NOTED A SHARP RISE IN THE NUMBER OF UFO'S RE-
PORTED, 928 DURING THE LAST SIX SPACE-CONSCIOUS MONTHS OF
1957.
BUT, IT REPeated A STATEMENT MADE IN 1953 BY A PANEL OF SIX
SCIENTIFIC CONSULTANTS. THE STATEMENT SAID THAT " THE EVID
ENCE ON UFO'S SHOWED NO INDICATION THAT THESE PHENOMENA
CONSTITUTED A DIRECT THREAT TO NATIONAL SECURITY".

THE AIR FORCE SAID THAT DURING THE 13 MONTH PERIOD, REPORTS
EXPLAINED INCLUDED 353 ASTRONOMICAL PHENOMENA, 290 AIRCRAFT
194 BALLOONS AND 224 OTHER OBJECTS, SUCH AS LIGHTS BIRDS AND
HOAXES. *********** end if UP I story.

That wire service "routine denial" was too much for the editor in view of
the following and he felt that he couldn't let the AIR FORCE "COVER-UP"
continue unanswered. Following is the UNITED PRESS answer to our letter
asking for a UFO photo that was taken by the Brazilian Navy:

United Press Associations
INCORPORATED IN NEW YORK

GENERAL OFFICES
NEWS BUILDING, NEW YORK CITY

Written from
UNITED PRESS NEWSPICTURES
461 EIGHTH AVENUE
NEW YORK 1, NEW YORK

July 21, 1958

Mr. W. Gordon Allen
Radio K-GAY!
Salem, Oregon

Dear Mr. Allen:

We are pleased to acknowledge your letter of July 12
in which you inquired about United Press photos of a
UFO over Trinidad.

> "Rio de Janeiro...Above is one of the phto-
> graphs of a "flying saucer" taken recently
> aboard the Brazilian Navy survey ship
> Almirante Saldanha. The Brazilian Navy
> Ministry vouched for their authenticity Feb.
> 25th, in a statement which stated that the
> pictures were made by a photographer Almiro
> Barauna while the ship was cruising off
> Trinidade Island, 700 miles off the port of
> Victoria, Espirito Santo State."

In ordering our photo kindly refer to our file number:
RIO 1151512.

Yours truly,

Peter A. Sansone
UNITED PRESS INTERNATIONAL

Here is the reproduction of the United Press photo and certainly is available to the US AIR FORCE. It then appears that the AIR FORCE was not keeping faith the tax payers who foot the bill. Placing its faith in the SAC massive retaliation is a macawbre JOKE which someday may find the US at the mercy of the nation on this planet that solves the problem of ELECTRICAL FLIGHT. Certainly "some-one" already has.
HERE IS THE ANSWER TO THE AIR FORCE "COVER-UP" GIVEN TO UPI.

SALEM---LEBANON AND SALEM BROADCASTER W. GORDON ALLEN TODAY ACCUSED THE U.S. AIR FORCE --IN THESE WORDS--" OF WILLFULLY DUPING THE U-S TAX PAYER BY ITS PERIODIC DENIAL OF UNIDENTIFIED FLYING OBJECT PHENOMENA".

A REPORT FROM THE AIR FORCE (quoted above) RELEASED TODAY SAYS THERE ARE "NO AIR FORCE DOCUMENTS WHICH PROVE THE EXISTENCE OF FLYING SAUCERS OR SHOW THAT THE EARTH IS BE-OBSERVED, VISITED, OR THREATENED BY MACHINES FROM OTHER PLANETS".
ALLEN--WHO IS PRESIDENT OF RADIO STATION KGAY IN SALEM AND KGAL IN LEBANON SAYS HE HAS INVITED THE AIR FORCE TO SEND REPRESENATIVES TO HIS OFFICE TO SEE WHAT HE DISCRIBED AS "SOME OF THE BEST PICTURES OF FLYING SAUCERS IN EXISTENCE."

THE AIR FORCE REPORT ADMITS THAT IT HAS BEEN UNABLE TO EXPLAIN 21 REPORTS OF UNIDENTIFIED FLYING OBJECTS DURING THE 13 MONTHS ENDED JULY 31ST.

ALLEN SAYS THAT HE HAS A PICTURE RELEASED BY THE PRESIDENT OF BRAZIL OF AN OBJECT PURPORTED TO BE A FLYING SAUCER OBSERVED FROM THE BRAZILIAN IGY SURVEY SHIP ALMIRANTI-SALDANA WHILE IT WAS OFF THE ISLAND OF TRINIDAD.

ALLEN, AN ELECTRICAL ENGINEER, AND PUBLISHER OF A PUBLICATION CALLED " SPACE-CRAFT DIGEST" SAYS THAT --IN HIS OPINION ELECTRICAL FLIGHTS WITHOUT PROPELLORS OR JETS USING THE FREE SPACIAL ELECTRICITY THAT RUNS THE UNIVERSE IS POSSIBLE AND THAT THE MANY UFO REPORTS SHOW THAT "SOMEONE" IS NOW USING THIS METHOD OF INTERPLANETARY TRAVEL. ALLEN SAYS--"I HAVE THE PICTURES TO PROVE IT".

THESE PICTURES have been published in the past issues of the "Digest" and of course our subscribers are familiar with them. BUT, to demonstrate on how high a level the "cover-up" goes as the battle for the slice of the budget goes on while the tax-payer is saddled more and more under foolish military budgets--we quote further. We feel we can pretty well in this issue "prove" that the AIR TECHNICAL INTELLIGENCE COMMAND is guilty of outright lies to the public. It issues them thru such AIR FORCE releases as we quote. Here's another letter:

DEPARTMENT OF THE AIR FORCE
Washington

Office of the Secretary 30 July, 1958

Dear Mr. Allen:

Your letter of 2 July 1958 addressed to the Air Technical Intelligence Center concerning unidentified flying objects has been referred to this office for reply.

From time to time we have so-called unidentified sightings on our defence radar screen but these sightings have been eventually identified as normal military training flights, commercial flights or phenomena that can cause radar returns.

For your information I am enclosing the Department of Defence Fact Sheet on unidentified flying objects dated 5 November 1957, which clearly outlines the Air Force's position regarding this subject.

Sincerely,

LAWRENCE J. THACKER
Major USAF
Executive Officer
Public Information Division
Office of Information Services

NOW IN THAT NEWS RELEASE WE QUOTE JUST A PORTION ------

SPACE-CRAFT DIGEST   p. o. Box 768   SALEM, OREGON, USA

NEWS RELEASE
PLEASE NOTE DATE

DEPARTMENT OF DEFENCE
Office of Public Information
Washington 25 D.C.

Fact Sheet   November 5, 1957   No. 1083-58
                                                               LI 5-6700 Ext. 75131

Air Force's 10 year Study of Unidentified Flying Objects

In repsonse to queries as to results of previous investigation of Unidentified Flying Object reports, the Air Force said today that after 10 years of investigation and evaluation of UFO's no evidence has been discovered to confirm the existence of so-called "FLYING SAUCERS".

Dr. J. Allen Hynek, professor of Astrophysics and Astronomy at Ohio State University is the Chief Scientific Consultant to the Air Force on the subject of Unidentified Flying Objects.

THE REPORT CONCLUDES WITH THIS PUBLIC PROMISE:

T$_h$e Air Force, assigned the responsibility for the Air Defence of the United States, will continue to investigate, through the Air Defence Command all reports of of unusual aerial objects over the US, including objects that may become unidentified flying objects. The services of qualified scientists and technicians will continue to investigate and analyze these reports, and periodic public statements will be made as warrented.

----- END -----

THE SPACE-CRAFT DIGEST charges that this is outright falsehood. Such an investigation is NOT being carried on as promised. Instance after instance of UFO violation of the air-space of US has gone uninvestigated such as these we have noted on the preceding pages. But more than that---Dr. HYNEK, who is on the public payroll to do a job, doesn't even asnwer a query from our radio stations concerning the UFO problem.   His secretary wrote, but from the "feather-bedding" doctor there is no reply because he apparently is one of the Ph.D's hired by the Air Force to produce a "public whitewash" of this fantastic world-wide phenomena.

As a former Naval Radar-radio officer, a graduate electrical engineer the editor realizes that these charges are serious. BUT--at the same time-- the possibility that the USSR or Red China discovering the secret of electrical flight is also serious. While the giant armed forces budget fools with rockets to the bankruptcy of this nation some voice must speak out. The least the fumbling military can do is to stop ignoring those who do fly in space with the vain hope that "they might go away".

SPACE CRAFT DIGEST   SALEM, OREGON, USA   po Box 768   page 7

SMITHSONIAN INSTITUTION
ASTROPHYSICAL OBSERVATORY

SECTION OF UPPER ATMOSPHERE STUDIES
IGY OPTICAL SATELLITE TRACKING PROGRAM
60 GARDEN STREET
CAMBRIDGE 38, MASSACHUSETTS

August 13, 1958

Mr. W. Gordon Allen
P. O. Box 768
Salem, Oregon

Dear Mr. Allen:

In the absence of Dr. Hynek, who is in Europe until September 9, I am acknowledging your letter of the 3rd and inclosures.

I will be happy to pass on your letter to Dr. Hynek upon his return in order to answer further your inquiry regarding the UFO over Trinidad last January.

Yours truly,

(Miss) Lois T. Callahan
Lois T. Callahan
Secretary to Dr. J. Allen Hynek

/lc

WELL...today is November 20th and still no answer from the Dr. of Astro-physics who is lapping at the public trough. His negligence having the effect of proving for the AIR FORCES of the U. S. that the UFO can be ignored.

NOW, it just so happened that your editor was also in Europe last Summer and it seems that if Dr. Hynek was really earning his money he COULD HAVE run down some mighty interesting UFO reports. If he was REALLY interested in solving the UFO problem.

It seems that the AIR FORCES and their "fly boys" like to ride their "hot rod" obsolete bombers making spectacular vapor trails in the sky rather than doing some quiet thinking.

BUT the strangest situation of all occured in October in New Mexico. It seems that the AIR FORCE reached back to the hottest news of 1783 and dusted off a balloon ascension and publicized it under the tricky name of the "MAN HIGH PROJECT". They managed to use a balloon and hoisted a gondola some 100,000 feet into "space". The newspapers across the country dutifully gave it publicity while the tax-payers "marvelled" at what wonders they were getting for their tax dollar.

They got what they deserved, but it seems that even this project had its SPACE-CRAFT watcher from other portions of the cosmos. Your editor called Mrs. Romero and KGAY has the tape recording of the interview. Certainly Mrs. Romero's husband in the lower echelons of the Air Forces hadn't been checked-out yet, for he told the truth! And so did she!

HERE"S THE WIRE SERVICE STORY: (UNITED PRESS INTERNATIONAL)

A CIGAR-SHAPED UNIDENTIFIED FLYING OBJECT HAS BEEN REPORTED SEEN LAST NIGHT NEAR THE PLACE WHERE THE "MAN HIGH" AIR FORCE SPACE BALLOON LANDED WEDNESDAY AT ALAMAGORDO, NEW MEX. THE OBJECT WAS REPORTED BY JOHN ROMERO..... WHO WAS IDENTIFIED AS " AN ASSISTANT ENGINEER" AT HOLOMAN AIR FORCE BASE, NEAR THE WHITE SANDS PROVING GROUNDS. ROMERO SAYS IT WAS FAN-SHAPED AT THE TAIL AND FOUR PI N POINT SPOTS OF LIGHT ON THE SIDE LIKE FOUR PORTHOLES. ROMERO SAYS HE SAW THE OBJECT THROUGH BONOCULARS FOR ABOUT SIX MINUTES. IT HOVERED ABOUT 10 DEGREES ABOVE THE HORIZON AND THEN VANISHED OVER THE SAN ANRES MOUNTAINS NEAR ALAMAGORDO.

CX 940A 10/11

NOW..... someone like Senator Byrd ought to ask the AIR FORCE just what goes on and how much it costs.... and how much longer are we going to put up with this military SNAFU and conceal the RAPE OF THE US TAX PAYER.

13th U.S. Satellite Shot Fails

CAPE CANAVERAL(UP) America's 13th attempt to launch a satellite ended in failure early today because of some difficulty in the upper stages of its launching vehicle. The Army disclosed it gave up hope that the Beacon Balloon satellite had orbited only two hours and 40 minutes after it Jupiter "C" launcher blasted off late Wed. nite. BRIG. GEN. JOHN A. BARCLAY, COMMANDER OF THE ARMY BALLISTIC MISSILE AGENCY AT HUNTSVILLE, ALABAMA SAID THERE WAS SOME DIFFICULTY, BUT THAT HE DIDN"T KNOW PRECISELY WHAT WAS WRONG!!!!(My God!Ed.)

SAUCERS OVER PORTUGAL
by Sr. Marciano Alves

Port. Pilot Lt.

LISBON...In the Spring of 1958 four jet pilots of the Portuguese Air Force on a problem between Granada and Lisbon first noted four glowing saucers cavorting and called to each other on their communications gear. The four brightly glowing saucers were from a cigar-shaped "mother" ship, they observed. The four excited pilots abandoned their problem and watched the mother ship and the saucers for some 45 minutes. They told of their "sighting" and Sr. Marciano Alves of Lisbon personally interviewed them. The story was covered in the papers for a couple of days and then their senior officer told them that it might "be better" if they did not talk too much about what they "saw".

Sr. Alves became interested in the UFO phenomena because of the following story reported to him by a young friend of his from the South of Portugal who is an engineering student. Sr. Alves reports to the SPACE-CRAFT DIGEST...

"In its humble kind of popular observation, I will tell it to you as if I myself have lived it; because the testimonial of my friend F. is that of a friend never misguiding a fellow, and his experience as a student finishing a course, having already accomplished his military, exceptionally cheerful and intelligent, is a guarantee that he did not mistake balloons, birds, or jets for the flying saucers.

'He was spending a day with his bride and some other friends in an estate in the country. They were walking and chatting when suddenly they heard a strange, growing noise which forced them to peer the sky in search of a plane. But they could see nothing from the site where they stood, and then the interest grew because the sound was now strong and it did not seem to him to be the proper sound of an airplane.

According to his description, there were two sounds after one another-- one of them like a sharp whistle and the other one like a "roar", but completely different from what his military ears were familiar with.

They both made up their minds to discover the origin and in rapid agreement they defied one another, although without the remotest idea of flying saucers, which they had read some articles about in the newspapers!

At this occasion the case of Ota base was not yet known to the public.

They ran out of the hall ground, but on their way the strange noise stopped suddenly and my friend stopped, too, making in his mind the hypothesis of an aircraft accident.

Then he saw them!!!!!!----------

Shining, very shining, like a mirror reflecting the sunlight. There were four flying saucers before him at a height of about 40 degrees.

Then his bride grew frightened noticing his watchful expression, and then she discovered them also. Then they shouted, calling the familiar people of the estate: "Flying Saucers! Look up! Here are the Flying Saucers! Finally they do exist! Come and see! Quickly..."

About twelve people came up, and they all did see.

In a part of his report he wrote: "They seemed to be formed by two parts, though we could not distinquish them perfectly--a higher one like the upper part of a Mazzantine hat, and encircled by a narrower ring."

And deeply moved he added:

"I was like dazzled...then I felt a pang to run and tell every body that the Flying Saucers did exist, that they are a reality, that they were in front of me going down and up and furthermore, my friend, I am sure that they did it vertically and at such a quick speed it was rather difficult to follow them with our eyes! I assure you I am not exaggerating!"

Please notice: "going up and down vertically at a tremendous speed"! But there are further surprising details of these evolutions, as you are going to see.

"The regaining of speed (in opposite directions) after the falling took only a few seconds during which we could not see them on account of the natural relief of the ground there. The extraordinary acceleration they must have to be able to go down and up again at the same rate is inexplicable."

"And everything in front of my eyes!!!"

"It seemed that gravity laws did not exist, or else the direction of their force was acting crookedly, as time consumed between falling and recovery was about five seconds."

But those evolutions were not for the four of them at the same time sheer fancy. They formed a line, and only the first and the fourth were moving, while the two in between were not moving!

This see-saw movement repeated during about four minutes and at last one of them described a curve with great inclination and actually feeble speed as to show better his circular shape.

In these positions it lost the reflection of the sunlight and its color was dark, opaque.

My friend F. tells also that since it stopped at the beginning, he could hear no other noise afterwards. And now I make an addition: This fact may have been made on purpose to attract their attention, and if I had been there it might have happened that I would have gone to a lonely place in the hope of a "contact", like Adamski.

Then they disappeared in profoundness Northwards, and after three or four minutes they returned again, only to again disappear completely in a few seconds.

Sr. Marciona Alves, LISBON, PORTUGAL--Aug. 1958

EDITOR'S NOTE---- I spent some time in the Summer of 1958 with Sr. Alves and his friendly family. We took a tour to the convent of Mafra, near Lisbon, and on a delightful Sunday afternoon I had dinner with the family. During this time I satisfied myself that the reporting of Sr. Alvez is of the highest type of integrity in nature and that his background is such that his word is to be respected. I had the feeling that he is a gentleman of the old school that is fast disappearing in our fast moving modern society--a man of high principles.

BEST UFO PICTURE NOW AVAILABLE ---------
Mail 1.00 to the SPACE CRAFT DIGEST for this 5x7 glossy print
SUITABLE FOR FRAMING

OR GET IT FREE WITH AN ORDER FOR "SPACE-CRAFT FROM BE-
YOND THREE DIMENSIONS" See back cover..........

ADVANCE EDITION IN PRINTING---
"WHY WE ARE HERE"

The SPACE PEOPLE tell the dynamic TRUTH about themselves and our planet and their real intentions.

A "BEING FROM JUPITER-----tells Gloria LEE

What's wrong on our planet, WHY, and what we can do about it.
****

Revelations about themselves and their etheric world........
****

Earthman's misconceptions about SEX and their attitudes on it.
****

PLANS of the space people to help us and keep us from the fate our planet seems headed for.
****

WHY we will not fly to the moon or other planets.....how to govern- according to the cosmic law of space
****

WHAT THE FUTURE HOLDS
****

MAIL $2.75 to GLORIA LEE......4449 Ranchview Rd.
WHY WE ARE HERE!   Rolling Hills, California

"TRIP TO MARS"

(From Prince George, B.C. CITIZEN)

AS TOLD TO EDITOR Ron Powell-----"...Iwas working for the U.S. occupation army in Austria on May 15th 1951. I was driving for QM Colonel Cousin. He asked me to drive a Mr. Haster from Linz to Salzburg and back where he was teaching in an Army school. It was on one of these trips that the following incident happened:

Suddenly someone came out of the bush and came close to me. I could see only an outline in the dark, but he seemed to have a helmet on. He was about my height, maybe a little shorter. He had something in his hand and pointed it to me. I thought it was his finger, but it made a click.

After the "click" he waved his hand quickly and I went to put my hand in front of my face, but I was paralyzed. I felt like falling down, but I didn't. He put a black, square plate on my chest and strapped it around my back. I could hear a dog bark in the distance, but I couldn't hear him walking. He must have walked very easily. I could see his outline as he walked around me.

COULDN'T MOVE OR WALK-After he strapped the plate on me he walked in front of me and he pointed the thing in his hand at the plate on my chest rather than at my head like before. He walked away and pulled me after him. I couldn't move or walk, but he just pulled me along after him. I wasn't actually in the air, but my full weight wasn't on the ground. It seemed as if I was light.

Behind the brush was a small field. In the field, hidden from the road was a round object about 150 feet in diameter. It was dark and I couldn't tell what it was. My first thought was that a Russian spy had captured me for some reason.

THE THING (MAN?) THAT LED ME SORT OF ROSE FROM THE GROUND THE TOOK ME AFTER HIM TO THE TOP OF THE OBJECT. HE DID SOMETHING, EITHER STEPPED ON SOMETHING OR PUSHED SOME BUTTON, AND THE DOOR OPENED AND HE PULLED ME AFTER HIM DOWN INTO THE DARK. I WAS PLENTY SCARED AND I WONDERED WHAT WOULD HAPPEN NEXT. I GOT DOWN INTO THE DARK AND FINALLY COULD FEEL A FLOOR UNDER MY FEET.

I knew that I was underneath either a plastic or glass-like canopy because the stars were shining thru above. Then, I saw the outline of what looked like a door and he pulled me through into what I later found out was a room of glass or plastic. He kept his finger or what I later found was a pencil shaped object pointd at me until I was inside the room, but he took it off me and I sank down to the floor.

I next had a sensation of rising up into the air. In a few minutes I could see half of the moon shining. I was scared, but I got a feeling that I was dreaming. Then I started to feel my hands and feet again. By the time I finally got to my feet we were in the sunlight. I looked across the ship and I could see the person that had brought me. He was standing over by a wall with some levers on it. Even tho he looked much like a person as we are-- at the time he looked to me like the Devil!

He had no hair at all that I could see thru a sort of glass helmet. His head was a sort of sylinder form--a very high forehead with big eyes. You could see lots of little eyes in the two big eyes. It seemed to me that it looked something like the eyes of a fly. There was no nose at all, just two holes. He had a very small slit for a mouth. It seemed that his skin was very white. His very large skull had two holes for ears, with no eyebrows at all. His torso was very round like a tin can. The legs were of a proportionate length His arms seemed a little bit shorter than our arms, in proportion. His hands had three fingers. I couldn't see ny neck and he was dressed in material that seemed silvery in color, but not shiny. This material covered him except for the head part that had on the helmet.

The main part of the ship that I could see from the room seemed to be round. The walls were glass like, but I could not see through them. The floor was of glass or plastic. In the middle of the floor, under the plastic, was also a square box, a kind of bigger model of the one that was strapped to my chest. From the corners of the black box or plate (about 10' square) beams ran to the walls of the craft. I could see under the black plate and there seemed to be a duplicate room on the other side of the ship. I could also see the same kind of levers to control the ship in the duplicate room.

As soon as we came into the sunlight I could feel an intense burning heat, but he pulled a control and a covering like blue water came over the transparent roof. Then, the sunlight was more "normal" but I could still see the sun.

I first thought that I was dreaming and then my second thought was that I was dead and that my soul was rising up. The ship was not rotating or going sideways, but was rising straight up. I could see the sun like a ball of fire and the moon like a silver ball, but the rest of the "sky" was quite dark. As I looked up the moon was large and seemed to be setting right down on us. Suddenly we appeared to be standing on the roof about a quarter of a mile above the moon. I could clearly see the many craters on the surface of the moon. The "ground" seemed to be grayish in color and I could see large rocks and hills. We were first in the sunny part of the moon but then the ship glided to the darker part of the moon. As the driver stopped the ship the sun still seemed to shine into the ship and we seemed to be "waiting" for something. I saw him take one of the pencil-like "things" that he pointed at me and point it downward. Then, I thought that he might be from the moon and might be signaling to "some-one" on the moon. However, there was no noise from the ship or from the signal instrument. After a time we moved again to the right. I then had the thought that we might be moving back to earth. But I looked above me and could see the big ball that was the earth and I could see the outline of the North and South American continents. I could also see clouds and part of the outline of Asia.

THEN THE EARTH AND THE MOON STARTED TO MOVE AWAY FROM ME VERY FAST AND IT WAS THEN THAT I BEGAN TO FEEL THAT WE WERE GOING TO ANOTHER PLANET.!

Suddenly, the other planet began to loom up so fast that I thought we were going to crash into it. The driver stopped in time with no jerk, but then I could see we were still quite a ways away and we then glided sideways into a landing on the "ground". THIS LAND LOOKED LIKE PARADISE TO ME!!!!!!

AS WE WENT DOWN I LOOKED AT THE LAND ON ONE SIDE AND COULD SEE THE RED FIELDS. I COULD SEE STRAIGHT RIVERS WITH BLUE WATERS IN THEM. ON THE OTHER SIDE THERE WAS WHAT LOOKED LIKE GRAY-GREEN FIELDS------SOME PLACES IN THE FIELDS I COULD SEE CHIMNEYS RISING FROM THE "GROUND". It was a bright day and the sun was shining with no clouds in the sky.

We were approaching the red fields and I could see much more plainly the straight rivers with the blue water and at intervals there were bridges across these rivers. The bridges were just like our bridges. From as high as we were I could see no definite sign of life.

Then we glided up to a field that was filled with saucers just like the one I was in. There appeared to be hundreds of them. They were of many many colors, but no black or red ones---gray, gold and silver etc.

The driver stopped the ship about a quarter of a mile above them by just pulling one of the control levers. Then we went straight down until we were about 20 or 30 feet above the ground and the ship was PARKED ON A HIGH PLATFORM! (Ed. this might have great significance as it might have been an insulated platform)

When we got stopped on the platform the driver slid back the "glass" and then he stepped outside. Then he put the pencil-like "thing" to his chest and he floated down like a falling leaf. He then started to walk very fast along to a third or fourth saucer. He again pointed the "pencil" to his chest and jumped up into the ship. He stayed in that ship for about ten minutes and I then had a chance to look around. I could see that the "man--or--thing" in the other ship was a little smaller than the man from "my" ship.

Quite a 'ways away around other saucers I could see the same type of people. I also saw two ships further away that had some earth people aboard. One ship, kind of dirty looking, had two kids and one man and woman in it. In another that was kind of golden I saw an earthman and earth woman in it. I was too scared to wave to them and they did not wave to me. After I had seen them I thought that I would have to stay there with them now. I then looked off in the distance at a river where I could see things moving. They were dark and I could see really what they were, but I thought they might be a herd of beef. On the ground I could see big red flowers growing that looked like our sunflowers. There was some earth between them, but the flowers grew as far as eye could see. The earth could be seen in patches and it looked about the same as our earth. It was then that I got to thinking that I must be on Mars. I remembered having learned in school that it was red and had canals, but I wasn't sure because I had kind of lost my directions since we had left the moon.

The driver then came back, hopped into our ship, and we took off again in the direction of the moon. ("A" moon? ed.) The moon that we went by looked like a tin ball, was not very big, and had no craters on it. I didn't know where we were then going and I thought we were going on to another planet. AFTER 10 MINUTES I COULD SEE THAT WE WERE APPROACHING THE SUNNY SIDE OF A HALF BALL, "OUR" MOON, AND THEN I COULD SEE "OUR" EARTH. I WAS GLAD TO SEE THAT IT WAS "OUR" EARTH, BUT THE TERRIBLE SPEED WAS SO GREAT THAT AGAIN I THOUGHT WE WOULD CRASH!

The driver stopped the ship when we came close enough to near our atmosphere and again glided gently through it without a sound. I then seemed to feel that he was going to take me back to where he had found me.

I did have the impression that he was going to kill me just to keep my trip a secret. We went into the darkness and came down to the ground and I knew that it was the exact, same place at which he had picked me up.

NOW, I was really afraid that he was going to kill me. He took the pencil "thing" out and pointed it at me and then took me out the door back to the road where he had found me. At that time I could walk, but was very light and he was pulling me along. HE THEN TOOK THE PENCIL FROM MY CHEST AND POINTED IT AT MY HEAD.

AT THAT MOMENT A DOG BEGAN TO BARK!
It must have startled him because the "click" came, but nothing happened to me. I knew that I should "pretend" to be paralyzed and I acted so and he took the black plate off my chest. He returned to his ship.

I waited until I saw the ship rise into the sky and then I returned home. My wife saw I was quite upset and I just told her that I was "sick". I was home at 12:20 and that the whole trip had taken an hour!

I feel that the "thing" pointed at my head was to make me forget---because if he were to kill me he could have just as easily done that at any moment on the trip.

I HAVE KEPT STILL FOR THESE YEARS BECAUSE I KNEW THAT NO ONE WOULD BELIEVE ME. BUT NOW THAT MY HEART IS ACTING UP I AM NOT AFRAID THAT PEOPLE WILL THINK ME CRAZY WHEN I TELL THEM WHAT IS REALLY HAPPENING IS SPACE.

From this experience it is easy to see how far ahead their scientific knowledge is and that they don't need satellites to travel in space. With our two satellites now circling the globe I feel that now some-one will believe me.

---------30----------

COMMENT BY ED. This was a story told to the editor of this Canadian newspaper. The banner story was four inches high across the front page and set in bold type in the inner pages. AT NO TIME was the informants name used. HE CERTAINLY DID NOT DO IT FOR PERSONAL PUBLICITY......matter of fact, THE SPACE-CRAFT DIGEST could not make the newspaper divulge the name of the man who gave them this story. Further, we feel that Canadian journalism is quite conservative and that the editor must have been impressed by the sincerity of the man enough to risk his position and the good name of his paper. Technically---from our understanding of "how the saucers fly" this is certain within the realm of reason.

Big Green Flash Lights Channel

November 1, PLYMOUTH, England, (AP) A bluegreen light blazed over the Western end of the English channel Saturday night. The brilliant light lasted about 5 seconds and was sited by dozens of ships and coast guard units. It set off a flurring activity of Royal Air Force sea rescue units and authorities reported that no plane was reported missing. A meteorological office spokesman in London said "..IT IS UNLIKE THAT IT WAS CAUSED BY A LIGHTING BOLT OR SOMETHING ELSE OF METEOROLOGICAL ORIGIN..." A coast guardsman in S.W. Cornwall said..."for a few minutes the whole sky was lit up with a great big blue glare that was nothing like a rocket or anything else I know...."

WELL, WHAT IS THE ANSWER OF OUR DOGMATIC SCIENTISTS TO THIS?

INTELLIGENCE DIGEST

BULLETIN-----Just about the most serious intelligence report that we have received is from a former intelligence officer of the South Korea (ROK) who reports that the USSR already has electrical flight operational!!!!!--------
KILSOO HAAN reports that the USSR has flown a space ship to the heighth of 1 4 0 miles and that it stayed aloft for three weeks. Members of the ROK underground in Red China have provided information in definite quanitites which can be definitely assessed to be reliable, he added. At least one Red Chinese General witnessed the space ship in action in MARCH I 956! He called it the world's first air platform. It can take off vertically, hover anywhere over the earth indefinitely.

Mr. HAAN stated that he had other information that showed that Red Chinese participated in the experimental flights and told of the event on their return to Pekin in 1957. The speed of the ship was reported to be incredibly fast and that it had missle launching equipment. The missile platform was said to be equipped with an "anti-missile missile" destroyer.

MR. HAAN further revealed that his informants in Red China state that the USSR also has four atomic powered space ships. Mr. Haan, said that in 1954 the US atomic energy commission was informed of the USSR work on a space satellite (Sputnik) nearly a YEAR before the soviets made public announcement of the project. At that time he forewarded a resumé of a SECRET September 1956 meeting between First Deputy Premier A. Mikoyan and the "Powerful Standing Comittee of the Chinese Peoples Republic" in which Mikoyan concluded that war between the East and the West "was inevitable" and that more atomic weapons would be provided for the peoples armies.

THE USSR is helping China to build a string of rocket and missile bases which are scattered along the Chinese Coast facing Korea and Formosa. The Red Chinese Armies already have four atomic equipped divisions and in the next four years 3 6 MORE will be equipped. Mr. Haan told the SPACE-CRAFT DIGEST that this information was forewarded to the defence department in 1957.

TIE-IN EXCLUSIVE.... The Editor is reliably informed that a "CONDITION RED" alerted ALL CARRIER BASED AIR in Formosan waters in October and that planes with atomic weapons were "ready" and that only a last minute order from the Pentagon stopped this atomic attack on the Chinese MAINLAND by minutes!

HELSINKI FINLAND (EXCLUSIVE).... A Finn who sells to Russia writes of the USSR "secret" of how Sputnik was launched so successfully and with a 1200 pound payload. A MAGNETIC CANNON OR CATAPAULT was used which launched the rocket some 100,000 feet into the air doing away with the necessity of a "monster" first stage which we use ...and still have fail at Cape Canaveral.

NEW GUN..by Bofors... A radically new type of artillery gun is being developed by the AB BOFORS armament concern (Swedish). It will fire shells which are constructed in a form resembling that of ARROWS. Prototype experiments have eliminated rifling. The arrow form gives the smooth bore projectile a precise trajectory. (From an English member)

INTELLIGENCE DIGEST, cont'd

FROM ENGLAND......A statement by a British Scientist that the British are now working on a magnetic catapault!
** ***********************

FROM PORTLAND OREGON.....The release that a Portland electronics Company has been invited to bid on sub-contracts for THE MOLE...an atomic disintegration of solid matter device that will burrow THROUGH THE EARTH TO ITS TARGET.
****

This last device is rather interesting from its connection with an occult standpoint as occultists who have investigated the civilization of the lost continent of ATLANTIS have told of the ATLANTEAN MOLE which burrowed tunnels under the ocean to carry Atlantean commerce and communicating groups of colonists. One termination is supposed to be near the great pyramid of Cheops.

NOW ABOUT OCCULTISM AND OUR POLICY...... even tho the editor has a scientific background he feels that the occult must not be ignored because science cannot explain it. Which brings us to our next bulletin which is a rumor that has not been checked out yet. However it is so reasonable that we feel it might well be based on fact.

THE US HAS A SECRET OCCULT project off the coast of Maine that was brought into being because the US Intelligence Agencies found out that "the enemy" knew the contents of secret scientific and other meetings whose proceedings had not even been written down. The only explanation was that the USSR or some other group selling information to the USSR was using a form of ASTRAL PROJECTION to obtain infformation. So the US searched the world to obtain adepts at this type of intelligence projection that is not held back by time or distance. These "adepts" are now gathered on the unknown or un-named island and being checked out with our intelligence demands............THIS IS AN UNCONFIRMED RUMOR........BUT to those who know the story of the Polish Count Korzypski, who later taught semantics at Penn State and who is an authority it is NOT fantastic, but probably true! Count Korzypski used this method to stall the Germans on the Russian front in the first world war--when he had nothing to fight with. But he always knew the German movements in advance and could roll with their blows effectively. ASTRAL TRAVEL is well known in occult circles and there must be many adepts in the world. THERE ARE NO SECRETS as those with other clairvoyant abilities are used by police forces of the world to seek out criminals and altho the information in court is inadmissible---still the French Surete The Royal Mounted and Scotland Yard have solved many many crimes by use of those with ESPabilities.

It is well known that peoples of peasant stock who live close to nature have these abilities to see manifestations beyond science's ability to explain. In Northern Russia and Finland these unknown "magic" arts which have been "lost" for a hundred generations are still known. It is from these groups that the adepts could be gathered, trained, and launched into their Astral Spy network. TOO FANTASTIC?.....well, if you think it is too fantastic to try---your type of thinking will lose this vital conflict to come.

UFO OVER PHOENIX, ARIZONA!!!!..... taken IN
COLOR on Sunday March 24th 1957 by Agnes Sanborn.
You can get a copy of this copyrighted picture for $1.00
for the 3x4 1/2 size or $3.50 for the 5x7 color picture
in a folder. Certainly one of the best examples of how
the highly charged, whirling, fields of a UFO will cause
the cloud to form around the outside of a UFO. The
space-craft is shown hovering about 30 feet above the
housetops of a housing development on the outskirts of
Phoenix Arizona, USA. The COLOR pictures of this
saucer are the most beautiful that we have seen and we

certainly recommend this "buy" and you can get them by writing AGNES SAND BORN at 1516 HOOD AVENUE in PHOENIX ARIZONA--USA. Meteorologists will confirm that this cannot possibly be JUST A CLOUD FORMATION and certainly even the lowest clouds do not come within 30 feet of the ground. Further, such a phenomena does not occurr when there are no other clouds in a desert sky--such as on this day. AGNES SANDBORN is to be congratulated on being at the right place at the right time and with a loaded camera.

REFERENCE OUR EDITORIAL "CHARGE" THAT THE U.S. Strategic Air Command is a "JOKE" and that elsewhere we mention that it is a "Macabre Joke" because it is obsolete, expensive, a military "toy" giving the public a false sense of security while the fantastic budget of the would-be military dictatorship grinds us under the millstone of national bankruptcy. WE ARE NOT alone....dispite our "proof" of the existence of electrical flight in the universe by other than earth entities it seems that there are other reasons why SAC is an obsolete military "toy" to enable them to play "world fighter director games"...... Political columnist Joe Alsop says:

> RED CHIEFS MAY FEEL THEY CAN STRIKE THE
> FIRST BLOW BY 1962.........

"........When President Eisenhower took office, the American Strategic Air Command still had the power to strike the first blow, but soviet neuclear striking power was already growing fast, and the Eisenhower administration decided not to make the great effort to maintain the American lead. Hence SAC lost its true offensive capability rather shortly there-after. The Dulles doctrine of "massive retaliation" became MASSIVE NONSENSE not long after it was proclaimed......."

As if this emphatic statement by the nation's foremost political columnist is not enough we have elsewhere in this issue THE ADMISSION from a Pentagon Public Information major that the DEW Radar is NOT effective!!!! i.e. it responds to other PHENOMENA THAT CAN CAUSE RADAR RETURNS....like UFO's!

ERUPTION ON MOON SEEN BY SOVIET ASTRONOMER

MOSCOW(AP) A Soviet scientist Wednesday reported there was an eruption in the mountains of the moon November 3rd. He said it prooved that the moon was not a dead celestial body.

Dr. N.A. Kozyrev told the Tass News agency the Crimean Astrophysics Laboratory witnessed the nearly double light intensity for 30 minutes in the center of the moon crater Alphonse. He said it began shortly after 3 AM.

Dr. A.A. Mikhailov of the Soviet Academy of Sciences commented that Kozyrev's findings rule out the present views of the origin of the moon "and demonstrates the similarity of the moon and the earth processes"

Kozyrev, who is attached to Linengrad's Uulkovo Observatory said brilliant fields of carbon and carbon compounds appeared simultaneously in the spectrum after the phenomena ceased.....that is they appeared and then after the "eruption ceased" the spectrum was "normal"..the crater was as usual. The story became a little uncertain here as is the usual newspaper reporting of scientific phenomena..... 20 photos were taken of the crater spectrum in three weeks ....end..... THE SPACE-CRAFT DIGEST has repeatedly pointed out that these and other moon phenomena indicate that the "dead planetoid" theory is not practical. BUT still journalism seems amazed each time something NEW is observed on the moon and then springs back into its cave of dogmatism to forget the many many lights, moving spots, domes that seem to come and go, and other phenomena that indicates that there isplenty of activity on the "dead" moon.

SPACE CRAFT DIGEST po Box 768 SALEM, OREGON, USA page 20

DANISH AIR FORCE CAPTAIN ASKS PERMISSION TO QUOTE------

From: Captain H.C. Peterson
Præstegaardsvej
Vojens, DENMARK

Dear Sir:

"....first I would like to tell you a few things myself that I have seen about the UFO. Since 15 December 1957 I am the leader of an organization called SUFOI which has 19 groups with over 200 members. In the last few months we have handled some 1 2 0 reports on the UFO.

I have read a few copies of the SPACE-CRAFT DIGEST and I would ask your permission to quote from them. Many people feel that Denmark needs a magazine about UFO's and are asking me to get one started. So 1 November we will publish a magazine called UFO news in Danish and that is why I write you..

Sincerely yours,
H.C. Petersen

COMMENT......of course we are happy to have Danish Air Force Captain Petersen join the fold. But we point out that in this single issue of the SPACE-CRAFT DIGEST that we have reports from The Portuguese Air Force, The Brazilian Navy, The Danish Air Force, and many other groups but still it seems that the US Air Force that controls a goodly portion of the World's air space and has a budget of some 30 billion dollars more or less can't seem to SEE ANY UFO's...but to quote a Pentagon major...they do SEE PHENOMENA THAT CAUSE RADAR RETURNS!

****

ANOTHER REPORT of a sighting from people we are personally acquainted with is from Lebanon, Oregon. Mr. and Mrs. Jack Lemon (business people of the community) sighted a most amazing UFO toward the end of August of 1958 at 2:30 in the morning while they were up with their youngest child. The "fiery ball" about a size smaller than a full moon hung between them and a nearby butte near Lebanon, Oregon. They watched this strange sky phenomena for about 20 minutes. It was orange to green-yellow in color and "seemed to be just a large ball of fire". We certainly wager that this highly charged body would be of the type that "would cause radar returns" but it is these same "balls of fire" that seem to move under intelligent control and to appear everywhere in the world.

****

A BRIGHT SILVERY UFO hovering over Uraguay on May 5, 1958 created such an intense heat in the cabin of a plane that the pilot was forced to open the windows and door and remove his jacket.

Carlos Alejo Rodriguez flying his Piper aircraft from San Carlos to Montevideo, saw the brilliant object approach on an Easterly course and then stop and wobble slightly. He flew to within 800 yards to see the metallic appearing, "top shaped" object both its top and bottom symmetrical. The object then took off at fantastic speed toward the sea.

LET'S TALK ABOUT GRAVITY.......

THE UNIVERSE in which we live is organized according to principles of measure, number and balanced harmonious relation. NATURAL LAWS follow a pattern that can be RE-discovered by human science of the NEW AGE. HUMAN intelligence and reasoning can again discern the rules and principles according to which the cosmos is built.

FASCINATED during recent decades by the intricate relationships inherent in the physical structure of matter, scientists have neglected the study and recognition of those forces which arrange matter into the SHAPE and FORM of living things-----THE FORCE FIELDS OF FORM!

Goethe's organic concept and Rudolph Steiner's imaginative idea of the FORMATIVE forces have inspired the workers at the GOETHEAN SCIENCE FOUNDATION at Clent, Stourbridge, in Worcestershire, ENGLAND to produce one of the World's great new thoughts. The plant is studied as to its form and its propensity for LEVITY. The title of this work is THE PLANT BETWEEN EARTH AND SUN. The price is 20 shillings.

The reader finds himself on the threshold of a new world; he begins to see the organizing principles in nature as an expression of reality which here-to-for were acknowledged only by artistic and aesthetic sense. These now become accessible to science.

The very concept of SPACE is enlarged, for the organic form is shown to contain more than mere outward three dimensional space!

NEGATIVE GRAVITY OR LEVITY The most elementary kind of ethereal force---a force of MUTAL ATTRACTION from plane to plane in polar analogy to the gravitational attraction of material particles of one for another---will naturally be discribed as NEGATIVE GRAVITY OR--LEVITY.   This term is again justified by the expansive forms and movements which arise if one imagines what will happen, say to a sphere Which is enveloped and permiated by planar entities between which such a levitational force is working. TO EACH planar entity, in such a case, a certain intensity must be given---analogous to the mass of a material particle. IT IS CALLED LEVITATIONAL INTENSITY. According to their intensities and geometrical distribution in the ethereal space to which they belong, a number of planar entities have have a resultant PLANE OF LEVITY, analogous to the center of gravity of a material system.

The hypothesis that the negative Euclidean spaces and planar forces play a real part in LIVING NATURE, imply that vast reaches of the spacial cosmos will have quite another function in this respect than in the merely point-wise mechanical aspect of the world. LEVITY then has a planar and NOT a "POINT WISE" focus.

We will not attempt to develop the whole theory of LEVITY as based upon Goethean Science. BUT, we will have to say that again there are examples around us that do levitate. Might we just point out that a plant grows UPWARD--IT LEVITATES, does it not?

To understand the new mechanics of this phenomena or phenomenom is to understand that man need not be forever earthbound. There are schools of thought in the world that are now making this attempt.

SPACE-CRAFT DIGEST   po Box 768 SALEM, OREGON, USA

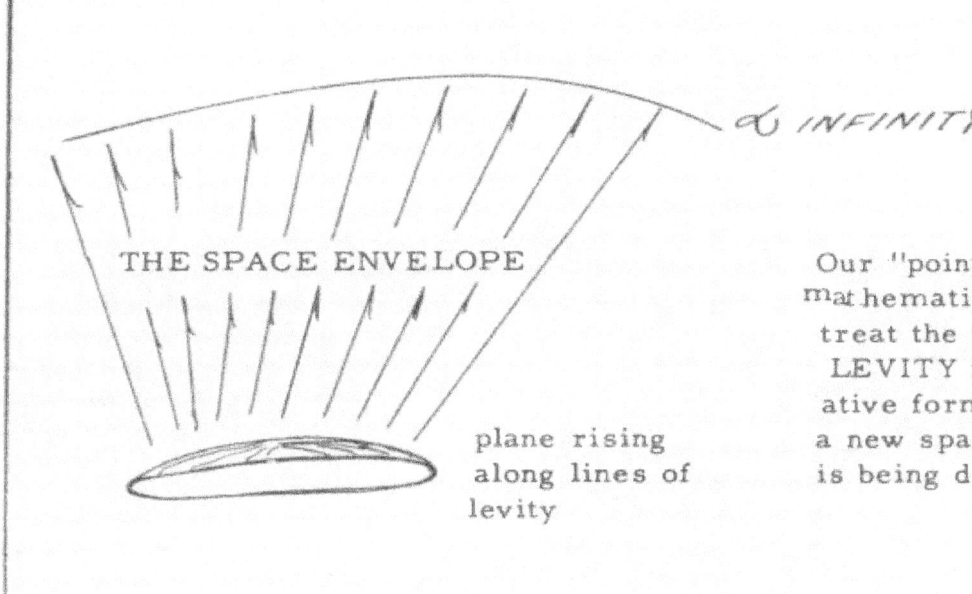

A "plane" moving in a LEVITY force field ...(all of its components or particles moving outward.. i.e. not point centered as in a gravity field)

WHAT IS GOETHEAN SCIENCE?..... Goethe's method of approach to scientific phenomena was to array his manifold observations and experiments so that Nature might reveal to him at least some of the letters of the alphabet of her language. His scientific work, largely neglected by the main trend of 19th century science, was edited by Dr. Rudolph Steiner, who took Goethe as the starting point of much of his own work and showed that a truly modern philosophy of science will be confronted with the very same principles which Goethe was discovering through his imaginative perception. The most important of these is that the "unifying idea" behind whole groups of related phenomena in Nature is objective reality, accessible to human intelligence by direct observation....provided our faculties are fully used and developed.

THUS a modern GOETHEAN SCIENCE must learn to perceive QUALITIES in the same objective way in which science has hitherto has learned to measure quanities. It must be able to lead from the realm of number, measure and weight into the realm of the supersensible forces from which life itself develops...all life proceeds.

It is interesting to note that the Encyclopedia Brittanica in its biography of Goethe lists him as a great German poet. It does mention his long arguements with Isaac Newton on the nature of light. But it does not mention his 140 volumes of scientfic works. It says that Goethe thought that this was his most important work...in a grudging two lines... but in no manner was the nature of these 140 volumes examined to impart the nature of the work that this great German mind thought most imortant. It is the dogmatic nature of the reference books of "our system" that must be attacked at every possible turn by those who can conceive new thought.

GOETHEAN SCIENCE FOUNDATION
Home Farm, Clent, Stourbridge
Worcestershire
ENGLAND

Dear Mr. Allen:

"...... Mr. Wilson and myself are at present working on a new book to replace "What is Colour?" but on more comprehensive lines; we hope to be ready in about a year or so. On the other hand we are expecting very soon to have copies of GOETHES COLOUR EXPERIMENTS reprinted from the Physical Society Yearbook (1958 London) which contains an account of a discourse given by Mr. Wilson at the Physical Society's annual exhibition of instruments and apparatus held in London last March. This contains a modern elaboration of parts of Goethes FARBENLEHRE(colour-study) and you shall have your copy in due course.

Mr. Adams and Miss Whicher who have been working on this problem many years have recently visited the Goetheneum in Dornach Switzerland where they staged large exhibitions of pictures entitled RAUM UND GEGENRAUM (space and counter space) --or physical and ethereal space........"

THUS ENDS OUR QUOTE FROM THE LETTER

We thought that the concept of "space and counter-space" is so important to an understanding of the UFO that it had to be included in this issue. CERTAINLY all admit that we must get away from our conventional concept of an all-inhibiting gravity if we are to travel in space as we can if we apply our abilities to observe nature.

There is also one other reason that we feel that this line of study is most important. This group in England is a small private research group that has labored for years on this and similar concepts. They are not bound by dogmatic military requirements. Their minds know no boundaries defined by the dogma that governs "our system" today. Their work then has a chance to be new and original.

In the United States with its fantastic military budget that dominates all industrial and educational research there is little chance for developments like the thoughts above. This is the tragic truism which binds our efforts in the US. At the moment with failure after failure at Cape Canaveral and at other places in our expensive program--we are certainly in a rat race. Our only hope is that our "ENEMY" is in the same "rat race" of dogmatism. If he is not--then it appears that we are destined to lose the race for space.

THE REASONS appear to be simple when outlined as we have noted in this issue of this publication. An amazing visitor is IGNORED with the hope that it "will go away" because our thinking at this time, when analyzed by the postulates of our dogmatic science, cannot explain the UFO!

by W. GORDON ALLEN

BULLETIN from the FLYING SAUCER REVIEW.......
excerpts from a letter from the Hon. Brinsley Le Poer Trench
64 Pont Street
LONDON S. W. 1, England

Dear Gordon:

The story and pictures were sent to me by Miss Lou Zinstag, UFO researcher of Basle, Switzerland. The pictures are small in size, but are the only copy I have left and I hope you can get them enlarged.

You have probably heard that George Hunt Williamson has been over here lecturing. Actually his visit has been a great success and he was well received everywhere. I introduced him from the platform at a big London meeting of about 500 persons. He had some interesting colored slides with him.... his talk was excellent. In the course of his lecture and repeatedly in private conversation he said that the UFO's were not only appearing over atomic bases but were also appearing over spots that they had come to thousands of years before! He said that saucers were appearing frequently over places on South America and other parts of the world where there were very ancient rock sculptures. The theory is that these rock sculptures, usually of animal or human heads are some points of reference for reservoirs of energy over the earth. The saucers occupants know this and are over these areas to "refuel" from the earth. The amazing thing is that people in these ancient times should have carved these figures for the saucers (probably done in Atlantean or Lemurian times) and it means that there were saucers in the sky then who were in contact with inhabitants of the earth. That is roughly what Williamson said in this connection. He produced very interesting slides pointing this out.

Now some time after Williamson left England, I waslooking at the Monguzzi photos again and recalled what Williamson said. I wondered what would come of studying the saucer photos from all angles... then I saw it!

I bet that even Monguzzi Himself, does not know this. Look to the right of the antenna or mast sticking out of the saucer and you will see a cherubic human face looking toward the sky. What do you think of that!

I am greatly looking foreward to reading your book and know that it will be a sizzler.

We must watch out for a spate of sightings again because Mars will soon be in opposition.

Meanwhile my best personal regards,
/s/ Brinsley le Poer Trench

COMMENT.....first a rather tragic thing happened to Geo. Hunt Williamson while on tour. His wife contact a mortal fever while he was absent and died in the interior of Peru. Friends had to care for his young son.

****

THE SPRING ISSUE OF THE SPACE-CRAFT DIGEST points out how the markings in the Andes were made to be seen ONLY from the sky. Further, it is the feeling of the editor that mountain ranges are not "raised from within" but are due to "FORCE FIELD FAULTS" which hold the planet in its orbit in the solar system. These are the very force field concentrations that are used to form the "space hi-way" between the planets of the system by the UFO's. Many many sightings are around the high mountains that have been "pulled up" by these fields.

THE CONTROVERSIAL MONGUZZI UFO PICTURES-----

Following the letter from Editor TRENCH of the FLYING SAUCER REVIEW we are reproducing the pictures with the following comment:
FIRST.... From the mimeographed TEES SIDE UFO RESEARCH GROUP
96 Russell Street Middlesbrough, Yorkshire, ENGLAND.......quote-------
"...In the Sept/October issue of FSR there is an article by a Mr. Lou Zinstag called the FLYING SAUCER PHOTOGRAPHS OF THE CENTURY...which show a saucer on the ground with a figure standing next to it and also a saucer taking off. It is claimed that a Sr. Giampiero Monguzzi of Milan took these pictures while on holiday in the Bernina Mts. with his wife. Yet back in 1952 when the incident was recorded Sr. Monguzzi sold a copy of this photograph to a French magazine. It was discovered that the saucer was made of painted cardboard and the spaceman modeled of clay. In the background some pebbles had been placed to represent mts......"

It is very regretable that an "impartial" circular on UFO's should print this kind of material. We ask THE NAME of the French magazine and the editor. We have examined the pictures very carefully and find that the background is NOT pebbles. It appears to be either a lava formation or a very close approx.-imation.....so close...that if these are fake the Italian Gentleman is to be complimented on his excellent modeling job. Certainly with the data available it is just as easy to believe the pictures as it is the undocumented "out of the blue" accusation we quoted.

We would invite the SPACE CRAFT DIGEST readers to compare these UFO pictures with UFO pictures for sale elsewhere in the magazine. Certainly it is almost exactly the same type of saucer that appears in the work of the editor SPACE CRAFT FROM BEYOND THREE DIMENSIONS....(see back cover) which was taken by a Marine Air Group photographer over Korea.

There has been little in UFO literature about spacemen in space suits BUT " THE USSR ACADEMY OF SCIENCE and Space Research indicates that UFO's are INTERPLANETARY and have gone so far as to say that the planet VENUS is the originating point of 90% of the UFO's. They conclude that some UFO's have crashed in earth and that the pilots have been killed...."

OTHER UFO OBSERVERS.. Dr. Clyde Tombaugh (discoveror of Pluto) Professor Hall of the Lowell observatory in Mass. Dr. Seymour B, Huess of the U. of Florida; Dr. G. Duncan Fletcher of the Astronomical society of Kenya, South Africa.

It is our belief that this issue of the SPACE CRAFT DIGEST covers about every good photo in the field of "saucerdom". The next issue will bring to public eye some very interesting information on RAUM und GEGENRAUM (SPACE AND COUNTER SPACE) which we believe, is the FIRST, attempt to provide a theory of LEVITY which some day might possibly be quanitized in the manner that even the mathematicians can handle. There will also be a further development of the editor's FOUR FIELD conception of the ENTIRETY which could account for life and intelligence ANYWHERE in the cosmos.
SPACE CRAFT DIGEST po BOX 768 SALEM, OREGON USA page

THE FIELD OF ELEMENTALS----indicating that there is SPACE-LIFE from "Beyond Three Dimensions" which "lives" nearly beyond our powers to detect it is not one that should be neglected by any scientific investigation with an open mind. "THEY LIVE IN THE SKY" gives us the Amoeba as shown, but ever since there has been photography there have been pictures of Fairies. These have been suppressed in the last decades, but there are those that believe in "the little people"----to the Irish, descendants of ATLANTIS--they are REAL!

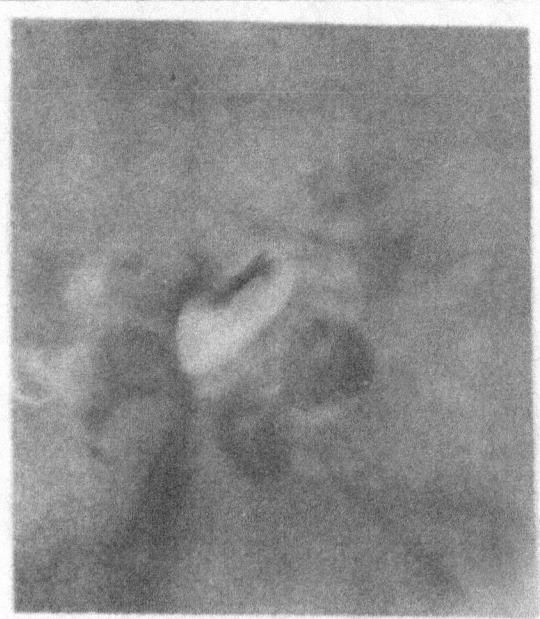

LIMERICK, Ireland, (AP) The Fairies of Ireland are amiable people as is well known, but not when they get their Irish up.

And since that is where their Irish is now, goodness knows what is to be done about extending Shannon's Int'l. Airport runway. Ambrose McInerney, who has the contract to do a bit of earth-moving for the extension told about his troubles Saturday.

The Irish Government sent him orders NOT to disturb the fairy fort on top of Trade's Hill. Troubles is that the Fairies have their fort where the airport people want to extend the runway. Quite a useless order, he observed, because his Irish workmen never would molest a fairy fort anyway. As soon as play patty-cake with the Devil, himself, they would. A Fairy Fort is a sort of a headquarters and community Hall. That's where the fairies give their parties and kick the Fairy gong around. Farmer Frank Fahy said that many a midnight the Fairies can be heard "champing and chattering at the 'fort'." A farmer was known to die when he took stones from a fairy fort to make a wall. "His hands swelled and he never lived to finish the wall," Fahey said. People wouldn't even cut brush off a fairy fort. So, how is the airport authority ever to extend the big jet runway?

Darned if McInerney knows, even if he did ignore the Government orders and tried to level the hill with the fort on it, his workers would strike. The airport engineers have decided to leave the hill as a minor obstruction and light it.

SUPERSTITION?.....Well, behind many superstitions of this psychic type there is a basis of truth. WHAT is the story behind the elementals known as Fairies. Do THEY REALLY EXIST beyond our senses? Shown above is a "thought-camera" picture of a Fairy who has told Lord Dowding that his name is NORMUS. He inhabits the garden of Lord Dowding (former Air Marshall of England) and asked to have his picture taken. ABOVE is the little ectoplasmic entity. NORMUS was a bit unhappy with his picture, but stated that certainly they could do better. NEVER-THE-LESS.....very real things do happen to people in certain parts of the world. The psychic backgrounds of "superstitions" that are laughed off by less sensitive three-dimensional scientists are not to be so easily discounted.

SPACE-CRAFT DIGEST P.O. BOX 768, SALEM, OREGON, USA

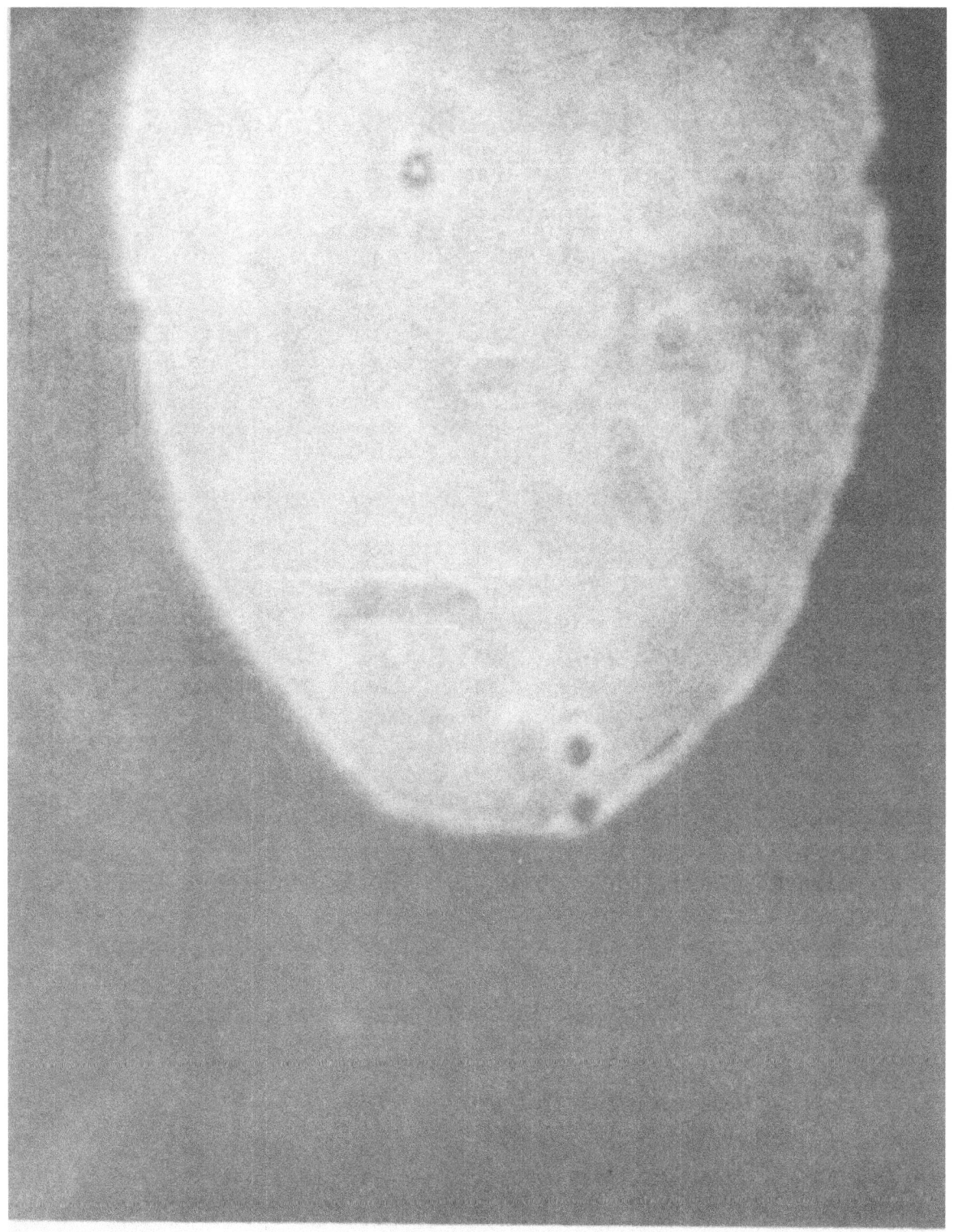

THE AMOEBA is the name given to this invisible flying animal photographed with infra-red film by Trevor James, author of the book "They Live in the Sky". Using infra-red film and an e.s.p. method, James took six successive photos of this strange and invisible airborne animal, which has its own light source. James, who has also photographed four of these creatures in a flock, states that their presence in our atmosphere, hitherto unknown to science, undoubtedly accounts for many reports of UFO's (unidentified flying objects).

"Space-Craft From Beyond Three Dimensions"

by W. Gordon Allen. (ILLUSTRATED)

FROM THE JACKET In this challenging and provocative work, W. Gordon Allen, owner of several radio stations, a graduate electrical engineer and a former U. S. Naval radio-radar officer — seeks to prove conclusively the existence of Unidentified Flying Objects and offers an UNPRECEDENTED number of pictures to substantiate his claims.

The author's investigations over the last seven years indicate that "extra-terrestial" entities using electrical spece-craft propulsion "are all around us".

The mystery, Mr. Allen continues, is why this attention seems to be paid to earth at this time—unless this space traffic has always been with us. If it has—and certainly there are indications that the UFO has always been with us—then the ruling powers-that-be who have oppressed the mind of man over the last few thousand years on this planet have been guilty of the universes' MOST INCREDIBLE CRIME AGAINST HUMANITY!

BEYOND THREE DIMENSIONS constitutes a challenge to conventional 20th century physical science to re-consider its "proved" conclusions and to re-evaluate the atomic theory. As the FIRST comprehensive attempt to reconcile Western scientific knowledge with the fantastic phenomena of the UFO, it is a scholary and important work; as an exploration of flying saucers and their mysterious brethren, it is a true to life adventure story—as timely as tomorrow!

CHAPTER HEADINGS . . . TOWARD NEW DIMENSIONS OF THOUGHT . . . COSMIC-MIND RECEIVERS AFTER NEWTON . . . ATOMIC THEORIES AND PRE-HISTORIC CATASTROPHY . . . FROM COLD-WATCH to MOON-WATCH . . . (Space craft in our skies) . . . FIRST PRACTICAL THOUGHT RESONATOR? . . . THE POST-WAR PHANTASMA OF THE UFO . . . LUNAR CHANGES AND THE EARTH'S HALO . . . SOME EXTRA-TERRESTIAL VISITATIONS . . . A NEW VISTA OF THE ENTIRETY . . . and four essays on the space-vortex atom by C. F. Krafft. (Many UFO photos)

ORDER TODAY AS FIRST EDITION IS NEARLY SOLD OUT.

Name...

Address..

City...

State..

Exposition Press Inc.
386 Fourth Avenue
New York 16, New York

Mail me "SPACE-CRAFT FROM BEYOND THREE DIMENSIONS" by W. Gordon Allen
$3.60 POSTPAID

SPACE CRAFT Digest

SPRING & SUMMER ISSUE 1959

Theories of Electrical Flight

published by the PACIFIC LEMURIAN SOCIETY

EDITORIAL . . . . . My Dear Lemurians:

You who live all over this planet, in nearly every country, have in this issue received your last copy of the SPACE-CRAFT DIGEST. At some future date we may revive as a philosophical society. But our function was to solve the "secret of the saucers" and with this last issue the "secret" is pretty well solved. Sufficient information is given for any member to go ahead and continue his study of the "mysteries" either from a philosophical standpoint or to build his own model of an electrical flight device.

Without doubt, in the decade of the '60s, various countries will manufacture machines which climb the electrical LATTICE WORK of SPACE. It is our feeling that in these issues we have not only been among the first of modern man to make these postulates; but also, we have shown by pictures many of the first SPACE-CRAFT to explore our planet from other planets and other dimensions. Of course, *ALL* of the dimensions of the cosmos are to be found in our own mind! This seems to be the mental barrier of many technical "scientists". When these people are required to have a philosophical conception before they call themselves "scientists" much of our dogmatism will readily evaporate. We therefore, have ceased publication because we have solved the problem of the UFO.

RECOMMENDED . . . . as the best of the UFO magazines is that of our friend The Honorable Brinsley Le Poer TRENCH'S *FLYING SAUCER REVIEW* of 1 Doughty Street; LONDON. We do hope that every LEMURIAN will mail $3.50 to him. It is issued 6 times a year. The magazine is outstanding and will carry articles by your Founder from time to time.

McChord C-118 Falls In Flames

McChord Air Force Base, Wash. (AP) A military transport plane trailing, a long plume of flame, plunged to earth 15 miles east of this sprawling air base Wed. night (April 1, 1959) shattering on impact in a sharp explosion. The Air Force told a Pierce County Sheriff's office that four men were believed to have been aboard the four-engined Military Air Transport Service C-118 when it plunged to earth.

The Air Force said one man might have parachuted to safety but has not yet been located. The pilot, in contact with the McChord AFB tower as his doomed plane went to a fiery death, told the radio operator seconds before the plane hit: "this is it". They were the last words he uttered. McChord is 40 miles south of Seattle....."

Now that is what the Air Force public relations office in collusion with Associated Press finally gave to the newspaper wire-service. But one very significant story that did appear on the UPI radio wire had, by the time of the above release, been killed and it contained the quote: "we have hit something in the air"...the first words of the pilot at the beginning of the disaster. We called Colonel King of McChord Air Force Base near Tacoma and he confirmed that these words were the first words of the pilot.

Col. KING also stated that the accident board of inquiry investigating the accident determined that there were "no odd or bizzare" circumstances surrounding this particular plane loss, but that the report had gone to "higher echelons" and he could not release the actual reason for the crash.

He further stated that in "his personal opinion as a pilot" he was not concerned about SKYQUAKES or "sonic booms" and he had been experienced in flying near them.

NOW WE QUOTE FROM.....pp 206 from Trevor James' THEY LIVE IN THE SKY....."..... What information is known publicly about air force plane losses? Not much, but it is enough to be significant when viewed in the light......of these figures: (Brig. Gen. Joseph Caldara, Director of Flight Safety Research, USAF (1955)

> "..There were 1664 major accidents to US Aircraft. In equivilant terms, 18 squadrons of jet fighters (794 planes) and five squadrons of bombardment aircraft (75 planes) were lost. Over 20% of these losses were from UNDETERMINED causes (!) This represents over 150 jet fighters lost from undetermined causes in the year 1955 (or three per week). One might ask, "where's the war" so large does this attrition seem to be........"

In April, 1959, it seems that the Air Forces are still up to their old tricks. If there is real reason that the taxpayers who foot the bill and buy these expensive airfoils for the military to play their little games with, should not know the truth? The "misleading of the public" goes right to the top. Here is an editorial from the morning STATESMAN in Salem, Oregon:

> MISSILES NOT ON GUARD -----
> Ten months ago we were assured that Thor inter-mediate range missiles would be operational in Great Britain by the end of 1958. At the end of the year, missiles had been shipped to England and we were ASSURED by the national Defence Department that they were operational (ready to fire) earlier this year Gen. Nathan Twining, Chairman of the joint chiefs of staff, assured Congress the missiles were on guard in England.

When Senator Stuart Symington visited England recently, however, he could find no operational missiles. When pressed for an answer, Defence Sec. McElroy admitted the missiles were not operational. The reasons for this delay may be beyond his control because Britain shares in the responsibility.

The fact remains, however, that both Congress and the people were MISLED. McElroy should remember this the next time he asks with an injured air why people don't accept his estimates of the military situation without question......."

Now let's investigate another misleading news story. This one is of a couple of days after the crash of the plane that "hit something in the air".

Giant Meteor Lights Sky

A giant meteor flashed over Portland Monday night, sped southward over Redmond and Klamath Falls and broke apart over central California. William Elliot who lives on the slope of Squaw mountain near Estacada saw the fireball as he drove home at 8:45 p.m. "It was a big flame in the air and behind it was what looked like a trail of smoke." Other observers told of the "bright or blue-white light about 10 or 15 times as big as sputnik..."

The control tower at the Portland airport said that from its viewing angle the meteor appeared about like "a very pistol". In Redmond the control tower reported that "it was the brightest meteorite they had seen in 16 years experience"......"..the illumination was very brilliant in flashes of blue, white and bright orange...."

Other observers saw the fireball from Crescent City, Red Bluff and Eureka in California. Airlines pilots also reported the meteor.

Mather Air Force Base near Sacramento reported the object appeared to disintegrate in the air directly overhead. Many observers said it broke into three pieces..........end.

COMMENT by Ed.......Certainly this was NOT a meteor. The trajectory of a meteor is toward the center of the earth and not on nearly a horizontal line down the West Coast of the US for nearly six hundred miles! Further, what about the flashing lights? Was it a fireball, a meteorite, or meteor.....? ...all of these contradictory terms appear in this story as pieced together by the news service. "it disintegrated overhead"......but no pieces were found, rather at that point it might well have moved out of the visible spectrum.

However, our offering is that this is another "strange and bizzare" occurence that defys conventional explanation and so we must move to the analysis that is favored by UFO observers. But there is still more to the story:

SKYQUAKES....at this same time shook the San Francisco area in a manner that the city by the Golden Gate suffered smashed plate glass windows and a heavy bank vault door swung open on Mrs. Dewey Rayburn and knocked her down....the shock was felt from Martinez to Palo Alto....some 35 miles a part. We defy the air forces of the U.S. to create any SONIC BOOM which will react like this over a large area.

NOW......WHAT IS THE UFO OBSERVERS EXPLANATION?

That the tanker on the first day of April hit a stationary FORCE FIELD and that this field is of the nature of many left in the air during recent years which have caused a great number of air crashes. The force field is left stationary by the force-field of the UFO which was seen moving down the coast of the US and when it left the visible spectrum its 'mass' created the giant SKY-QUAKE or sonic boom, but it was not "one of ours" that did it, and we might as well look elsewhere for the explanation.

NOW, if the Air Forces looses planes at the rate of 3 per week, how about the Airlines? A Dutch Airliner crashed in the Atlantic last year killing 99 and the verdict returned by Dr. John Kennedy, an Irish pathologist was death by impact "...the nature of the injuries does not favor the view that they were caused directly by an explosion".... We have a story that we can begin to piece together for the news services that look at these happenings in the conventional manner that explain nothing.

NOW ABOUT CAPT'N KILLIAN..... at 7:10 PM on February 24th, 1959, an American Airlines four-engine DC-6 airliner took off from the Newark Airport, bound for Detroit, non-stop. At the controls was Captain Peter Killian a pilot for 20 years 15 of them logged in airliners for a total of over 4 million miles. His first officer was John Dee. The DC-6 was over Pennsylvania at 8500 feet when Capt. Killian saw his first UFO's.

IT WAS 8:45 HE REPORTED, WHEN I LOOKED OFF TO THE SOUTH AND SAW THREE YELLOWISH LIGHTS IN A LINE FORMATION. THERE WAS NO CHANCE OF A MISTAKE AS WE HAD VISIBILITY FOR ONE HUNDRED MILES. AT FIRST I ESTIMATED THAT THEY WERE NOT OVER A MILE FROM US. AT INTERVALS ONE WOULD MOVE CLOSER AND THEN FALL BACK INTO FORMATION."

After pointing out the UFO to the first officer Dee, Captain Killian notified his 35 passengers on the public address system.

One of the passengers had an aviation background--Mr. N. D. Puncus, General manager of Curtiss Wright's Untica division..... "I looked out and saw the objects in precise formation, he said, every so often one of the objects would glow brighter than the others as if it moved closer to the plane....."

Captain Killian called other aircraft when he was over Erie and two other American Airlines pilots answered quickly and one stated he had been watching the UFO's for 10 to 15 minutes.

Commenting on the sighting the Airline said that it had had considerable number of sightings in the Midwest.

-- 30 --

Now that's the summary of the story. BUT, what happened when the "dark forces" of the military began to move? Again, do we get HONESTY from our military?

AFTER THREE DAYS OF SILENCE.... this official opinion of the Air Technical Intelligence center at Wright Field in Dayton, Ohio, (who never saw the UFO's at all)..... "....had been misled by the belt of Orion...."

Captain Killian replied to that first story.... "I certainly know Orion when I see it, he said, it was not any brief look during those 45 minutes I saw Orion repeatedly and so did the other Airlines pilots....", When the Air Force, thru the New York Herald Tribune, accused the pilots of drinking he said"..Naturally I don't like it, they know we don't drink before flights, it is one of our strictest rules....."

Besides the Air Force statement the Herald Tribune article carried the following quotation from Captain Killian.... "I am sure there are people on other planets who have solved the problem of space travel. I sincerely believe their vehicles are coming close to earth...."

THE FINAL portion of the story is that the Air Force put so much heat on the American Airlines executives at top level that his own Airline finally told Killian to keep still about it if he wanted to keep flying and not argue any more with the government! ....

NOW WE HAVE THE TRUTH...... the military is to be permitted to mislead and falsify as they WISH to the taxpayers! But here in this last issue of the SPACE-CRAFT DIGEST are the sources of information that will tell the truth of the UFO to anyone who wishes to delve into the long hours of study that it takes to acquire the philosophical background necessary for a SPACE-CRAFT FROM BEYOND THREE DIVENSION explanation that is FACT and not the "belief" of Capt. Killian. But our greatest accolade goes to a fearless man who stood up to those who would tell him what he and many others saw in the air that night between Newark and Detroit. Capt. Killian didn't have pictures, but following is the story of a man who did!

LOOK UP!.... by Ray and Rex Stanford, 2629 Lynch Street Corpus Christi, Texas, which is worth $3.00 of anyone's money, is based on some color moving pictures of two air force jets chasing a UFO and the strip clearly shows the "force field" around the crescent shaped UFO! Further he has some affidavits quoted in his book from two police officers who were with him on another telepathic UFO contact near his home city.

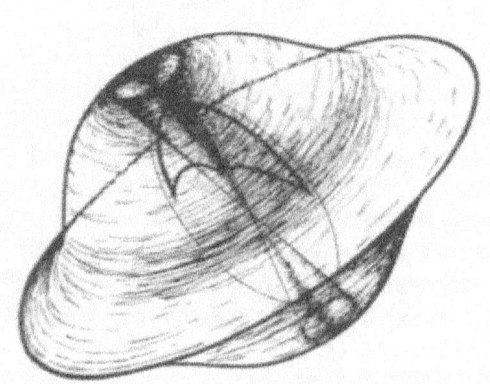

NOW FROM A LETTER TO THE SPACE-CRAFT DIGEST, WE QUOTE:

"Because you are so interested in the propulsion and force field of spacecraft, I should explain that the diagrams of the crescent-shaped craft and its field in Look Up are drawn by me exactly as I saw it at the contact. I could clearly see--it almost covered the whole field of the 8X binoculars--the motion of forces in the force field. It may truly be said to have been the most powerful and, perhaps, important thing I have ever witnessed. For many months I had wondered as to the real shape and motion of the spacecraft field, and on that date I saw this clearly in daylight. The sight of this great crescent-shaped ship and its fantastic force field was so beautiful that Ropczycki had to keep yelling at me to film it and the jets had to start chasing it before I could force myself to put aside the binoculars and start filming! I had wanted to wait until it was just above the hill and landing, so I could get the visitors stepping out of the spacecraft (so I'd have enough film for this.) You cannot imagine my recent thrill to learn that the field's actual shape is discernable in the movie film blow-ups.

I am particularly interested in the series of shots taken near Trinidad from ship Almirante Saldanha, because the object in these is shaped exactly like the force field of the crescent-shaped ship (see Look Up) on my movie film. (The diagram in our book shows the field in a contracted phase; note we said it contracted and expanded.) The photo of that series in your book shows the field (I think that is what the photo shows, rather than the ship itself!) expanded. You will be interested to note that it is more contracted in the photo of that series shown on the front of SAUCERS, Spring, 1958. It even looks a little contracted in the shot you present on page 5 of Fall, 1958, SPACE CRAFT

DIGEST. So, our Sept. 18, '56, contact and the movie I took and those photos from the ship off Trinidad confirm each other, and proves that the field of this type of craft (actually several different designs) is shaped as we reported and that its motion is an alternation of concentration and decentration (resonation) of the field. Much may be learned by study of this field.

Aside from the direct implications of the space visitation and aside from the other important information we have gained from them in our contacts, one of the things which interests me most is this force field and the mechanism by which it is "generated". Perhaps this is why the visitors saw to it that the field of the craft on Sept. 18 was intense to the point that I could see the effects of motion of forces within it. Several friends have suggested this.

The space visitors have indicated to us the general locations of certain of their bases on this planet. They have told us where actual spacecraft are buried. Some of these contain ancient records. Some are not too far away! We also know the locations--as a result of our contacts--of certain underground tunnel systems, entrances, etc., as well as the location of very old "magnetic beacons", as the visitors call them. These beacons were (some still are) used for navigation of spacecraft above this planet, just as water craft use lighted beacons as a guide at times--as a guide to certain harbors, bases, special points of interest, etc. We can hardly wait until the time is here for many of these things to be revealed to others....and for the time when the ancient spacecraft are taken out of their secret places for the fulfillment of their purpose.

One of the books I am writing will release accounts of several of my hitherto unreleased contacts and will relate certain contacts to special information given me by them in 1956. The other book will present proof that many Indian groups of this hemisphere were in contact with the visitors and will tell the effects of these contacts on their cultures and those following them. Both books will be well illustrated.

Sincerely,

Ray Stanford

....................."

In his book, Ray Stanford says that the Air Forces would not admit that their jets had "chased" a UFO, but he still has the pictures of the "fly-boys" defending our airspace.

In comparing the pictures with the TRINIDAD UFO we find that the "saturn-like" force-field explanation around the "real craft" is the best explanation yet of the difference in density between the UFO and the mountain of the island of Trinidad which is in the picture. The Brazilian Navy has given copies to Dr. Hynek of the Smithsonian Astro-physical Laboratory, but the good Doctor, being one of the Ph. D's "kept" by the Air Forces will come out with nothing constructive publicly.

However, we believe that this irrefutable repitition of instances shows that OUR MILITARY is willfully duping the hard-working U. S. Taxpayer and with this "head in the sand" attitude, we doubt if they are worthy of our blind trust and certainly they seem not worthy of 40 billion dollars worth of trust in the great military SNAFU that is shaping up!

-- 30 --

"Rep. William H. Ayres, Ohio: "Congressional investigations are being held on the problem of UFO's. Most of the material is classified; hearings are never printed."

****

"Dr. Harlow Shapley, former Director, Harvard Observatory: "We must now accept it as inevitable -- there are other worlds with thinking beings."

FORCE WALL..... photographed in Infra Red ..... of the type that when hit by our air-liners or military craft are like hitting a solid stone wall in the air! Photographed on the Mojave by Revor James on infra-red film these are offered in explanation of the mysterious air crashes that no one seems to want to admit. Obviously, the airlines don't wish to admit to passengers that they MIGHT hit a brick wall in the air. The Military can't tell their pilots about these hazards, but never-the-less they are hazards.

      HOWEVER, another more secret section of the military is already doing research in the "FORCE WALL PROJECT" that will attempt to build just such a force wall around the United States in the manner suggested some 23 years ago by cosmic minded NICOLA TESLA and which has been created artificially by private researchers in this nation and demonstrated to your editor. BUT---these people are not trustful enough of the military to submit the development to Washington, D.C.

----------30----------

WHERE PARTICLES ARE "CREATED" in the earth's VORTEX

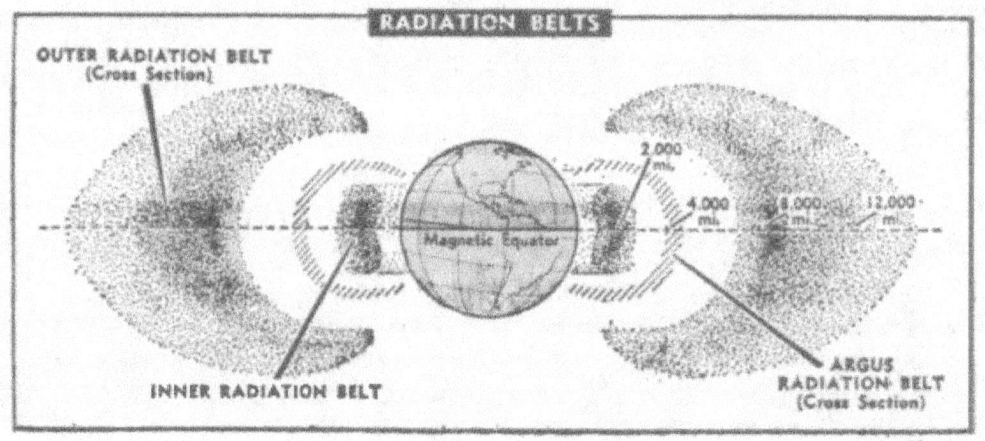

SPACE AND COUNTER SPACE
(Raum und Gegenraum)
by W. Gordon Allen

Possibly the most fantastic error that modern "science" has postulated is the EMPTINESS of S P A C E. The conundrum of space itself is psychological in nature..... "..a symbolic representation of our ability to perceive things or materiality in its separations......" matter of fact most every definition of space brings out the necessity of a conception which involves our poor and most incompetant "senses". Space might be defined as a conception of emptiness.

To be more material we might use the cosmologists definitions which say that SPACE, which we can plainly see for ourselves with binoculars any dark night, is a black void, near absolute zero in temperature with some shining bits of cosmic dust called stars, galaxies, universes separated by the "spaces" in between.
 The following offering of the SPACE LATTICE-WORK THEORY is an effort to point out the fallacy of any such conception as there do exist methods of "materializing" the reality of space so that even our poor senses can "see" what S P A C E is and thereby remove one portion of spacial conception from the area of the psychological and into the "material" for the possible purpose of quanitization. But, as mathematics never 'discovered' anything we must first have a qualitative understanding of the theoretical background before any attempt at quanitization. So, now we offer this marriage of the SPACE LATTICE THEORY with a theory of the qualitative understanding of the "flow" of force that is called GRAVITY.
 A FORCE FIELD dimensionality is fundamental to this conception. What are the 'lines of force' of the space-lattice in our solar system? Where do they originate and what do they "look" like?

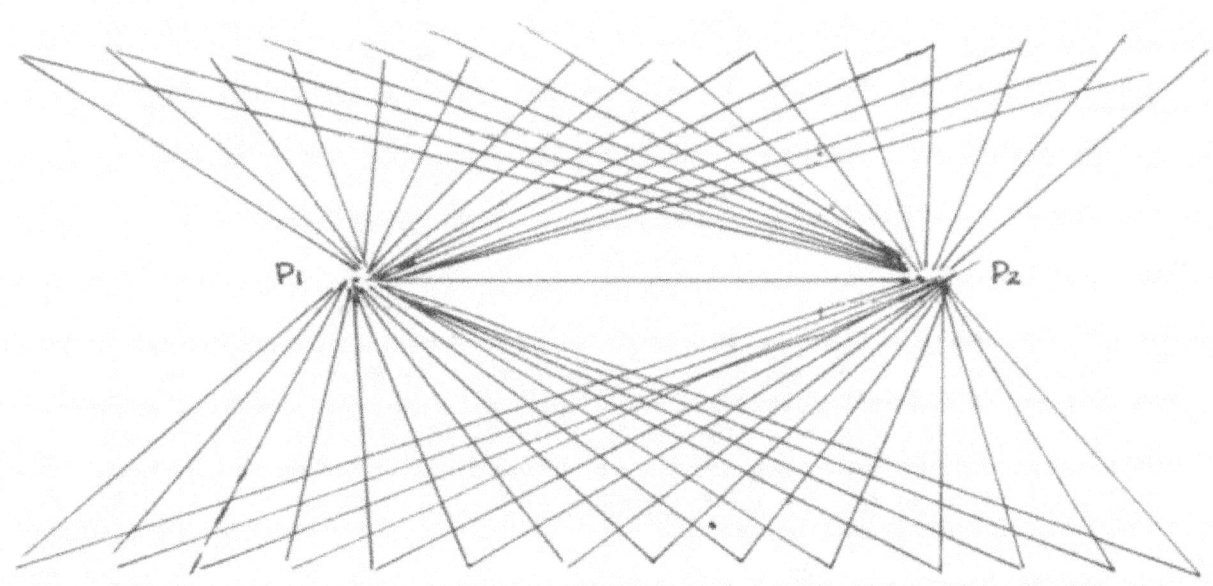

From the points (P1 and P2) or the planes of the various solar systems which can be taken to be finite between universes, and which surprisingly enough, are also finite in our Solar system we can postulate various points of intersection of a "lattice". We can conceive of a force "line" as that of the intersection of two planes. (What planes?)

PLANES OF SPACIAL DIMENSION:

In the Nebular hypothesis it may be noted that there seems to be a plane of stability in the pictures of spiral nebulae in the process of formation and this same plane of stability also appears in our own solar system as the planets revolving around the sun on their orbits are not at random points about the solar orb (and so far no cosmologist has postulated the reason for this stability) but are at points in their orbit ON A PLANE. This we call the "plane of spacial stability".

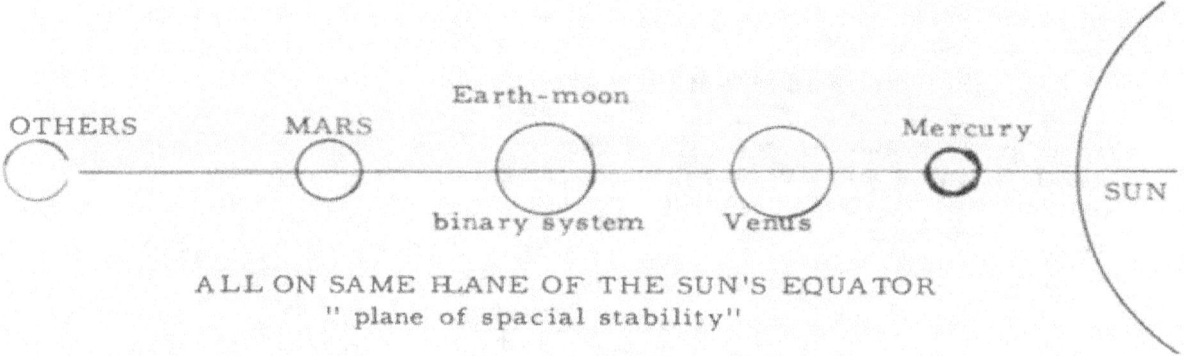

ALL ON SAME PLANE OF THE SUN'S EQUATOR
" plane of spacial stability"

All through the various universes we have billions of these planes of cosmic stability. But in "our" system we can definitely pinpoint the points of intersection and even the number of "lines" which this formation takes. We can do this by the study of the growth of crystal structures on this very same lattice work of space. This is the 3-D physical diagram that is provided for any observer of the force fields of form which give us a diagram at a certain narrow stage of the temperature scale of the SPACE-LATTICE of "our" solar system.

All crystalization on the earth (and perhaps thru-out the solar system as the crystal structure of meteorites should show) can be classified into the SIX units of the system.
1. cubic (like table salt)
2. Tetragonal
3. Orthohombic
4. Monoclinic
5. Anorthic
6. Hexagonal

Now, if we are to project these six finite systems one upon the other we should then have the lattice of "our" space in "our" system. Remember, and it must be continually spelled out, that the "lines" are but the limits of the 'force fields of form' of the non-animate crystal structure. The living plant and the animal bring other 'force fields of form' into being which are not as simple as the crystal lattice, but suffice for the moment to stick to the simple approach.

NOW.... what do we have, when we project as we mentioned, the 6 fundamental crystal forms of the space lattice composed of geometrical arranged ions or molecules occuring at these nodal points of the space lattice? The distances between these nodal points are 10^{-6} to 10^{-8} cm. Max von Laue discovered that X-rays give diffraction diagrams in these space lattices similar to diffraction phenomenom of light passing thru the same dimension of diffraction grating.

Von Federow and Scheinfliesz discovered that only 230 point systems (nodes or points of intersection) occur in crystalling substances which explain all physical properties of earthly crystals.

THIS FIGURE showing a portion of the projection that we mention demonstrates the condition that will provide a lattice with the 230 points of intersection of the 6 crystal forms. THIS IS THE SPACE-LATTICE.

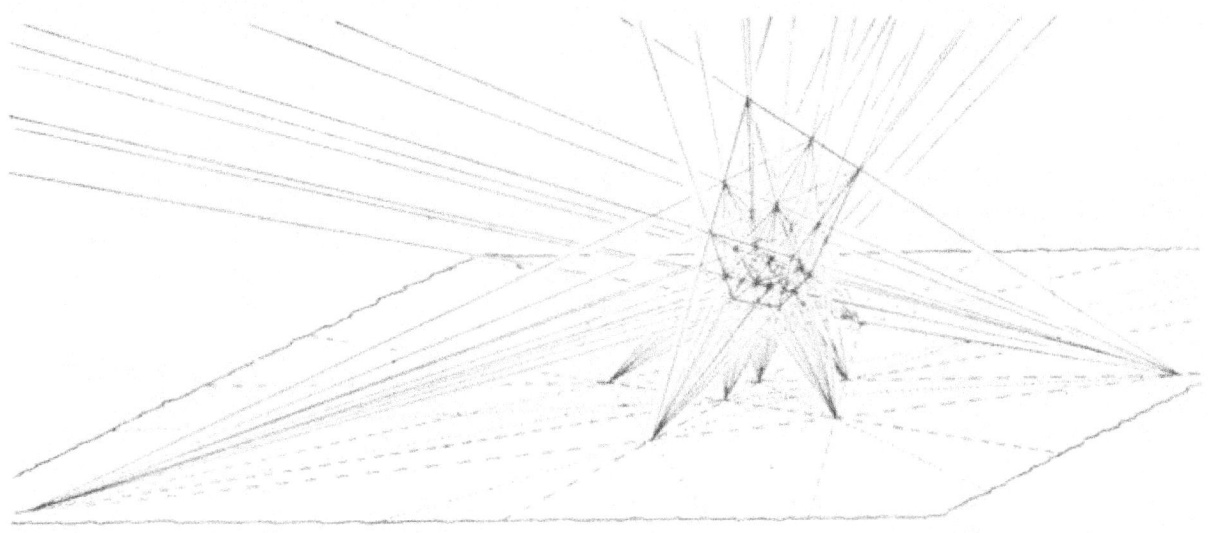

At a critical temperature and at a certain concentration a chemical compound will leap and grow along the lines of these electrically stable "force fields of form." The growth will be along the space-lattice lines characteristic of that compound. THE ART of "crystalography" is to classify these compounds by these graphic models of a portion of S P A C E.

Once the crystal has grown and become electrically stable it can resist the temperature change over a much greater range than that required to crystallize and this characteristic brings forth the possibility that heat should be investigated as a transitory form of matter or a catalyst of matter or materiality.

THE LATTICE WORK OF SPACE is not eletromagnetic or electrostatic in nature (it appears) however a voltage applied to a crystal causes the structure of the crystal to be stressed--just as does mechanical pressure which can cause a voltage to be taken off the stressed crystal.

E. Pfeifer (Kristalle)(1930) used the sensitivity of crystalizing solutions to register cosmic influences. According to his work a characteristic crystallization of Glauber*s salt prepared in the afternoon, changed during the night even tho the same temperature and concentration was used. The crystal structure changed completely during an eclipse of the sun.

This seems to show a solar distortion (lunar) of the spacial lattice. It is not the purpose of this treatise to develop all of the influences that tend to Materialize Space (nor would we presume to) but only to postulate the SPACE LATTICE THEORY as being true throughout the solar continuum.

As Bertrand Russel illustrated..."an electron is a wave of probability with nothing to wave in..." we maintain Electrons do not flow--electrons are not particles. So in the terms of Tesla and VORTEX ENGINEERING---how does OHM's Law need to be re-understood?

E=Voltage= a stress on space.

I=Current= "a flow of materiality" in which Heat is the transitory form.

R= still resistance and in ratio to the above. I^2R=watts or power to stress and move the material. NOW what else about a whirling vortex?

TESLA moved beyond materiality and 3-D with his alternating current conception and in this AC machine he needed no "flow of elections" he just "stressed space" at 60 cycles per second and at the rate of 3×10^{-10} cm/sec. the stress appeared at the other end of the conductor (power line).

Tesla and others then noted that it could be lagged or kicked by either inductance or reactance in the circuit. These QUALITATIVE phenomena were then quanitized in the conventional AC and Communications theory. BUT--it must be emphasized that the idea or conception beyond 3-D of Tesla was to stress space in a whirling vortex (armature in a magnetic field) and to convey it in the manner of the of the AC machine. The mathematics was then developed by means of ($\sqrt{-1}$ which is an imaginary "operator" needed to bring AC circuits from beyond 3-D to our reference of materiality or reality.

LEVITY....it is interesting to note that it is the plant world that responds in a positive and negative manner to this 'flow of space' that is gravity or the counter-flow outward that is LEVITY. This is known as orthogeotropism and plagiogeotropism. (see the last issue of the SPACE-CRAFT DIGEST for an illustration of levity).

So, even tho the problem of GRAVITY has been such that it has defied man's understanding one must admit that the Goethean qualitative approach offers the chance to visualize what happens beyond the 3-D of the materiality of our mathematics. In this sphere, dealing with energies that we cannot yet quanitize, lies that answer to the enigma of GRAVITY and the counter force of LEVITY......HEAT, again, is the transitory form of the state of change. Also, it must be emphasized that even Newton's law of motion applies...... "that to each action there must be an equal and opposite reaction." The force "lines" of LEVITY move outward from the planet in the same manner as the "lines" of GRAVITY or space-flow moves in toward to the center of the planet. HEAT is the transitory manifestation.

RAUM UND GEGENRAUM (SPACE AND COUNTER SPACE) then, become a qualitative reality as 3-D materiality is seized by this space-flow and moved to the center of the planet while certain life forces can be seized by the lines of LEVITY (such as the growing planet) and be projected outward upon still another dimensionality of the lines of LEVITY. (See THE PLANT BETWEEN THE SUN AND EARTH by Adams and Whicher) which illustrates the "force-fields of form" of a plant growing along these lines of LEVITY.

Certain plastics will also move along these LINES OF LEVITY as is known through experiments conducted by the author. However, as these plant stalks and plastics have mass and weight they also move along the lines of GRAVITY. With the proper space-positive charge the plastic can be made to move along the lines of LEVITY moving outward from the planet. It must be emphasized that this is not a phenomena that can be explained by electrostatic charges.

MATHEMETICS....it is unfortunate, indeed, that most of the study of the sciences gets side-tracked in the shoving of these phenomena into conventional mathematical theory and digital mechanics. So, it is said that "a mathematician never discovered anything--he just wrote it down...."

But one other phenomenom is of significance. When a crystal leaps into materiality and then is mechanically altered--what are its characteristics? The great RE-GENERATION CAPACITY OF CRYSTALS is demonstrated by the ALUM OCTAHEDROM which when polished into a globe, and then placed in a crystal growing supersturated Alum solution it quickly rebuilds into its original structure by developing the appropriate crystal faces.

It must be noted then that as the 230 point system is characteristic of the earth-moon binary system and that cosmic disturbances destroy crystal structure--now, if man goes beyond our "system" what will happen to his crystal structure--and the structure of his space-craft?......will it gradually change as it finds its space-lattice stressed?

NOW OTHER THAN THE SPACE LATTICE...WHAT ABOUT GRAVITY?

Gravity can be directly associated with no known force.....as a relation to it...or an affinity for any force or relationship. (says conventional science)

BETWEEN the lattice-lines there is the "SPACE" FLOW that holds the planet on its plane of stability--the action of this space flow on the molecule of materiality is the force of GRAVITY. This is the exceedingly simple conception that has been overlooked by investigators and those who mis-read Newton and insisted that he said much that he did not say in his PRINCIPIA.

Here now, is our simple QUALITATIVE DEVELOPMENT OF GRAVITIC FLOW:

The planetary distortion of the space-lattice causes the differential of space potential resulting in the "space-flow". This is proportional to the angular velocity of the rotating planet (or body). It was early recognized by Einstein (the Meaning of Relativity--Methuen, London ed. 5. 1951) and H. Thirring Physik Z. 19, 33 (1918) that a hollow rotating massive sphere tended to drag the inertial co-ordinate system around with it.

THE SPACIAL FLOW to the area of lesser spacial pressure(the center of the body) is CONTINUALLY INWARD and the energy (gravitic) is dissipated within the body as HEAT. This is another indication that HEAT is a transitory state of matter.

The van Allen bands lately re-discovered in the IGY research (known for a long time by the occultists as the 'arch of the firmament' and by others as the 'equitorial electrojet') indicates that the first phenomena of SPACE-FLOW toward the center of a sump area (such as the center of a planetary body) is to ionize and gather and form particles. As this velocity increases (the G-constant) the space-flow may well gather particles into a body of 3-D materiality and perhaps even form these particles from the fundamental neutrinos and hydrogen atoms and ions of "space". Even the direction of the whirl (above and below the plane of spacial stability) is noted as whirlpools flow into vortexes in different directions above and below the equator.

COSMIC MINDED Nicola Tesla was one of the few workers in the field of electrical machine design who possessed an understanding of the harnessing of SPACE-FLOW in what we might call VORTEX ENGINEERING. He understood that Ohm's law was but a ratio which quanitized this conception in a very crude manner. The fallacy was to think of the "I" or current as an electron flow. This was the mainstay of the direct current engineers of Edison generators which could only light about a square mile of city. It took Tesla's A.C. to make power available at 60 cycles for the whole planet with interconnection of power plants possible and also the much lower power line loss.

We must recognize that MATHEMATICALLY we can not yet quanitize an idea nor can we yet quanitize the SPACE-LATTICE until it is materialized for us to visualize in crystal structures, for instance. Then, we can develop a so-called science of crystallography, but as yet no tabulator of crystal forms can quanitize the spacial-lattice thus illustrated in 3-D materiality for us. We can, however, apply alternating voltages to this crystal structure of quartz and build our whole communications industry, but we must not forget that the mathematics of communications is just another attempt at the shoving of a cosmic phenomena into a familiar plane of reference.

IN VORTEX ENGINEERING, as Tesla conceived of it, we remove the barrier to conceptive thought found in the minds of conventional AC and DC machine designers bound to their mathematics devoid of an actual knowledge of what the whirling armature or pole-piece does with SPACE. The EMF (or voltage) or stress on space is whirled by the magnetic armature or pole-piece and we must understand that this is just a mechanical way to develop A SPACE VORTEX in the AC or DC Machine. We must also understand that we are dealing with just one vector of the space phenomena and that there are other vectors (Beyond 3-D) which also exist as a part of the action of the whirling vortex. We must understand that MAGNETISM FLOWS--and that SPACE FLOWS---and that there are several simple phenomenas that illustrate that space can be gripped in a mechanical device just as the spinning particle of materiality grips the space-flow to the center of the earth and is therefore subject to gravity.

GYROSCOPIC ACTION illustrates how a whirling gyro wheel grips SPACE along two dimensions and as long as it spins fast enought it will "defy gravity" but as soon as it looses it's "bight on space" it falls subject to the space flow of GRAVITY. THIS we offer as a partial development of a theory which accourts for GRAVITY, LEVITY and the theory of RAUM und GEGENRAUM which indicates that in our qualititive visualization of the problems of materiality we must have an open mind where space-vectors of energy are concerned. We bog down if we confine ourselves to conventional mathematics and conventional materiality because "counter-space" is everywhere manifested in electrical phenomena of which we use just the apparently "real" vector and ignore the flow of space beyond 3-D which holds our planet in its place. This "space" is seized by the gyro and flows through the lattice upon which crystals grow to materialize for us moemntarily to show that there "is something there" which we cannot yet quanitize and which is not yet materialized, but which nevertheless is "there" because atoms of materiality seize it and grow upon it. We cannot ignore its "reality" just because it is the lattice of COUNTER-SPACE or GEGENRAUM and is most illusive to our conventionality.

LEVITY is the flow of COUNTER SPACE or GEGENRAUM. Gravity is the lines of FLOW of Raum or the space of 3-D Materiality. The lattice-work of space is the force-field of "crystal form of materiality". The energy of Raum und Gegenraum is the flow of space and counter space.....gravity and levity. Heat, then appears, to be a transitory form of matter and magnetism a phenomenom of vortex-whirl and strain-on-space is an electrostatic in nature. BUT once a particle is "materialized" from counterspace it preserves the ability to move-in-space unhampered by the electrical nature of its instant of birth into materiality until it is again dissipated into counterspace as radiation. So we have the peculiar concept of the intertwining of SPACE and COUNTER SPACE with the instant of emergence or materiality governing the reality of the existance of the particle. This may be the fundamental outline of the conceptive difficulty that deters the development of the use of VORTEX ENGINEERING concepts for space travel.

SEE P. 24

SPACE CRAFT DIGEST   SALEM OREGON   P O BOX 768

AT
DORNACH
(near Basle)
SWITZERLAND

Dr. Rudolph Steiner's GOETHEANUM is the theater-university building of the THEOSOPHISTS which is the world center of spiritual science based on the lectures Dr. Steiner gave over most of Western Europe during the first quarter of the 20th century. Along with this Architectural masterpiece is a KLINIK whose healing methods employ the understanding of the spiritual forces which govern the human body and "mind".

    In the United States the Theosophical book list may be obtained from the ANTHROPOSOPHIC PRESS at 211 Madison Avenue in New York, New York. THE SPACE-CRAFT DIGEST is too limited a publication to attempt to present a summary of the work of Dr. Steiner, however, there is little doubt that he is a man whose abilities were similar to those of Swedenburg--both being thoroughly trained rational scientists who were at the same time at home in the realm of the super-sensible. Dr. Steiner's work and background of accomplishments are an intellectual wonder of this century. His actual achievements in connection with man's poor present day attempt at space-age learning have not yet been properly evaluated.

    BUT--we do recommend that Dr. Steiner's philosophy be carefully studied as it is the most concise and straightforward development of the influences of super-sensible forces on our everyday sense-world which is available to a student of either the occult plane or the mystery of the UFO.

    THEREFORE..... we strongly recommend to anyone seeking a philosophic understanding of the super-sensible that he study Dr. Steiner very very carefully. We also recognise that the group in Basle does not hold with "material" saucers. We do not feel that this schism between our thinking as put forth here in the SPACE-CRAFT DIGEST and that of the ANTHROPOSOPHISTS is not as different as they might at first think. We have long held that there were two types of "saucer" manifestations. That of the non-material or ETHERIC and the more conventional seemingly-solid type UFO of which we have printed many pictures. Now, one is just as "real" as the other. Further, if these are of psychic nature impressing themselves on our mental imagery in the form of a picture, they might well take different forms to different people viewing the same manifestation. These "hallucinations" are nevertheless REAL in that everything we view is just an illusion depending for its perceptibility upon the plane of reference of the viewer and the mental picture will be according to his scale of evolvement.

    As our friend, Miss Lou ZINSSTAG of Basle, says in her last letter to us......" The anthroposophists- at least the important group here in Basle are not interested in UFO research. They reject any idea of other planets being inhabited by human beings. They stick to a theorie (as far as I know) that other planets, especially Venus, are the home of etherial beings, living in other dimensions and with shapes vastly different from ours. They also

RIGHT out of "COUNTER-SPACE"... in Sicily these whirling "discs" demonstrate materialization into "our" dimensions. The whirling "VORTEXIA" manifestations are called by some FLYING SAUCERS. What causes them to whirl into material- ality is one of the mysteries of our time. They seem to be guided by intelligence and to perform amazing feats unexplainable by conventional science. BUT there is nothing NEW about these manifestations---they are as "old as T I M E ".......
THE U.S. AIR FORCES have repeatedly stated that these "things do not exist" and repeatedly ignore and ridicule those who see these performances. In this issue of the SPACE-CRAFT DIGEST we feel we have offered the first modern explanation combining science and occultism to give an explanation compatable to both schools of thought.

reject the idea that they need space ships in order to contact us; they feel sure that contact is established only through mediumistic channels." Now, etheric beings, exist to us. We have seen photographs of them and of course TREVOR JAMES has photographed the human ETHERIC DOUBLE or human Aura. "SCIENCE" cannot account for this "aura" and yet we can see it and photograph it. Spiritual Science accounts for all that conventional "science" does plus the nature of these baffling "force-fields-of-form" which are the real rulers of our natures. These are some of the reasons why we feel that every UFO student must know and understand Dr. Rudolph Steiner, one of this century's most remarkable incarnations.

EXPERT CITES STRONTIUM 90 DANGERS

WASHINGTON (AP) - Deadly strontium 90 is sifting down out of the stratosphere faster than expected, with its greatest fallout in the northern United States, Sen. Clinton P. Anderson (D-NM) said Saturday.

Anderson, chairman of the ment and the Atomic Energy Committee, put that interpretation on a series of communications from the Defense Department and the Atomic Energy Commission reporting on the effects of nuclear explosions by both the United States and Russia. The letters were released by the committee.

Anderson said a Feb. 19 letter from the Defense Department indicates that radioactivity remains in the stratosphere for shorter periods than the AEC previously assumed, and he continued:

"It also indicates that there is a latitude band of maximum dropout of the fallout from the stratosphere which occurs from 35 degrees-50 degrees north or south."

CONCENTRATION GREATER

"This area includes the northern part of the United States, and the letter states that "the concentration of strontium 90 on the surface of the earth is greater in the United States than in any other area in the world."

Strontium 90, taken into the body through food, damages the bones and in sufficient amounts produces bone or blood cancer.

"In layman's language," Anderson said in a statement, "it looks like strontium 90 isn't staying up in there as long as AEC told us it would, and the fallout is greatest on the United States. Perhaps this information may account, in part, for the recent higher readings of radioactivity in soils and plants.

"This new data appears to further contradict the official doctrine of AEC spokesmen as to residence time of fallout in the stratosphere and the theory that stratospheric fallout tends to drip out uniformly throughout the earth."

Anderson said the joint committee will look into these matters at fallout hearings in May.

Anderson complained about difficulties he said the committee experienced in getting the information before the public. He recently accused the Defense Department of "gagging" the congressional group against release of the fallout report.

AEC Commissioner W. F. Libby said in one of the letters he believed his previous estimate of the period in which radioactive debris would remain in the stratosphere "is too long and that it should be reduced"

He said evidence is increasing that stratospheric fallout occurs at maximum rates in a band of latitude lying between 35 and 50 degrees north and south of the equator. But Libby added "this old argument still is not quite settled."

-0-

(TORONTO) --AVRO Aircraft of Canada Limited has maintained official silence on a Washington report that the U. S. Army and Air Force are working on a project with the company which "we hope will be a flying saucer." However, it has been rumored for months that AVRO is working on a type of flying saucer and the Company has never denied it. A spokesman for AVRO said "we are exploring a new design concept," then added any further comment will have to come from the U. S. Services which control the program.

THE SCIENCE OF ATLANTIS

Based on the "time track" clairvoyant readings of the remarkable EDGAR CAYCE from the archives of THE EDGAR CAYCE FOUNDATION at Virginia Beach, Va.

For the purposes of this excerpt we shall not try to develop the proof that ATLANTIS existed. Most Naval hydrographic offices in the world know that it did from a land-mass standpoint. Whether "scientists" admit this is beside the point. Our space is too short in which to argue (see COLUMBUS HAD A MAP! in this issue). So now, from the time-compressing super-sensible "hallucinations" of Edgar Cayce, here is what he had to say about the forces of the universe which were everyday servants in Atlantis. These can be found by our present day researchers--if they keep their minds open and un-dogmatic. Matter-of-fact some of the primary development of the theory of the GREAT CRYSTAL or FIRESTONE is included in our development of the space-lattice and gravitic theory elsewhere in this issue.

"... The most notable scientific accomplishment of the ATLANTEANS was the harnessing of the sun's energy. Developed originally as a means of spiritual communication between the finite and the infinite the huge reflective crystals were first known as the TUAOI STONE. Later as its use was improved over the centuries its use expanded to become a generator of power or energy, radiating across the land without wires (as Tesla showed by experiment) .... "

"... set in the temple (or university) of the sun in POSEIDIA (Atlantis) the FIRESTONE was the central power station of the country. Basically, it was a large cylindrical stone or crystal of many facets capped with a mechanism at one end. It was suspended in the center of the building under an open dome and insulated with a non-conducting material. The concentration and the magnification of the sun's energy thru the power station created energy transfer of tremendous intensity. This space-energy was FREE energy that powered the air-ships, water ships and land craft (private vehicles).

Moderate application of this energy to the living body had a partial rejuvenation effect. (This legend handed down to the Spanish conquistadores started Ponce de Leon on his quest for the "fountain of youth" which still is said by Harold Wilkins to have been seen in a deserted city of the descendants of Atlantis in the Matto Grosso jungles of Brazil.)

The ATLANTEANS studied the creative energies of the universe in the resonance of the life vibrations of plants, metals and jewels--the latter in their actions on the psychic nature of man.

The priesthood in the Temples (UNIVERSITIES) was made up of the most learned men and women of the nation.

It must be emphasized that while our present Western World developed in the last few hundred years that Atlantis flourished for 200,000 years and disappeared about 12,000 years ago... more or less. It passed thru all possible phases of spiritual development and subsequent retrogression......."

ATLANTIS!....just as the secret of the "success" of our civilization is its source of power.... so it was that the SUN CRYSTALS were the secret of the source of energy that drove the space-craft, land-craft, and water-craft of the Atlanteans, and furnished the power to build gigantic stone structures and to bore tunnels thru the planet to act as the avenues of commerce. Some of these ATLANTEAN BORINGS still exist in out-of-the-way portions of the world. These construction marvels attest to the power of the Atlantean civilization which flourished for 200,000 years only to remain a wisp of a legend today. No matter what the power of mortal man, it is insignificant to the powers that shape the cosmos and hold the planet in its place in the universe. Insignificant too, when the powers of Vulcanism levitate portions of the earth's crust along the lines of space-flow in terrible eruptions that rip the earth's crust in such a manner that mountain ranges rise and continents disappear beneath the surface of the oceans--only to mysteriously rise a hundred thousand years later with accompanying cataclysm.

These forces could be loosed tomorrow----any tomorrow as today has no mortgage as security in the cosmos.

- 30 -

"Sen. Barry Goldwater, a jet-flying AF Reserve Colonel: "Flying saucers-- unidentified flying objects -- or whatever you call them, are real."

x x x x

"William Lear, winner of Collier Aviation Trophy, President Lear, Inc. (Aircraft and electronics equipment) who has sighted a UFO: "I believe the flying saucers come from outer space, piloted by beings of superior intelligence."

SPACECRAFT OVER MEXICO

by W. GORDON ALLEN

MODERN SIGHTINGS of flying saucers or UFOs over the plain of Mexico have been quite frequent, but in a recently completed study of the writings connected with the Spanish conquest of Mexico, it is found that the UFO performed for Cortez and Monteczuma just as it does today for us.

In the study of the stories and writings of the actions of the conquistadores in the Spanish conquest of Mexico, there were several omens that were taken as signs from heaven that the almighty Host would look with favour upon Cortez.

Further, on what is left of the public buildings of the Mayas and the Quiches who lived in Mexico from 20,000 to perhaps 12,000 years ago we also find allusions to " visitors from heaven." In the study of these writings are all kinds of references to the "lost" civilisations of Lemuria and Atlantis. The great plateau of Mexico was perhaps the buffer zone between these two great lands. Whatever the geopolitical position might have been, it is quite possible that the lands of Mexico and the two lost continents did have some sort of knowledge of each other and perhaps even regular contact. We won't say commercial intercourse because it is our suspicion that commerce and trade might be mostly an invention of a later type of psychology that made rule over others and personal acquisitiveness the compensation for the frustration of knowing little about the purpose of man and his growth after the deluge.

It was not necessary that trade and commerce and its resultant political rivalry develop during the time of the preceding civilisation. It might well be that the man of former epochs on this planet had other desires rather than personal aggrandisement or compensation for his inferiority through slavery of others by bondage or commercial debt.

These thoughts are brought out to indicate that civilisations can develop that do not have "modern" factors as the motivation.

Now, as to the place of the plain of Mexico in this development: we must admit that the relationship of these quotations to present understanding is esoteric in nature. In our opinions of their meanings we must of necessity look upon them with the doubtful benefit of a certain type of twentieth century mind. We might remark that we will have as much right to the interpretations as would the sixteenth-century mind of a Spanish padre or one of the priestly staff of Monteczuma. Nevertheless, we must admit that there might be a bit of truth in all three interpretations. There is little in the universe that is true or false, or black or white. Each mind arrives at some portion of the so-called " truth." The real " whole truth " is, of course, not yet for the mind of man to determine.

However, there have been manifestations of the appearance of UFOs over Mexico since the time of 20,000 years ago through the time of the Conquest right to present-day sightings of flying saucers.

One of the reasons that Hernan Cortez had such a psychological advantage over the ruling monarch, Monteczuma, was the ruler's preoccupation with the predicted " return of Quetzalcoatl." We know, now, that Cortez was not Quetzalcoatl; but the Aztec was not possessed of this knowledge and acted very strangely. However, the world air forces do not have the answer to the UFO and so they have also acted very strangely. We must understand the military mind —the Aztec military or the modern military— when we wonder how men act under stress.

The stress upon the ruling house of the Emperor Monteczuma in the year of 1519 was quite great when he heard the strange tale of white men from the rising sun who had landed on his shores.

The ruler was feared greatly by everyone in his empire. No one looked at him directly; he never set his foot upon the earth—his subjects carried him from place to place. He had the greatest contempt for the person of any of his subjects and his priesthood tore out tens of thousands of living hearts each year to keep the subjects duly fearful.

So, one can be certain that it was of no mortal man that the Emperor was afraid. So then, why was he so in fear of Cortez? Was it an omen? If so, what omen? Why was the interpretation of this omen of such significance that it destroyed one empire and preserved another?

It was in this year that a large green fireball trailing an orange tail performed for the subjects of this great ruler.

The fireball gyrated in the sky over Mexico City as the subjects wailed and screamed. The ruler made a definite inquiry of his priests as to just what was what. The group of priests who did not come up with an answer that would satisfy the Emperor knew they would lose their hides. (As we mentioned, Monteczuma feared no mortal— not even his priesthood.)

The priests went to the archives and came back to remind their monarch of some historical facts regarding the land he now ruled. Now it would be utter folly for us in the twentieth century to set down these historical "facts" from the archives of the Aztec priesthood as the mutterings of medicine-men with the fear of death upon them. Rather, it might be wise to take the "facts" of the priests as those writings kept as a state secret for tens of thousands of years. One of the secrets necessary to their power. Power, over each succeeding monarch and power over the people. The source of these secrets is, of course, conjecture, but nevertheless, the origin might be of a time before the deluge and of the esoteric school of the East. From the East they could well have passed through the hands of the Mayans and Quiches to the remote ancestors of the Aztec. The astrologers and priests of the Aztec had this to say [(We must remember that for the purpose of this writing, astrologer and astronomer have equal rank.) They told Monteczuma that the world in which he lived would fare no better than had the three worlds before him. Here is what they told the monarch and for the student of the UFO we feel these words are important]:

ATONATIUH . . . (Water Sun) the first world (or civilisation?) had been swallowed by a deluge.

> The fact that this appears in the book of ALL other religions over the world indicates that this fact seems pretty well known to every one of the ancient writers who attempted to preserve the legends that survived as religious literature. It seems somewhat remarkable that Monteczuma's astrologers knew this "fact" just as well as the Padre that accompanied Cortez.

TLALCHITONATIUH . . . (Earth Sun) had been quartered and divided again by earthquakes. Later, in other references we shall note that this was the great cataclysm that caused Atlantis to sink. How did the astrologers of the Aztec Empire know about this "fact" that seems not even to be widely accepted in the schools of the Western world even to this day?

ECATONATIUH . . . (Wind Sun) was very very interesting. This time great winds rose and killed all higher life except a few female monkeys.

TLATONATIUH . . . (Fire Sun) was, of course, the last world and that of the present Aztec Empire and that would be destroyed by fire. The Western bible predicts the same end for the planet.

Now, one would agree that we have two courses in lending credence to these declarations made some 450 years ago by Aztec priests. We can try to unwind the esoteric-psychological significance or we can just put them down to what ignorant savages told their ignorant monarch.

The latter course is the one that Western historians have followed until this writing. The author prefers to dust off these rather remarkable references and have "another go" at the problem of just what information these people had access to. It seems one devil of a lot more accurate than much we have used to build great hypotheses upon.

We might remark that our own astronomers have filled the public mind with what seems to be the most ridiculous of understandings of the cosmos. The International Geophysical Year discoveries have shown our own astro-observers to be not one whit better than superstitious savages —all their instruments notwithstanding.

We have long felt that astronomers were most exacting of scientists. Now we must admit that they are the most inexacting. So, our thought is to try to pay a lot more attention to the "historical facts" of the ancients. In the light of what we feel is our new knowledge we might find a much better fit to the jigsaw puzzle of the place where man fits in the universe.

What about the Water-Sun that swallowed the earth by a deluge? What caused the deluge? What cosmic disturbance could cause such a thing upon the whole planet?

The Aztecs say the deluge was caused by the explosion of the planet in the orbit beyond Mars into small parts. The largest now is the asteroid some 465 miles in diameter. There are thousands of other smaller pieces that make up the asteroid belt. This, perhaps, was the cosmic disturbance that brought about the first deluge.

Wind-Sun

Long eons after the deluge was the final settling of the earth's crust which could have been the cataclysm that sunk Mu, and raised both the Andes and the Rockies. Some very slight cosmic quake (disturbance of the planet's force fields) could have triggered this action. But the remarkable part of the tale seems to be that these ignorant savages knew about this happening eons before their time.

The Wind-Sun is the next earthly catastrophe that killed all higher life, but female monkeys are most interesting and at first reading seem like the mutterings of a witch-doctor.

BUT—there is reason to believe that the moon was once in an orbit between the earth and Mars. This satellite was either "pushed" out of the way of the Martians or "captured" by the "field" of the earth.

This could have caused the great winds that blew most of the life off the earth. The disturbance could have first been the "slight" cosmic disturbance that dropped Lemuria into the deep. Then the final result being the great winds around the planet as the atmosphere on the moon was "captured" by the earth when Luna dipped into its orbit around the bigger planet.

Why should our moon be by far the largest in the solar system in relation to its planet?

Now, these are truly remarkable situations which these astro-students of Monteczuma seemed to know about and brought out of their archives for his information at the moment when a ball of fire was performing over his empire. They had other omens on which they could build their case for the "Return of Quetzacoatl—a Spaceman" and, of course, they proceeded to give him their full performance.

The remarkable thing is that they seemed to have knowledge denied even to us today and, consequently, they were expecting a white god from the heavens.

The fact that Cortez was not this god indicates that they just didn't have their identification properly arranged.

But there is more record about this Spaceman. Yogi, or Christ-like figure that brought about the story of Quetzacoatl.

God of the Wind

He, as God of the Wind, "A man of good appearance and grave countenance with white skin, a beard, and dressed in a long flowing white garment." "He was called by some, Quetzacoatl, and by some, Huemac, because of his great goodness. He taught the men of that long past time the way of virtue by his word and deed. He hoped to save them from vice and to give them laws, and good doctrine and to restrain them in their lewd and lustlike ways, and he instituted fasting and care of the body (yogi?) among them. But, seeing how little they followed this doctrine, he vanished to the East, telling them that at some time he would return."

It seems as if this great and good man with a beard has visited every land. He told of a fine way of life, but it seems that men, being what they are in all lands, did not take his teaching to heart and they persisted in falling upon evil ways.

But why would this great Emperor be so concerned about this ancient legend?

Here is another detailed description of a very strange phenomena in the sky that many would call the appearance of a "flying saucer."

"A big 'comet' appeared in the sky that looked like a big flame of fire, very bright, which threw forth sparks. This 'comet' was in the shape of a pyramid, wide at its lower part, and becoming narrow as it rose, so that it ended at a point. It could be seen in the middle of the Eastern sky and could be seen during the day and at night."

We might think that this was a truly remarkable description of "something" that was in the sky and certainly was not a comet even though that is the translation. But there is more to indicate that, contrary to the action of a comet, this "thing" seemed to leave in its wake a very heavily charged "field" electrical in nature.

"The CU or temple of the war god was seen to blaze without any human reason for it and the flames came from inside of the beams outwards. The priests called for water to put out the fire but the more water they poured on, the more the 'fire' burned. The next portent was the lightning stroke which WITHOUT PURPOSE OR THUNDER hit the very war god himself (statue?). There was no thunder in this lightning stroke. The big 'comet' ran all through the sky of Mexico throwing off hot coals and big sparks and had a very long tail. The lagoon of Mexico (for the Aztec city was built on a lake) rose and boiled in fury though there WAS NO WIND!"

Well, read it two ways. Conventionally, the only explanation for this is that the writers were not to be believed. Such a thing is impossible.

IMPOSSIBLE unless it was a space ship and that it did have a highly-charged electrical field around it that could enable it to perform these "tricks" with ease.

This does, however, give us the basis of the reason that the Emperor of the Aztecs, his rule as absolute as that of any man on earth, was afraid of the advent of the "return of Quetzalcoatl."

The Omens

We can never know more than this which was without doubt the reason behind his strange actions. The mis-interpretation of the omens do, nevertheless, leave us with the interesting afterthought that the omens themselves might well have been the real return of a space craft with some "Quetzacoatls" aboard.

Now these sightings of typical UFO or "flying saucer" phenomena by the astrologers or soothsayers of the Aztec are one thing.

What was the other side seeing in the sky at the same time? What kind of an omen was it to them?

One Bernal Diaz del Castillo makes a passing remark to the very same appearance. He saw the same performance of the highly-charged body over the sky of Mexico over a period of time that would preclude its being a comet.

The Spaniards took this to be a message from their God that he looked with favour upon the venture to obtain this great new land for purposes of making ever greater numbers of catholic converts.

But, nevertheless, it did perform. It was not a comet. There is to this day no adequate explanation in our scientific world for this performance.

These things are mentioned in passing just as strange stories and are not particularly part of the narrative. Mainly they are valuable ONLY to those who feel that the history of Western man as told to us in school is indeed a fairy tale.

Other stories of the high plateau of North and South America tell of little people and giants. These indefinite tales tell of the little people who built pyramids in high places in the Andes of giant blocks of stone that we cannot lift even with today's equipment. We feel they were little people because the passages in the structures were for little people.

Tales of Giants

The tales of giants also abound. Giants came down from above and killed the Inca women when they had intercourse with them. We don't know if these were later Quetzalcoatls who had spent too much time aboard their space craft, or what. But this same Bernal Diaz del Castillo has this to say about the thigh bone of a giant that Cortez sent to the court of the Spanish King to demonstrate to the Monarch that he was indeed in a strange land with many wonders:

"They said that their ancestors had told them that in times past there had lived among them men and women of giant size with huge bones, and because they were a very bad people of evil manners they fought with them and killed them and that those which remained had died off. So that we could see how high and tall these people were, they brought us the leg bone of one which was very thick and the height of a man of ordinary stature (5 ft. ?) and that was the (thigh) bone from hip to knee. We were all amazed at seeing these bones and felt sure that there must have been giants in this country. Our Captain Cortez said to us that it might be well to send the bone to Castile so that his Majesty might see it, so we sent it with the first of our agents who went there."

The Mexican no doubt would have been happy to have the Spaniard believe that they were giant killers. But the bones themselves indicated that there were giants about this high plain of Mexico a few hundred years ago.

Then if we believe it to be true we might ask what sort of giant was it that appeared on the high plain of Mexico and also in the Andes some thousands of years ago?

As Cortez and his men had a lust for gold, and not for giants and UFO reports, we might take them at their face value.

"Rear Adm. D. S. Fahrney, Ret., former Navy missile chief: "Reliable reports indicate there are objects coming into our atmosphere at very high speeds. The way they change position would indicate their motion is directed."

****

"Capt. W. B. Nash, Pan American Airways, who with his co-pilot saw eight huge discs maneuver below their airliner: "I believe they were controlled machines from outer space."

******

COLUMBUS HAD A MAP!

The truth seems to be that Columbus didn't "discover" America, but that he had precision charts and just followed the well mapped trail to the double continents of the Americas. Here, unfolds the incredible story that was broken publicly in this country for the first time by the Georgetown University FORUM.

Through the generosity of Mr. Arlington Mallery, the GEORGETOWN UNIVERSITY FORUM is suplimenting the transcript of the broadcast entitled "NEW AND OLD DISCOVERIES IN ANTARCTICA" with prints of nine ancient maps referred to in the text. The addition of these documents to the stenotyped text of the program provides a very instructive monograph for study and reference.

PIRI REIS, a distinguished geographer and Turkish Admiral of the 16th Century, had as a slave pilot a man who had been with COLUMBUS on three voyages. The pilot, when captured, had WITH HIM A MAP USED BY COLUMBUS! Using this map and eight other Greek maps which had been handed down since the time of Alexander the Great (who was tutored by a product of the mystery schools of Egypt and apparently an Adept) Piri Reis compiled a WORLD MAP. This 1513 map of the world has only been partially found as yet--the map of the ATLANTIC OCEAN.

This ancient map, with precision, shows the coasts of South American, Africa, and a portion of the South Polar regions of Ant Arctica--called by the Greeks, Antithone. After being brought to a system of map projection by Mr. Mallery, the ancient map of Piri Reis proved to be amazingly accurate in many details. THIS FACT LEADS TO THE CONCLUSION THAT THERE WERE COMPETANT EXPLORERS AND MAP-MAKERS ALONG THE COASTS OF THE SOUTH ATLANTIC SOME 2,000 YEARS BEFORE COLUMBUS!

The section of ANTARCTICA is particularily interesting BECAUSE it shows the coast lines that are now under the ice cap, but which must have been SURVEYED presumably 20 centuries at least in the past by the authors of the maps from which PIRI REIS compiled his ATLANTIC OCEAN MAP.... used by Columbus.

These very old maps have been known for many years, (since 1931) but their real accuracy and significance were not appreciated in present day investigation until Mr. Mallery re-discovered the system of projection used by the original cartographers. It seems definite now, that these cartographers. It seems definite now, that these cartographers were part of a survey team that mapped THE ENTIRE EARTH. These men were not more adventurers, but were competent scientists, skilled in the art of the determination of astro-positions and traverses.

HERE ARE SOME EXCERPTS FROM THE BROADCAST OF THE GEORGETOWN FORUM

"..... studies of the ancient map of Greenland have turned up some remarkable facts which have been recounted in the book LOST AMERICA by Mr. Mallery. Some of the ancient maps show land forms which have been verified by seismic soundings of the ice capes of Greenland and Antarctica. The Rev. Daniel Linehan S. J., has made such seismic explorations in both polar regions of iced area and he has verified several items marked on these maps...." (including the fact that Greenland is two islands with a strait between---all now under the ice cap..... Ed.)

Further in the broadcast it was brought out that the U. S. Navy hydrographic office has checked the maps and estimated that the age of the conditions shown on the maps must be about 5,000 years ago. "... we were able to check, of course thru the hydrographic office and afterward by the seismic sounding of the French Polar expiditions, that these maps accurately recorded the sub-glacial topography of GREENLAND. About three years ago the chief engineer of the hydrographic office handed to me a copy of a map that had been sent to him by a Turkish naval officer. He suggested that I examine it in the light of information we already had on the ancient maps. After making an analysis of it, I took it back to him and requested that the office check both the latitude and longitude on the projection. When they asked why I asked that---I said, 'there is something on this map that no one is willing to believe coming from me, and I don't know whether they will believe it coming from you....". That was the fact that COLUMBUS had a map with him that showed accurately the Palmer Peninsula in the Antarctic Continent. Here is a two thirds copy of the map which shows that Columbus had with him a map that shows Yucatan, Guatamala, all of South America to the Straights of Magellan and of course the portion at the bottom of the world that we have mentioned.

HOW WAS THE PROJECTION SO ACCURATE? In the first place it was evident that there was very little ice, then. But secondly, they had a record of every single mountain range in Canada and Alaska...I checked the map and it had ranges on it that the Army map service did not have. THEY HAVE SINCE FOUND THEM!

> JUST HOW THEY WERE ABLE TO DO IT...YOU WILL RECALL
> THE ANCIENT GREEK TRADITION OF THE AIRPLANE (or Space-
> Craft...Ed.) MAYBE THEY HAD THE AIRPLANE. WE DON'T KNOW
> HOW THEY COULD MAP IT SO ACCURATELY WITHOUT THE
> AIRPLANE. NOT ONLY THAT, BUT THEY KNEW THEIR LATI-
> TUDE CORRECTLY---SOMETHING THAT WE DID NOT KNOW
> UNTIL TWO CENTURIES AGO..."

NORDENSKJOLD, the great Swedish explorer and cartographer spent some 18 years solving the puzzle of the projection of the curved surface of the globe on a flat chart in their grid system. (IT MUST BE EMPHASIZED THAT THE MAP IS PRECISE.....NOT JUST AN OLD MAP.....Ed.)

Thru the courtesy of Senator Neuberger's office and Walter Dodd the author was able to get from the Library of Congress a photostat of the full sized chart as sent out by the Turks after its discovery in 1931. After its publicity in that year in Germany the truth was let die and still it has not penetrated our school books. It is deplorable that truth after truth of this type cannot seem to penetrate into our school system and our children are still taught fables.

After the Spanish Conquistadores followed COLUMBUS into the "new" world in their mad search for gold and the good padres of the Roman Catholic Church, in their zeal to obliterate all records of the ancients, it became increasingly difficult to unfold the mystery of the descendents of ATLANTIS.

However, in the islands of the Carribean there were sub-terranian borings or caverns that led the way to vast underground cities. In the Andes, in the Matto Grosso jungles the bandits who hunted for gold found traces of the ancient colonies of Atlantis.

Harold Wilkins in his data-filled book THE ANCIENT MYSTERIES OF SOUTH AMERICA tells of the astounding things he found which indicate that Atlantis colonized South American even before it colonized Egypt and that their civilization lasted for some 200,000 years. The civilization (s) were destroyed finally by catastrophy after catastrophy which finally climaxed with a pole-switch about 12,000 (more or less) years ago. From that period it seems that the ice-caps grew. Certainly, by these maps, 5,000 or more years ago there were no ice-caps.

Elsewhere, we mention the development of our SPACE-FLOW THEORY OF GRAVITY which we shall call the ALLEN GRAVITIC THEORY because, to our knowledge, we are the first modern to develop it, we tell of the distortions of the space-flow that holds the planet in its orbit which causes great upheavals. BUT, what causes this distortion in the SPACE-FLOW and can it happen again?

It is our feeling that these catastrophies are heralded by gigantic sun-spots and other actions on the face of the sun. Many times in history this has happened and following is a few paragraphs of tabulation which indicates how even in the last 2,000 years catastrophies have been quite common. Always it must be emphasized that one could happen TOMORROW and that we are immune to the great power of the cosmos.

45 B.C. (the year Caesar died) the sun remained pale for a whole year and gave less than the usual warmth. The air was thick, cold and hazy and the fruit did not ripen.

33 A.C. (the year of the Crucifiction) from the sixth hour until the 9th hour there was darkness over the land.

385 A.D. 22nd of August a darkening for two hours, before a fearful earthquake distroyed several cities in the Greek and Asia Minor areas.

360 A.D.... When the light of heaven was suddenly concealed from the whole world and trembling men thought the light of the sun had left them. This lasted from early dawn until noon (much longer than any eclipse..... Ed.)

409 A.D.... so dark that stars could be seen by day.

536 A.D..... The sun suffered an "eclipse" which lasted a full year and two months and men said that something had clung to the sun.... a similar thing was observed in 1783.

567 A.D.... A flame of fire in the heavens by the North Pole which remained for a whole year.... darkness started at three o'clock and ashes fell over the whole world. (Ashes from which great upheaval?)

626 A.D.... the sun's disc continued to be obscured for 8 months.

733 A.D... the sun was so darkened as to excite terror.

840 A.D.... from the 28th of May until the 26th of August a moving spot across the sun's disc was observed.

934 A.D... for two months the sun was without brightness (Portugal)

1091 A.D..... on the 21st of September the sun was darkened for three hours and when the darkness had gone the sun's disc still retained a strange color.

1206 A.D.... On the 1st day of Feb. there was complete darkness for six hours in the morning.

1241 A.D.... So dark that stars could be seen at 3 P.M. on Michaelmas Day.

1547 A.D.... 23-25 April, Kepler says that for three days the sun was a bloddy color and stars could be seen in the afternoon.

Any of these catastrophies would be of panic magnetude if they were to occur today and certainly even with our modern instruments we might be hard put to explain them by our existing theories.

But, if we could eliminate the "fables" from our school system we might be able to develop enough scientists with 'open minds' who could supply us with the more correct theoretical understanding. However, strangely enough it is the occultist who is being born out by nearly every discovery of the International Geophysical Year.

GRAVITIC DEVELOPMENT--------
    The lines of SPACE-FLOW inwardly toward the center of the planet "seize" the particles of materiality (in our 3-D world) which are generated by the "vortex" that holds the planet on its plane of spacial stability and force the materialized particles to move with this SPACE FLOW. This is the action of G R A V I T Y. The "flow" of ultra-dimensional s p a c e (inward to the center of the earth in all directions) is transformed into another outward energy flow which we might liken to another vector and call it LEVITY. The dotted curve at the transition point is heat and this is the heat that is known as the heat of the "HOT" core of the planet---which we postulate in error as the cause of volcanic action...or Vulcanism.

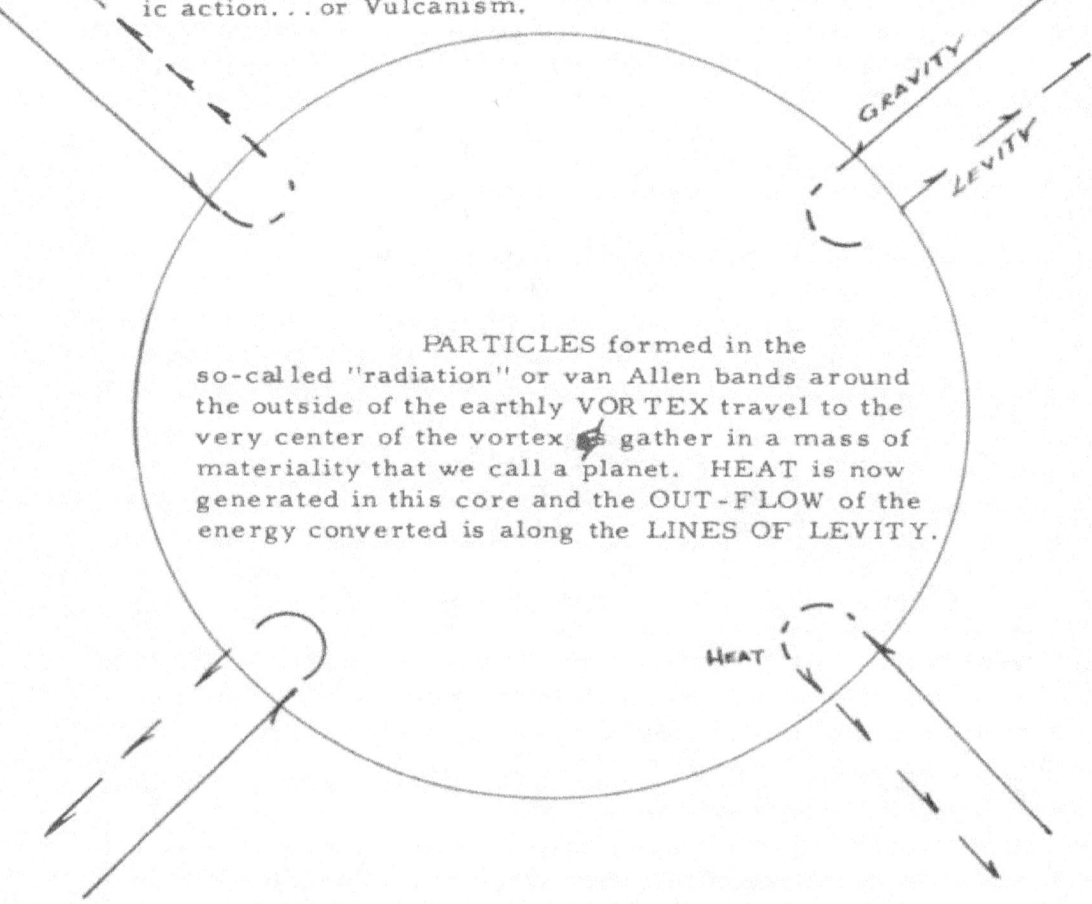

PARTICLES formed in the so-called "radiation" or van Allen bands around the outside of the earthly VORTEX travel to the very center of the vortex is gather in a mass of materiality that we call a planet. HEAT is now generated in this core and the OUT-FLOW of the energy converted is along the LINES OF LEVITY.

LEVITY....or LEVITATIONAL LINES are those along with the LIFE FIELD of FORCE (or the ODIC) flows and along these lines flowers and plants grow upward or LEVITATE.

THE FORCE FIELDS OF FORM....exist and we can see that along them the crystal structure of the mineral kingdom "grows"......force-fields of form using yet another "field-of-force" governs the direction of the growth and the three dimensional "form" of the plant and the animal kingdom.

FORCE FIELD REALITY....... is the elusive conception that we must understand if we are to comprehend the wonders of the multi-dimensional universe that is beyond the abilities of our senses or our instruments to detect. The very ancients and their wonderous civilizations that have disappeared in the great cosmic (earthly) convulsions knew of these forces. In late years there are those who have conspired to keep this knowledge secret. It must be emphasized that distortions of this SPACE FLOW causes mountains to rise, entire continents to fall beneath the seas. A rapid distortion of the lines of LEVITY is the explosion of a volcanic eruption like Vesuvious or Krakatoa.

SIR ISAAC NEWTON

GRAVITY RESEARCH FOUNDATION
NEW BOSTON, N. H.
founded by Roger W. Babson

Operated in connection with the Sir Isaac Newton Library of the Babson Institute

Following our development of the ALLEN GRAVITIC THEORY we think it only fair that we mention that each year Roger Babson's GRAVITY RESEARCH FOUNDATION offers the only prizes in this nation to those who attack this problem. There is a lot that we disagree on concerning his method of handling the project, but nevertheless the foundation certainly deserves the support of all groups as long as it does not become dogmatic. We are inclined to feel as illustrated in the reprint of the release following that the foundation seems to have gone pretty far up the trail of scientific dogmatism.

(a) We especially object to the fact that the foundation will not accept a modification of a theory of VORTICES. Certainly Newton's PRINCIPIA (as it was altered) is no basis on which to reject any theory! (see...a.)

(c) GYROSCOPIC ACTION is significant to a gravitic understanding..... if we understand just what relation this action has to the space flow.

(e) If neutrinos are a vortex motion of space then, certainly the error of the remarks in (a) following are born out.

But all in all--read the following release and then judge for yourself the track that conventional science in the United States is taking. We feel that too many categorical statements have been made in this release and our GRAVITIC explanation shows why we feel this way.

GRAVITY DAY 1958

Tenth Anniversary of the Gravity Research Foundation
New Boston, New Hampshire
August 16

At the morning session beginning shortly after 9:30, Mr. George M. Rideout, president of the Gravity Research Foundation, gave a cordial welcome to all those in attendance. This was followed by a brief review of the progress of the Foundation during the past ten years. At the first meeting there were 22 present. This year there were 278 present. Fifteen of the original 22 attended the tenth anniversary meeting. Greetings were received from friends in Moscow, Peru, and many points in the United States. He called attention to the meetings on Gravity at Chapel Hill, and also the meeting of the Institute of Aeronautical Sciences in New York, which was led by Mr. Charles Tilgner Jr. of the Grumman Aircraft Engineering Corporation, that had an attendance of over 500. As further evidence of the growth of interest in gravity he pointed out the Research Institute for Advanced Study at the Martin plant in Baltimore. In addition General Electric Company and most of the larger airplane manufacturers are interested in discoveries and theoretical advances in the field.

The second speaker of the morning was Dr. Igor I. Sikorsky. He called attention to the fact that the fundamental nature of matter and radiation was fairly well understood but there was very little if anything known about the fundamental nature of life and of gravitation. At present there seems to be no agent to transmit gravitation.

Little was known about gravitation until the time of Galileo. It was Newton's Law of Universal Gravitation which formed the basis for accurate computations in many areas of mechanics and astronomy until the time of Einstein. The English scientist Wherwell called the Law of Gravitation the greatest scientific discovery ever made. (Is it a cosmic law? Ed.)

Dr. Sikorsky looks on Einstein's General Theory as an extension of Newton's Law into a few very special cases. Newton's Law is still adequate for nearly all problems in mechanics and astronomy to which it applies.

The magnitude of the gravitational force between the earth and the sun is such that a steel cable nearly the size of the earth in diameter would be needed to hold the earth in its orbit were it not for gravity. As a further illustration of the magnitude of the force of gravity he considered what would happen to a steel sphere the size of the earth as it approached the sun. At a distance about 400,000 miles the greater attractive force on the side nearer the sun over the attractive force on the distant side would tear the sphere apart.

To illustrate the importance of gravity he pointed out that an interruption of the light of the sun for one hour would do no serious damage to the solar system, but the interruption of gravity for one hour would result in the disruption of the solar system as we now know it. His talk was followed by a motion picture on the usefulness of helicopters. (He always gets his pilch in......Ed.)

The third speaker of the morning was Professor Howard O. Stearns, physicist and Chairman of the Board of Trustees of the Foundation. He called attention to the great increase in the number of papers devoted to the subject of gravity since the inception of the Gravity Research Foundation. Twenty-six of the 30 papers in the July, 1957 issue of Reviews of Modern Physics were devoted to some aspect of the problem of gravity. Among the contributors are DeWitt, Dicke, Wheeler, Bondi, Bergmann and Weber. The latest book that gives a mathematical approach to the subject of gravity is Geometry of Einstein's Unified Field Theory by Vaclav Hlavaty of the University of Indiana.

During the year we have received at the Foundation hundreds of letters and papers attempting to "explain" gravity. These fall into six groups with a few that cannot be classified. Parenthetically there are two major pitfalls into which many of the writers fall. Some attempt to start from scratch, with a mind uncluttered by knowledge, to develop a wholly new theory. Most of their original ideas have been known to scientists for from 50 to 2000 years. There are others who stumble over the need for dimensional consistency in statements and equations.

    a. One group of writers attempts to revive some form of the theory of vortices put forth by Rene Descartes. Newton in the Principia pointed out the fallacies of any vortex theory.

    b. The inflowing ultramundane-particle theory of LeSage, or some modification of it, is attractive to a large group of writers. The defects of such a theory were pointed out by G. H. Darwin some 70 years' ago.

c. Many have the idea that by treating a gyroscope in the right way it may be induced to take off into interstellar space. This is as probable as the chance that the inventor will be able to lift himself to the moon by means of a pull at his bootstraps.

d. Since Gold, and others, have pointed out that the only way anti-matter could accumulate in a steady-state universe would be for it to exert a repulsive force on ordinary matter some writers have hoped to use anti-matter to counter the force of gravity. However, since anti-matter unites with ordinary matter destructively, annihilating both of them, there is naturally no way of containing it.

e. Neutrinos are being investigated as a possible explanation of the mysteries of gravity. Dr. Leonard Schiff of Stanford University is exploring the possibility that gravitation may be due to exchange forces among neutrinos and matter.

f. Professor Dicke of Princeton and others are working on the possibility that gravity may be the result of some kind of second order effect of electromagnetism.

The mathematical complexities encountered in the exploration of the possibilities of each of the last two ideas are so great that it will be some time before their value is determined.

At the close of the morning program an illuminated citation was presented to Mr. Babson by the Trustees of the Foundation. The citation praised his foresight in the formation of the Gravity Research Foundation and pointed to the likelihood that he would be more readily remmebered for this organization than most of the others he has founded. Mr. and Mrs. Babson were then presented with an anniversary cake.

Those attending the morning session were guests during the noon hour of Mr. and Mrs. Roger Babson at a buffet luncheon. This afforded a pleasant intermission for the renewal of friendships and for informal discussions about the morning papers.

The first speaker of the afternoon was Mr. Fred Vacha, engineer and trustee of the Gravity Research Foundation. He reviewed the five prize-winning essays presented this year.

The paper to achieve the first prize was one by Professors Giuseppe Cocconi and Edwin Salpeter of Cornell University. They pointed out some aspects of present theories that must be shown to be deficient in order to develop a more inclusive theory. They suggested an experiment by which anisotropies in the inertia of terrestrial bodies could be detedted.

The second prize went to Mr. Quentin A. Kearns of the Radiation Laboratory of the University of California. He described a laboratory method for measuring the propagation velocity of gravitational interaction. The velocity measurement can be achieved by a precise determination of the phase difference between electrical signals derived from a pair of electromechanical transducers.

The third prize this year went to Dr. Joseph Weber of the University of Maryland for a paper on New Experiments in Gravitation Physics. He suggested new experiments for testing the General Theory of Relativity; a means of generating gravitational waves, and other experiments for studying the invariance of intervals in accelerated frames.

The fourth prize went to Dr. Winston H. Bostick of Stevens Institute of Technology for a paper on Stabilization of the Elementary Particle by Gravitational Forces. He considered the consequences of a torus model of the elementary particle. With such a model it can be shown that self gravitational effects can be comparable to electromagnetic effects in the elementary particle and that the electron and proton can therefore be stabilized by self gravitational forces.

The fifth prize went to Dr. Fritz Zwicky of Mount Wilson and Palomar Observatories for a paper On the Breakdown of Newton's Law of Gravitation at Great Distances. He showed that the ;nonexistence of clusters of galaxies and the smallness of the velocity dispersion among neighboring clusters of galaxies proves that Newton's Law is not universal but breaks down for bodies separated by more than a few million light years.

Mr. Joel E. Fisher of New York and Professor W. J. Hooper of Principia College then gave A Progress Report on Gravitational Research. Mr. Fisher described the new apparatus he has developed since last year consisting of 153 soft-steel rods varying in cross section but symmetrically mounted about and parallel to the shaft, and held in place by four, one-inch thick aluminum discs. Around the core, 12 inches in diameter and 40 inches long, were would 1480 turns of No. 12 insulated copper wire, connected to slip rings. Measurements were made with a Worden Gravity Meter. This instrument has a detecting mechanism which is made entirely of fused quartz. The meter itself is completely enclosed in a light aluminum case. With this equipment a reading of 4.7 milligals was obtained which is 27.6 times the reading obtained with last years's equipment.

Professor Hooper described his theory which is based on the idea that the vector electric field resulting from the motion of a uniform magnetic field past a conductor (or the reverse) cannot be shielded any more than a gravitational field can be shielded, hence it becomes possible to express a relationship between the v x B field and the gravitational field.

Further tests of the theory and the apparatus are planned as soon as Worden instrument, being purchased by Mr. Fisher, is delivered this next month.

The third paper of the afternoon was given by William S. Alcott on The Ups and Downs of Gravity. He described, on the basis of a search of the catalogue of the Library of Congress, the number of books on the subject of gravity which have come out over the past three hundred years. He exhibited a chart that showed how intermittent the activity in the field had been. There were long periods with no activity at all. As a means of stimulating interest in gravity he suggested the establishment of a Journal of Gravity Research.

In a few minutes before the close of the session Mr. Babson reported on the question of the physical reality of the examples of levitation mentioned in the Bible. Christian Scientists and Roman Catholics accepted the physical reality, while the Protestant clergy he asked considered the phenomenon to be due to mental or spiritual agents.

NEED FOR INSTITUTE OF PHSYCHIC PHYSICS

In the news releases of the last few days it appears that a demonstration for the graphic and striking need for such an institute as Professor TROMP proposes is illustrated.

THE RAND CORPORATION at Pal Alto, California, recipient of government brain-storming contracts, has just sent a memorandum to the U. S. Space Planners stating that an attack on the space travel problem via the anti-gravity or contra-gravitic--or some similar term---route does not seem practical at this time. They worded their high-cost communique more definitely, but suffice to paraphrase and say that this was the gist of the public release. We cannot believe that such is really true, because certainly this dogmatism cannot be so universal even in the confines of a commercial concern which prides itself on being un-dogmatic.

Here is another release which we will quote verbatum and then we shall comment upon it.

Crude Radiowaves 'Death Ray' Kills Monkeys in Government Experiment

WASHINGTON (AP)... Government scientists reported Friday (April 24th, 1959) that at least 10 monkeys have been killed in recent experiments by a crude "death ray" derived from certain ultra-high frequency radio waves.

But Dr. Pearce Bailey, who made the report, indicated a belief that it would be unlikely that such a thing could happen to a person listening to the radio or working a radar set.

However, he also said that while " we feel certain that radio and radar are not dangerous....we HAVE HAD MYSTERIOUS AIRPLANE ACCIDENTS ON THE OTHER HAND...."

It always is assumed that with the ordinary frequencies these things could not happen, he said, but it appears here that if you use a certain frequency and have the head (monkey's) in a certain critical position, it can happen.

Bailey reported, what he termed a remarkable phenomenom, in testimony before the house appropriations committee released Friday. Bailey is director of the National Institute of Meurological Diseases and Blindness.

Describing one experiment, the doctor said that waves that killed a monkey emanated from a radio antenna pointed toward the monkey's head and in line with his central brain stem, the central and vital part of the brain (Medula Oblongata.... Ed?) He said the monkey was killed in five minutes.

The radio frequency used was 388 megacycles. Radio experts told a reporter this was within the band of frequencies used in ultra-high frequency line-of-sight radio communications between airplanes and is also used in some types of specialized television and radar.

In contrast, commercial radio broadcasts are in the range from 600 kilocycles to 1600 kilocycles (or .6 to 1.6 megacycles) and FM and TV are about 100 megacycles while radars go up to about 1000 megacycles.

Bailey reported the deaths of a number of monkeys were apparently related to something other than the heating effect of the radiowaves---which would be a new twist in the line of possible hazardous duty from certain radio waves.

Several scientists have reported in the past that radio beams can be dangerous from their heating effect. Dr. John R. McLaughlin of Glendale, California, reported in 1957 that a man died in 1954 as a result of exposure in a radar manufacturing plant in Los Angeles.

But Col. George M. Knauf, a flight surgeon of the Air Force missile test center at Cape Canaveral, has said that the present day radar equipment poses no great threat to personnel other than those engaged in operating and maintaining the equipment.

A SCIENTIST AT THE NATIONAL BUREAU OF STANDARDS SAID THE POWER USED ON THE MONKEYS MUST HAVE BEEN TREMENDOUS IN ORDER TO PRODUCE SUCH AN EFFECT. (END OF QUOTE) Now a later dispatch from the same news service states that instead of being tremendous the power was a very small 100 watts which is very low where radar powers are concerned. This brings us to the very apt illustration in these "hot" full-coverage, front page news stories out of Washington, D.C. The "scientist" from the Bureau of Standards made a very juvenile remark and unknowingly the reporter in his good reporting caught him on it.

If these "scientists" had bothered to read TROMP'S PHYSICS that we think so highly of (and we were first introduced to it in the Library of the Bureau of Mines Laboratory in Albany, Oregon) they would have known about the response of nerve cells and other living cells to radio frequencies. It has been known for almost a half a century that cells respond to certain resonant frequencies. This is what the scientists encountered, but due to the narrow specialties of their "educations" they were not aware of the phenomenom and their ignorance received world-wide publicity. This must have been humorous to researchers in Europe who have much broader learning. . . . in most cases and whose pay is but a fifth of what these men are getting.

But there are other principles involved besides the resonance situation which these men ran into, and it has to do with the medula oblongata itself... We believe we know the answer but we will just pose this question---what is the only organ, which cannot be punctured, without leading to instant death--- I call it an "organ" purposely---and the answer is the Medula Oblongata.

Now, these statements are amazing from the standpoint that there is nothing NEW in the allegations made to astound and confuse the lawmakers in the never-ending battle for more money for "research" for the step into "space". However, it seems nothing short of tragic that "scientists" should let themselves be prostituted in to performing this type of subterfuge. Unless of course--they really didn't know better and if the latter is true then we shudder to think of what sort of hands our "space-race" is being entrusted.

AN INSTITUTE OF PSYCHIC PHYSICS

One of the most significant books in print on the subject of the influence of subtle forces on the human body is S. W. Tromp's PSYCHICAL PHYSICS published by the ELSEVIER PUBLISHING COMPANY of New York, Brussels, London and Amsterdam. S. W. Tromp is on the faculty of Faud the 1st University in Cairo. There is enough data in the book to suggest research on on the subtle forces of nature which would keep all of the world's scientists working on this one project alone.

In the bibliography, many of the references are in French and German publications of limited issue and obscure reference. Matter of fact, the bibliography in the back of the book covers pages 441 thru 503 and is the most complete reference on the subject that we have seen anywhere.

Here are some of the sections: Bio-electricity; Structure of the Cell; Electric properties of Cells; Cell Radiation; Sensitivity of Organic Crystals to Physic-Chemical Influences; sensitivity of collodal substances to volatile matter and electric fields; . . . . . to magnetic forces; to radio-active radiation; Sensitivity of protoplasm to Homeopathic Concentrations; Sensitivity of solutions to cosmic influences; excitation of plants and animals to tropism and nastic movements and so on.

Truly, this book is the world's most complete text on the subtle forces that influence life. Basis can be found in this book for the action of the divining rod and even the Thought Camera. From the jacket: ". . . . . . This publication presents an analysis of the influence of electromagnetic fields on psychic phenomena. The author, being a geologist, met many dowsers in his work, and has always been skeptical of their powers, since the results he had seen had never been convincing. However, important data collected in 1940 seemed to indicate that divining phenomena were just as real as electricity and other physical phenomena.

During recent years, experiments with artificial magnetic fields and string galvanometers indicated that divining phenomena really exist, that they can be explained by normal physical and physiological laws, and that a careful analysis of these phenomena might prove of great value in medicine.

In the first chapter of the present publication, an analysis has been given of the electromagnetic field in and around living organisms. In the second chapter further evidence has been gathered to support the assumption that the existence of divining phenomena can be suspected even on theoretical grounds and a summary is given of the different influences of electrostatic, electromagnetic fields on living organisms. In the third chapter the divining phenomena have been analyzed scientifically and the author's experiments fully described.

A summary of the basic conceptions and units has been compiled in the appendix for those readers who are not sufficiently acquainted with electromagnetic terminology....."

Of course this development of the subtle forces that rule living cells and the sensitivities of the human bodies to force fields that lie beyond the abilities of our instruments leaves some of the subtle sciences of the ancients less open to doubt---much more open to belief. To those who pose that the "natural life" is best...minus drugs and other violent therapies of the allotropic doctors.... we offer this corroboration.

TROMP recommends that world-wide institutes of PSYCHIC PHYSICS be set up (a recommendation that the SPACE-CRAFT DIGEST hopes to pursue) with teams of at least ten open-minded scientists: A physicist (with technical experience) a pharmacologist (specializing in physical chemistry) a biologist (specializing in electrophysiology of plants and animals) a physiologist (specializing in electroencephlographic research) a neurologist and a psychologist (specializing experimental psychology) a para-pshychologist; a geophysicist (specializing in meteorology) and a scientific co-ordinator. Now, we come to the crux of the whole UFO matter. As far as conventional Western science is concerned it is easy to note that any specialist "sees" but one (his) little portion of the picture.

When these phenomena "materialize" out of "beyond 3-D" there are at least ten different explanations of the "REALITY" of the UFO....just as the ten specialists in our institute of PSYCHIC PHYSICS would see "their" portion of the "saucer phenomena" thru 'their' eyes backed with "their" separate disciplines and trainings.

It is our hope that such a pilot institute can be set up somewhere in the world. It would then be possible to carry on basic research along the lines outlined and suggested by Tromp and others. Not only would the problem of the UFO see some constructive work, but the resulting benefits to mankind would be enormous.

At the present stage of his development in the Western World, man, seems now to know that there is m re to the cosmos than western science has admitted. He is also certain that the miriad schisms of religions offer only their distorted dogmatic views of the "truths of the cosmos". So, out of the various world institutues of PSYCHIC PHYSICS could come some well coordinated "answers". These answers have been there since the time of the ancients but they have been suppressed by the various political and religious systems that man has allowed to rule over him.

Even tho such a re-examination of our "learning" seems badly needed today, it is unlikely that the political systems of today would allow such an institute to effect any cures for the ills befalling our present societies.

SAME SHIP OVER AUSTRALIA..?..asks Herb Clark, secretary of the Vancouver Area Flying Saucer Club (p.o. Box 720 Vancouver, Canada) who sent us this colored slide of the "saucer" over an Australian sheep flock. We had this enlargement made and certainly it appears on the glossy pictures before reproduction here as the very same type of craft. The California picture on the right as shown was obtained from United Press International.

In this publication we have presented the TWO main types of manifestations. The "etheric" aeroform "materializations" from counter-space and the more "solid" types of circular craft which we have also shown.

ACTUALLY, when these first modern sitings of the UFO were made by military intelligence during the last war, the race was then on to "cover" until we could get our own SPACE PROGRAM into being. The satellites were brought about by other "etheric" satellites showing up on our radar and visual detection systems. We then, pushed ahead our own "earthly" satellite orbit programs -- in the meantime following the old-as-time military trick of duping the civilians.

UFO near Bakersfield, California, U.S.A., which appears to be about 1,000 yards away. Weston, a passing motorist, saw the UFO as it made its first pass. He leaped out of his automobile in wonderment . . . with his camera. The UFO then sped back down the same track and the result was recorded in this picture . . . an excellent UFO documentation.

"Space-Craft From Beyond Three Dimensions"

by W. Gordon Allen. (ILLUSTRATED)

FROM THE JACKET In this challenging and provocative work, W. Gordon Allen, owner of several radio stations, a graduate electrical engineer and a former U. S. Naval radio-radar officer — seeks to prove conclusively the existence of Unidentified Flying Objects and offers an UNPRECEDENTED number of pictures to substantiate his claims.

The author's investigations over the last seven years indicate that "extra-terrestial" entities using electrical spece-craft propulsion "are all around us".

The mystery, Mr. Allen continues, is why this attention seems to be paid to earth at this time—unless this space traffic has always been with us. If it has—and certainly there are indications that the UFO has always been with us—then the ruling powers-that-be who have oppressed the mind of man over the last few thousand years on this planet have been guilty of the universes' MOST INCREDIBLE CRIME AGAINST HUMANITY!

BEYOND THREE DIMENSIONS constitutes a challenge to conventional 20th century physical science to re-consider its "proved" conclusions and to re-evaluate the atomic theory. As the FIRST comprehensive attempt to reconcile Western scientific knowledge with the fantastic phenomena of the UFO, it is a scholary and important work; as an exploration of flying saucers and their mysterious brethren, it is a true to life adventure story—as timely as tomorrow!

CHAPTER HEADINGS . . . TOWARD NEW DIMENSIONS OF THOUGHT . . . COSMIC-MIND RECEIVERS AFTER NEWTON . . . ATOMIC THEORIES AND PRE-HISTORIC CATASTROPHY . . . FROM COLD-WATCH to MOON-WATCH . . . (Space craft in our skies) . . . FIRST PRACTICAL THOUGHT RESONATOR? . . . THE POST-WAR PHANTASMA OF THE UFO . . .LUNAR CHANGES AND THE EARTH'S HALO . . . SOME EXTRA-TERRESTIAL VISITATIONS . . . A NEW VISTA OF THE ENTIRETY . . . and four essays on the space-vortex atom by C. F. Krafft.   (Many UFO photos)

ORDER TODAY AS FIRST EDITION IS NEARLY SOLD OUT.

Mail me "SPACE-CRAFT FROM BEYOND THREE DIMENSIONS" by W. Gordon Allen
$3.60 POSTPAID

KGAY
P.O. Box 768   Salem, Oregon

www.ingramcontent.com/pod-product-compliance
Lightning Source LLC
Chambersburg PA
CBHW080635230426
43663CB00016B/2885